# DESIGN CULTURE

## AN ANTHOLOGY OF WRITING FROM THE AIGA JOURNAL OF GRAPHIC DESIGN

*Edited by Steven Heller and Marie Finamore*

## ALLWORTH PRESS
### NEW YORK

Co-published with the American Institute of Graphic Arts

Published by Allworth Press
An imprint of Allworth Communications
10 East 23rd Street, New York, NY 10010

Co-published with the American Institute of Graphic Arts
164 Fifth Avenue, New York, NY 10010

Designed by Woody Pirtle, Pentagram, New York, NY

Page composition/typography by Sharp Des!gns, Holt, MI

ISBN: 1-880559-71-4

Library of Congress Catalog Card Number: 96-79696

This book is dedicated to

**CAROLINE HIGHTOWER**

executive director of the AIGA from 1977 to 1994,
without whom there would be no *AIGA Journal*.

# CONTENTS

## IDENTITY AND ICON

## ARTS AND CRAFTS

## MODERN AND OTHER ISMS

## DESIGN 101

## FUTURE SHOCKS

## FACTS AND ARTIFACTS

## LOVE, MONEY, POWER

## PUBLIC WORKS

# PREFACE

*Richard Grefé, Executive Director, American Institute of Graphic Arts*

T he American Institute of Graphic Arts is dedicated to advancing excellence
in graphic design as a discipline, profession, and cultural force. The AIGA
provides leadership in the exchange of ideas and information, the encour-
agement of critical analysis and research, and the advancement of education
and ethical practice.

      This anthology is an important contribution to our role in educating,
enlightening, and informing current and future generations of designers. It serves
to extend the reach of an eclectic range of critical writings on the trends and
issues of graphic design, previously available only to AIGA members and a few
individual subscribers. It validates the decision of Caroline Hightower to revive
the *Journal* and Steven Heller's editorial leadership, without whose indefatigable
quest for yet another angle on design this anthology would have been consider-
ably thinner.

      *Design Culture* demonstrates the AIGA's commitment to being a thought-
ful and provocative design advocate on behalf of its ten thousand members, the
design community as a whole, design educators and students, and a much broader
audience interested in visual communication and popular culture.

# ACKNOWLEDGMENTS

**W**e would like to thank everyone who has contributed articles and illustrations to the *AIGA Journal* over the years, as well as the various supporters who donated services and materials.

The *Journal* has been the result of a fruitful collaboration of the above-mentioned contributors as well as editors, managing editors, art directors, designers, and typographers. At different times, the following (in order of appearance) have been invaluable to its smooth operation:

### EDITORS
Wylie Davis (1982–1983)
Rose DeNeve (1983–1985)
Steven Heller (1985–present)

### MANAGING EDITORS
Shelley Bance (1982–1985)
Marilyn Recht (1986)
Ruth Toda (1987–1990)
Philip F. Clark (1990–1993)
Marie Finamore (1993–present)

### ART DIRECTORS
Elton Robinson
Kit Hinrichs
Susan Limoncelli
Lisa Naftolin
Laurel Shoemaker
Michael Ian Kaye

### DESIGNERS
Margaret Wollenhaupt
Lisa Bernich
Terri Driscoll
Callie Johnson
Susie Leversee
Julie Riefler
Jaye Zimet
Dimity Jones

Brett Gerstenblatt
E. J. Smith
Leslie Goldman

## TYPOGRAPHERS
Susan Schechter
Ira Ungar
Rick Binger
Karen Krimmel
Boro Typographers
Jennifer Lawson
Alexis Siroc
Tammi Colichio
Tobias Frere-Jones

## GUEST CO-EDITORS
Richard Saul Wurman
Nathan Gluck
Michael Bierut
Paula Scher
Randy Hipke
Rick Poynor
Samuel Antupit
Jessica Helfand
Ellen Lupton
DK Holland
Michael Rock
Sylvia Harris
Matthew Carter
Juanita Dugdale
William Drenttel

# INTRODUCTION: TIME WELL SPENT

*Steven Heller, Editor,* AIGA Journal of Graphic Design

Fifteen years ago, the *AIGA Journal of Graphic Design* was an eight-page tabloid. Today, it is a seventy-two-page magazine. Although you might assume that this alone is a major accomplishment, in 1948 the first issue of the bimonthly *AIGA Journal* (the words *graphic design* were not yet included in the title) was a magazine—and a fairly good one, too. Throughout the 1950s the format continued, and in 1966 it was expanded to include catalogs of the AIGA annual competitions. In the early 1970s, it folded—the casualty of economic crisis—and lay dormant until 1982, at which time the AIGA published a newsletter that gradually evolved into the *Journal.*

The revivified *Journal* had a lot of living up to do. The *Journal* of the forties and fifties offered the AIGA's one thousand or so members broad-based reportage and critical coverage of the graphic arts. It included essays by such luminaries as Herbert Bayer, Alvin Lustig, Paul Rand, Leo Lionni, Alexey Brodovitch, and Fritz Eichenberg (who was also one of the early editors). In unflattering contrast, the editorial content of the eighties *Journal* was initially at the press release level. Nevertheless, this was also a period of considerable change for the AIGA. In the institute's tidal shift from a small, exclusive club to a large professional organization with nationwide chapters, the *AIGA Journal* could not afford to be merely a parochial newsletter. Somehow, it had to become a forum for design issues.

The notion of graphic design criticism had been discussed for some time as a panacea for the graphic design field's netherworld status between art and commerce. For the editor of the *AIGA Journal,* the somewhat nebulous term pointed toward a new direction. In 1986, the *Journal* switched from its exclusive AIGA orientation to more incisive analysis, reportage, and criticism of the field as a whole. Borrowing an op-ed page model, the *Journal* became an outlet for numerous viewpoints solicited from design practitioners, academics, and journalists as well as nondesigners, among them social critics and popular historians. Within a short time, the *Journal* was transformed from an AIGA house organ into an AIGA-sponsored distillery of ideas.

In the 1970s, most professional (or trade) magazines had become instruments for promoting designers and their work. Since *Graphic Design USA,* the omnibus launched in 1980 that includes each year's award-winning work, satisfied the membership's need for colorful reproductions of successful design, the AIGA could afford to allow the *Journal* to be both text heavy and concept driven. Entire issues of the *Journal* were devoted to rarely scrutinized themes, including information design, the future of magazine design, designing for children, myths of corporate communications, the bridge between theory and practice, design for the public sector, paradigms of typography, the annals of book design, design preservation, fashion and style, design in the real world, political design, cultural iconography, vernacular design, and the history of graphic design. With such special issues as *Dangerous Ideas* and *Love Money Power*—the articles for which were collected from two contentious AIGA national conferences—the *Journal* became a platform for heated debate. Most important, the *Journal* introduced issues that crossed disciplinary boundaries, including one on the First Amendment (featuring an interview with the embattled curator of the Cincinnati Museum of Art, who mounted the controversial Robert Mapplethorpe exhibition), which focused on the graphic designer's responsibility to the doctrine of free speech.

Of course, not everything in the *Journal* was this weighty. The editorial challenge was to maintain a balance between serious analysis and comic introspection, while making the *Journal* accessible to its readers. In this regard, "Dear Tibor," a quirky advice column by Tibor Kalman, was introduced as much to encourage interactivity between the *Journal* and its readers as to add acerbity to the mix. In addition, comic and satiric articles on the nature of design practice deflated the taboos, conventions, and canons of the field. Thematic issues devoted to the practice of humor in design and the eccentricity of designers further exposed our alternative passions.

Before the *Journal* was reconstituted in 1982, most graphic design publications failed to address the culture of design, the factors that make design function in the overall environment. Design coverage was introverted rather than introspective. As the *Journal* grew to represent the internal and external workings of design, it also helped to expand the vision of designers. Through a marriage of journalistic and academic criticism, the *Journal* blazed a trail that others soon followed. It provided a primary outlet for authors who pushed the standards of design writing. Indeed, good writing became increasingly important to the field, which had traditionally been criticized from within and without for lacking fundamental communication skills. The *Journal* proved that designers could write intelligently, and often humorously, about their own culture and its impact on the broader culture. For purposes of this anthology, these essays are organized in somewhat culturally thematic sections.

By 1994, the *AIGA Journal* had grown out of its tabloid skin. Despite a number of changes in the overall design, editorial space was excruciatingly tight. But, more important, the *Journal* simply looked too ephemeral. Not only did readers call it "the AIGA newsletter," which was somewhat deflating, but librarians (especially art school librarians) were not preserving it. This was the primary reason for the decision to transform it into a magazine. The new size and format allowed greater flexibility and tighter coverage. It also clarified a sometimes confusing editorial scheme. The grand themes, which were clear to the editors, were sometimes lost on the readers who found the thematic articles scattered throughout the issue. In the magazine format, a dedicated thematic editorial feature well is distinct from, say, the Talk of Design (or op-ed section) in the front of the book; and both are separate from the back-of-the-book columns (Letters, Professional Practice, The Student, Book Monitor, and the like). With its new color cover, advertisements (which were not accepted until the last couple of tabloid issues), and AIGA Communiqué, the magazine is a much more substantial-looking document than ever before.

In the fifteen years since the *AIGA Journal* went from an eight-page tabloid to a seventy-two-page magazine, design publishing has also changed. There are more design writers, a wider range of subjects being covered, and a higher level of editing. Design criticism, though still in its adolescence, has found acceptance in leading publications, including *Eye, Print, Communication Arts, I.D., Design Issues,* and *Emigre.* And various academic graphic design journals have also contributed to the "design discourse." Over time, the *Journal* has certainly helped shape this discourse and it continues to help define the issues. The mission of the *Journal,* like the AIGA itself, has been to inspire designers to think seriously about their impact on the worlds of art and commerce—and how they serve society as a whole. But, in the final analysis, the readers of the *Journal* must decide whether this has been time well spent.

# BORROWED DESIGNS

# MONDRIAN AS A MARKETING TOOL

*Philip B. Meggs*

A visual style is not just an attractive surface decoration: it is often an expression of a philosophy, an ideology, and the spirit of its times. This is precisely why art nouveau or the psychedelic poster, for example, remain fascinating for contemporary designers and the general public. The mania for historical revivals during the last decade has often detached the visual appearance of an earlier style from its symbolic meaning and social context, rendering it neuter. This process can corrupt and debase the original, robbing it of its historical potency.

The debasement of Piet Mondrian, a founder of the de Stijl movement, is a classic illustration of this process. From the founding of de Stijl in 1917, until his death in 1944, Mondrian dedicated his life to the quest for absolute visual harmony and purity of form. But this mission was not seen as an end in itself; rather, Mondrian believed that pure art could have great meaning for society.

De Stijl began during World War I, when the politics of Europe were being reformed. Many artists, writers, and political activists believed that the old order of European society would be destroyed and replaced by a new society. Kaiser Wilhelm II of Germany was deposed in 1918 and replaced by a constitutional democracy that only survived until the rise of Nazism. Socialism and communism were steadily gaining ground throughout Europe, spurred by the Bolsheviks' triumph in Russia.

As the old social order was clearly passing, Mondrian sought nothing less than a new art of pure form and color. He believed that art could become a beacon pointing the way toward a new order in society. In his writings he spoke of achieving the universal in art as a sign of the "new age." He wrote, "It is the spirit of the times that determines artistic expression, which, in turn, reflects the spirit of the times. But at the present moment, that form of art alone is truly alive which expresses our present or future consciousness." His compositions were restricted to horizontal and vertical lines, rectangles, and squares, and a palette limited to black, white, grays, and the primary colors of red, yellow, and blue. This universal vocabulary of form was arranged in compositions achieving dynamic equilibrium. Mondrian saw his art as a metaphor pointing toward a universal harmony and order that might be attained in human society and daily life. This new spirit of art could be integrated into life by its application to architecture, product design, graphic design, and urban planning. Theo van Doesburg, cofounder of de Stijl, worked tirelessly to apply this universal language of form to applied design.

Seventy-three years after de Stijl began, how should we interpret the appearance of L'Oréal's Studio Line Daily Express Shampoo, packaged in a white container decorated with Mondrian's black horizontal and vertical lines and his squares of pure red, white, and blue? The advertising copy says, "Raise your styling consciousness with Studio Line's New Daily Express Shampoo. Express away residue in one lather to illuminate clean hair." It closes by urging the user to "gently prime hair for infinitely better styling, wet maneuvering, and expressing yourself."

The new formal vocabulary wrested from thin air by Mondrian, van Doesburg, and their confederates is pressed into service as a marketing tool for shampoo. Is this the extension of universal principles of harmony and unity into daily life? No, it is the shameless usurpation of serious art forms, seizing the style while leaving the content and the context behind. Shampoo is given the luster of high art. To make sure the magazine reader (or perhaps *marketing target* would be more appropriate) makes the connection, the red, yellow, and blue configuration from the package hangs on the wall in the background as a work of art.

Art is a form of language, and its manipulation to accomplish predetermined objectives is consistent with the contemporary manipulation of spoken and written language. As Louis Danziger once said, a corruption of language began during the Eisenhower presidency when the Department of War was renamed the Department of Defense. This doublespeak is still with us. President Reagan named the proposed MX missile "the peacekeeper"; the Department of Defense took "protective action" when it invaded Panama. And the purist forms of Mondrian's paintings are "appropriated" for L'Oréal's shampoo, offering "one lather clean; lightweight conditioning; and easier styling." Even the word *appropriation* is doublespeak, a palatable substitute for *plagiarism.* Plagiarism is regarded as a form of piracy, the stealing of someone else's work. Appropriation, on the other hand, is now regarded as making sophisticated use of existing material.

These issues become very complex. Not all appropriation is plagiarism. It is possible to extend an existing formal vocabulary, to continue a tradition, or to revive forms that have been cast into the dustbin of graphic history. When, in the 1890s, William Morris revived typefaces from the incunabula at his Kelmscott Press, he was restoring excellent typographic forms that had perished in the industrial revolution. Paula Scher's typographic posters for Columbia Records did not merely mimic Russian constructivism; they synthesized visual attributes from that movement with other design properties, such as the spatial compression of nineteenth-century wood-type posters, to make masterful and original designs. I have heard designers and architects ridicule contemporary housing developments continuing the tradition of Victorian farmhouses. The Greco-Roman architectural style of marble buildings lined with columns lasted from the seventh century B.C. to the third century A.D. One is forced to wonder whether the Victorian farmhouse style can't be viable for two hundred years, if its functional use of space, economy, appropriate use of materials, and overall function and appearance satisfies the physical and emotional needs of its occupants.

In many instances, the preoccupation with graphic design history during the last decade has been a form of homage, respecting and honoring past masters and movements. But when appropriating forms from the past, each designer must carefully assess whether he or she is continuing a tradition, honoring the past, or debasing the original by separating it from its symbolic meaning and historical context. Historicism has often occurred at the end of an era or movement, signaling that the period is closing and a new period will begin. We are in a period of flux. Radical changes in Russia and eastern Europe, along with renewed concern about the environment, are altering culture. The historicism and appropriation of the 1980s may well yield to new visual forms in the 1990s that express a new age, just as Mondrian and van Doesburg sought new forms to express a new age seventy-three years ago.

*Originally published in Volume 8, Number 2, 1990.*

# THE POLITICS OF CULTURAL OWNERSHIP
*Fath Davis Ruffins*

**W**hile people often suffer the consequences of being legally or socially defined as belonging to an ethnic group, they have no legal right to own or even control how their culture is portrayed or exploited. Individuals, corporations, and even state and local governments can own trademarks and copyright ethnic portrayals, such as the Washington Redskins, yet cultural groups do not have such legal authority. There is no single definition of the term *cultural ownership* that would be universally accepted across the various disciplines of art history, anthropology, or political science. However, in light of the complicated social history of the United States, the main issues in the concept of cultural ownership have to do with longstanding contradictions between *cultural definition* and *cultural control*. Cultural definition involves being identified by oneself (and by others) as belonging to a distinctive cultural group. Cultural control involves members of a specific cultural group exerting social, economic, and/or political influence over laws, issues, and representations of that group.

The contradiction between cultural definition and cultural control has been apparent since the early years of the republic. However, such conflicts became particularly contentious when the rise of mass media and mass marketing collided with the growing political power of the modern civil rights movement. Movies, radio programs, and mass-marketed product advertisements were key ways in which humorous, sentimental, satirical, and stereotypical attitudes about American ethnic groups were portrayed, perpetuated, and transmitted to new generations and incoming immigrants. Efforts to resist prevailing negative portrayals have occurred since the Civil War era, but protest efforts gathered speed in the early twentieth century. While no group has the legal power to control its portrayal, some groups have grown more effective in using political and economic tactics to protest offensive imagery.

In 1915, two unrelated events occurred that galvanized certain American communities. The innovative but deeply racist film *Birth of a Nation,* directed by D. W. Griffith, was released. Shown to an adoring public and given a White House viewing by President Woodrow Wilson, *Birth of a Nation* is still remembered for its technical innovation and the pathological depth of its racist portrayals of African-Americans, especially men, and its images of rapacious and corrupt white Yankees. The NAACP, then four years old, made strenuous efforts to boycott, picket, and disrupt the showings of this film, more or less in vain. In the era of silent film, it became the first major success, characterized by such technical innovations as outdoor and long panoramic shots along with a cast of thousands. Also in 1915, the Atlanta merchant Leo Frank, a Jewish man whose grandfather had fought for the Confederacy, was lynched. He had been convicted of the murder of an Irish girl working in his factory. Although he was clearly railroaded, and the governor of Georgia had pardoned him, Frank was eventually taken from his jail cell and hanged before a jeering crowd of hundreds of white Georgians. The anti-Semitic propaganda stirred up by his sensationalist murder trial and wrongful death spurred the founding of two different important Jewish organizations: the American Jewish Committee and the American Jewish League. Each in distinct ways immediately began to protest the portrayals of American Jews in a variety of popular media, with little success until the Cold War era.

These two examples can demonstrate the earlier difficulties of counteracting virulent stereotypes, even those with murderous consequences. Yet much changed in the years following World War II. Economic boycotts such as the Montgomery Bus Boycott of 1955–1956, which brought the Reverend Dr. Martin Luther King, Jr., to national attention, began to reveal the buying power of heretofore ignored ethnic groups. The development of new outlets, such as the publications empire of John Johnson, produced new ways for advertisers to reach a certain segment of the African-American community. After World War II, the NAACP targeted the entertainment industry, especially movies and television, to change the portrayals of African-Americans in these media. The popular TV show *Amos 'n' Andy* was pulled off the air in the early 1960s because of these protests.

Perhaps an even clearer example of the assertion of cultural identity issues had to do with the elimination of a rather successful character, the Frito Bandito, introduced by Frito-Lay (a part of General Foods) in 1968. Sales of Fritos were reinvigorated by the introduction of the animated Bandito character, who stole Fritos from other characters on television and in print. As described by a journalist, the Frito Bandito "was a sneaky 'toon, part Speedy Gonzalez, part *duende*, that got into people who munched on Fritos and made them grow pencil-drawn mustaches" (Enrique Fernandez, "Ay Bandito!" in the *Village Voice,* October 13, 1992). Although the character had a very high rate of recognition among the public, Frito-Lay dropped it in 1971 in response to the protests of Hispanic groups, including the Mexican-American Anti-Defamation League, founded by, among others, Ricardo Montalban, the noted screen and TV actor. Over the last twenty-five years, many large-scale American companies have been forced to pay attention to the interests, sensibilities, and consumption patterns of groups of Americans who had routinely been stereotyped in earlier product advertising.

Each of these examples illustrates the growing power of various interest groups to assert both economic and political desires. In recent years, Quaker Foods has redesigned Aunt Jemima to make her more like an African-American suburban matron, consulting with Dorothy Height, the longtime chairman of the National Council of Negro Women (NCNW). Such changes point to the durability of images that companies knew demonstrated extremely high consumer recognition. At the same time, the death of the Frito Bandito and Sambo's restaurant chain indicate the susceptibility of companies to consumer reaction. But are such instances examples of cultural ownership?

While it is undoubtedly positive that ethnic groups are now better able to protest stereotypes of their culture and effect change, the question of cultural ownership remains problematic. With the exception of certain Native American tribes, most "cultures" still have no legal definition in the United States. Many ethnic groups now contain watchdog organizations that focus on the various aspects of politics and the media. Yet, problems of consensus inevitably arise within the group: Who is a "legitimate" spokesperson? Who appointed that person or group to "represent" the feelings of all Arab- or Japanese-Americans? Such issues become much more complicated when well-known members of the group take dissenting or even opposing positions on such questions. Should there be different rules when the owners of the advertising agency, film production company, or recording studio are themselves members of the ethnic group being portrayed? Perhaps the most vehement differences of opinion on this topic concern the images and lyrics of gangsta rap music. In the name of communicating the realities of ghetto life, black rappers have presented controversial images that certainly would be considered racist if created by whites.

Arguments over substance and style, content and form, are raging in contemporary American society, and the idea of cultural ownership per se is not that helpful in guiding us through the ethical thicket raised through the commercial use of ethnicity, or in analyzing the meaning of patterns of imagery. Regardless of the aesthetic choices that designers, agencies, or companies make, they must inform themselves about the history of that imagery. Individuals may feel that particular ideas or images have emerged directly from their own unconscious, with no intention of offending anyone, but run into major opposition when those ideas become public. For example, the Italian company Benetton prudently withdrew some of its magazine and transportation ads in the United States when protests were mounted. Advertisements showing an African-American woman suckling a white child, or models dressed in Catholic nuns' habits, played in the European market, but were too offensive in the American context.

The long development of American (indeed, international) consumer culture means that many, many images have an earlier history. That history is not only aesthetic, but also contains the racial and ethnic pieties and conflicts of earlier generations. Before an image goes before the public, it is imperative that its creators research its sociopolitical history as an image as well as its aesthetic appeal.

Those responsible for selecting imagery operate in an environment in which cultures may not "own" images, but can assert the power of their historical interpretations of imagery and use their socioeconomic power to force changes in commercial presentation. Knowing the social and cultural history of ethnic imagery could easily prevent key errors (and lawsuits) in this era of tremendous visual sensitivity. Researching the history of a particular image can prevent a company from muddying its commercial presentation by introducing visual elements associated with prejudicial attitudes unrelated to its contemporary commercial purposes. Intentional efforts to draw attention to previous stereotypes need to be produced in a clear-cut manner, probably more suitable to documentary presentation than direct advertising. In any event, the complicated history of visual imagery in the United States cannot be ignored as one of the key elements in choosing a final design or company presentation.

*Originally published in Volume 14, Number 1, 1996.*

# RAINBOWS, CLOSETS, AND DRAG: APPROPRIATION OF GAY AND LESBIAN IMAGERY

*Stuart McKee*

With a long history of social exclusion, lesbians and gays have until recently kept their cultures steadfastly private. During the last quarter century of "gay liberation" and "out" politics, however, we have recognized the value of legitimizing our presence within the public spaces of American print culture. Affirmative images of lesbians and gays are now flourishing within our own print channels, where we have made significant political gains by establishing our identity within the cultural margins.

And corporate America has been paying attention. It is now difficult to browse any of our media-saturated marketplaces without finding carefully veiled appropriations of lesbian and gay identity. Though such representation gives us public exposure, it also co-opts our culture and fuels a contention that has divided the lesbian and gay communities throughout our coexistence with the cultural mainstream. Should we aim to assimilate with the dominant culture, risking eventual acculturation, or will we make greater political gains by remaining culturally distinctive?

Unlike most other cultural groups, lesbians and gays fit into every pocket of the American demographic, crossing lines of gender, ethnicity, age, class, and religion. It is thus difficult to define what types of imagery are lesbian or gay, let alone whether such images are being appropriated. Critical queers have denounced the white, prosperous gay cultural elite, which they claim overshadows more marginal lesbian and gay interests. Other, more specialized factions, such as the bisexual, transsexual, and activist communities, are frequently criticized for overadvertising their subcultural idiosyncrasies. Finally, to assert that lesbian and gay cultural imagery exists is to imply that all other imagery is essentially "straight," and thus politically stigmatizing. Many within the gay community would uphold that a straight designer could never successfully replicate the lesbian or gay identity, no matter how positive his or her articulation of gay concerns.

Lesbians and gays are naturally suspicious of the appropriation of their imagery. Having had to lie and hide throughout our collective past has made recovering our own history a difficult task. Certain themes that have been primary to our experience are becoming culturally common and hence up for grabs, including the ritual of coming out, the metaphor of the closet, and the gender play of drag. Camp expression, one of the most ingrained gay cultural traditions, first came into widespread contention in 1964 when Susan Sontag published her influential essay "Notes on Camp." By de-emphasizing camp's status as lesbian and gay territory, Sontag instigated one of the many cultural border wars that rattle lesbians and gays to this day.

The advertising industry, for example, has become prolific at appropriating the alternative, underground chic of lesbian and gay visual language. A "life"-sized placard of Joe Camel, the cultural chameleon, stands within a store window near one of the busiest street corners in San Francisco's Castro district, pumped up and decked out to cruise gay passersby. Marketing professionals, in their recent recognition of our capacity to influence capital, have incorporated lesbian and gay lifestyles in their advertisements in hopes of attracting our distinctive audience. In the early 1990s, Banana Republic released an ad campaign presenting a variety of same-sex couples in intimate proximity. Corporate advertisements placed within the lesbian and gay media have even begun to appropriate our political voice, as when Anheuser-Busch declared, "Labels belong on beer, not people" in a recent ad for Bud Light.

No strangers ourselves to crossing cultural boundaries, lesbians and gays have been adopting the strategies of corporate communication to market our own identities. Lesbian and gay identification can be bought as a variety of symbols, most notably the inverted pink triangle and the rainbow sequence of colors. These commodities function as corporate markers to label ourselves, the things we own, and the spaces we inhabit. One company, Shocking Gray, offers a four-color mail-order catalog entitled Pride, which specializes in articulating the rainbow as a commodity. All told, it advertises more than fifty rainbow-emblazoned items, including clocks, screen savers, suspenders, and picture frames.

Much of what lesbians and gays have created as our own culture has been appropriated from the mainstream. The symbolism of many lesbian and gay institutions, such as the Gay Games, the Pink Panthers, and the Sisters of Perpetual Indulgence, are fashioned after established cultural models. ACT UP, Queer Nation, and a variety of other lesbian and gay pressure groups before them have recognized that sampling from the print status quo undermines the values that delineate cultural boundaries in a language they know society will understand. Queer Nation, for example, has invaded public shopping malls with queer declarations disguised as back-to-school fliers. Appropriation, for the lesbian and gay community, becomes a powerful mechanism for mocking the systems of representation that have been established by America's social institutions. Appropriation repositions print's cultural boundaries, introducing lesbians and gays into a variety of places—the public square, the workplace, and the home—where we have been refused recognition.

*Originally published in Volume 14, Number 1, 1996.*

# ANGELA AND THE NEHRU JACKET

*Natalia Ilyin*

**N**ehru jackets remind me of being fifteen years old in that baking Marin County summer, the summer that Jonathan Jackson, seventeen, shot a judge to death in the parking lot of the Civic Center. In that shoot-out, Gary Thomas, assistant district attorney, was paralyzed from the waist down by a bullet from a .30-caliber carbine owned by Angela Davis. Four people died that day, including Jackson, Judge Haley, and two of the convicts Jackson was trying to free. The TV news carried muddy, blown-up, black-and-white photos of victims and suspects, caught at birthday parties or in front of new cars. I especially remember a picture of Angela Davis speaking to the crowd, wearing love beads and a Nehru jacket.

I'm sure that Jawaharlal Nehru, India's first prime minister, had not expected his jacket to land on the back of Angela Davis. At first, in the early sixties, it had symbolized a muddled belief in the value of Indian spiritualism to Western culture. The Beatles, after all, had returned from India with long hair and Nehru jackets, and they were the hippest thing imaginable. But after all those pictures of Angela Davis, and the pictures of the shoot-out, the jacket carried a meaning of ascetic radicalism.

As soon as a cultural image like a Nehru jacket or a love bead is replicated in the press, it comes under the purview of the graphic designer. It can be manipulated, used to sell laundry detergent, separated from its original meaning, and filled with new meaning, or, interestingly enough, with nonmeaning.

Ms. Davis, once the quintessential radical, now makes a quiet living on the college lecture circuit, speaking to the huge cool darkness of university auditoriums for a flat fee. In the early seventies, her image symbolized intellectual vision, then the violence that blurred that vision. In the eighties, she told people to get MBAs, while Jane Fonda, another radical icon, made fitness videos. Like Jane, she has reinvented herself many times. Like Jane's, her face is a recycled image.

Now, in the mid-nineties, when our middle-parted, mini-skirted assistants are wearing their Max Mara Nehru jackets made of a lovely chocolate-brown worsted wool, women my age want to take them by the shoulders and scream loudly into their benign and intelligent faces: Why?

We believed in the culture that was concurrent with the jacket; we believed in what it represented—in that feminism, in that antiwar movement, in that civil rights march. We believed that things would get better, but they did not. The dreams of the sixties culminated in the violence of the seventies, and America turned, as one, away from war and intellectual rhetoric and toward the power of money. Now we look in vain to the wearers of Nehru jackets for a flicker of recognition of a meaning that has long evaporated.

I have found that there are two kinds of people in the world: those who understand the ramifications of a sentence or an image or a typeface and those who do not. No amount of hiding behind a pose of insouciance, irony, satire, or ambiguity can save dullards who do not understand the ramifications of what they design, wear on their back, or repeat in smoke-filled bars. It is the denial of ramification that makes the stylistic use of old symbols painful for those who believed in their meaning.

Nostalgia twists truth out of its socket. We accept a false simplification of the past because we have forgotten the details, because it is convenient to forget.

The recycling of the imagery of the seventies for use in the nineties is really a shift from politics to consumerism: we are selling people a cleaned-up image of ourselves, of what we wish we had been. The emphasis is on the way things look, on how to attain that look, rather than on what things mean and how to symbolize that meaning. Angela, who had become the mediated icon of radicalism, depoliticizes herself, reinvents herself as a product, in order to survive in the public eye, in order to stay on top.

People always say that the history books are written by the winners—by the people on top in a society. It's true: a construct of past images may be created by the winner, but a hoarded knowledge of the real facts is often the strength of the losing side. The images of the Holocaust are kept from fading by its survivors, not by the governments who won the war. My Russian aunt in her two-room Moscow apartment lived through Stalinism and purges and perestroika by burying herself in history: she recites to me 1,133 years of Ilyin patronymics. These people survived the false historical construct perpetrated by a dominant order by clinging to the facts of their experience.

And we are in a similar spot. Survivors of "discovered" eras are caught between the truth of their own memories and the commercialization of their culture's past. They watch symbols that meant something to them become marginalized, become fashion. They note that Jane Fonda got implants. They grouse about kids and what they're wearing, but their real argument is not with the kids. Of course not. It is with the loss of detail, with the changing of fact that comes with selling aspects of the dream back to the twenty-year-old. Young people pick what they want to use as symbols, true. But their choice, today, is highly influenced by the narrowness of the mediated palette. The fewer details shown, the fewer used. It is in detail, not in broad-brush nostalgia, that meaning survives.

When we rely on recycling a shrinking stock of recognizable images (the one of Marilyn on the subway grate, the one of the Kennedy brothers in shirtsleeves, the one of the bloodstained body of Martin Luther King, Jr.), we narrow our focus away from the details of the real—of what these people were, of what they said fully, of what they meant in their context. When we design by picking and choosing from Charles Spencer Anderson's image books or other predigested sources, we leave out so much information that the past is unrecognizable. We weave the fabric of our culture from a shrinking supply of threads, and the truth is forgotten, in favor of the simple.

*Originally published in Volume 14, Number 1, 1996.*

# CEASE AND DESIST: ISSUES OF CULTURAL REAPPROPRIATION IN URBAN STREET DESIGN

*Interview by Kevin Lyons*

Located on the margins of postindustrial society, urban youth of all races have had to face political and social alienation, truncated opportunity, and economic oppression. At the end of the 1970s, urban youth were forced to create their own cultural networks by reshaping their cultural identities in a hostile, technologically sophisticated, multiethnic urban terrain. Through dissemination and reappropriation of sampled sounds, styles, and images, urban artists brought Afro-diasporic cultural priorities to bear on advanced technology through rap music, break dancing, and graffiti, in turn creating urban street culture. Often criticized and misrepresented by uninformed academics as purely rip-off design, hip-hop and rave design, drawing inspiration from both pop art and graffiti, have come to graphically represent this culture and are executing the most creative and complex forms of reappropriation of cultural imagery.

As both a graduate student in graphic design and a practicing designer within this unique artist group, I sat down with four of the more influential urban street designers—Eric "Haze" of L.A.–based Haze Graphics; James Jebbia, owner of New York/L.A. Union stores, as well as New York City's skate store Supreme; Ssur Russ, owner and creator of SSureal Visuals; and Joseph Melendez, store manager of Union in New York and creator of the clothing line Rock Hard—to discuss their views on reappropriation and issues of cultural, commercial, legal, and moral ownership.

**KL:** Denied certain opportunities, educational and economic, urban youths have a history of turning to art for a way out—as a means of self-employment. By taking familiar or powerful imagery from corporations, products, and films, reappropriation has become a method of crossover and thus a source of finance, survival, and success in a society once closed to us. When confronted with issues of ownership and rights to imagery, how do each of you respond to critics who simply say that we are rip-off artists?

**Haze:** The way I see it, there are no original ideas anymore. Everything is based on a familiar cultural reference to something in the past. *Biting* [a street term for "appropriation"] is a way of life. It has a longstanding tradition. It is, in essence, an extension of pop art.

**James:** I believe it is hard to judge ownership in the case of a big shoe company that actively pursues legal suits against small, cutting-edge companies while, at the same time, it sends video cameras to New York City playgrounds to observe how kids wear clothes and rock styles.

**Haze:** Urban youth make up their most profitable market group. All of those companies draw inspiration from the streets. We are simply stealing back what they took from us.

**James:** Yeah, I don't believe any imagery should ever be given so much power that it cannot be played with.

**Haze:** In many ways, we are killing our icons—our heroes. From childhood on, we are overwhelmed by name brands and product logos. By playing with them, you can go toe-to-toe with the giant. The little guy eclipsing the big guy.

**James:** I have to laugh. It costs them more money in lawyer fees to tell me to *cease and desist* [a legal term informing a company to stop producing certain products on grounds of copyright infringement] than I make doing it.

**Haze:** I believe 100 percent, though, in legal ownership. If a company sues me, I own up. I went for it, and they caught me.

**James:** The new reappropriation, though, must be as strong graphically as the one it was taken from. It must be able to stand on its own.

**Ssur:** So much of what I do, even my knockoffs, no one understands. So it is important that the logo looks so good that it can sell itself even if the reference is unknown.

**Haze:** That's why we only do certain logos. I only do logo bites if I like and respect the logo to begin with.

**KL:** Then, like sampling, by appropriating old symbols and images, we are, in effect, paying homage to the originals—a form of cultural archeology. We reformulate, change the context, and make kids recognize and rethink logos and images. The new reappropriated symbols take on new cultural identities. What about in the case of using exploitative imagery? Or what about artists who use imagery outside of their own immediate racial makeup or culture?

**Haze:** Inner-city urban youth culture is made up of many races and cultures.

**Ssur:** And that is not to say that we are *multicultural.* That denies our individual histories and backgrounds. Academics have made multiculturalism into the new melting pot. Urban street culture now has more to do with economic inopportunity and sociopolitical nonrepresentation than race.

**Joseph:** African-American culture has been exploited for hundreds of years. Reappropriation is part of this tradition. But now some of us are turning it around and using it as a source of pride and awareness, rather than exploitation and shame. Of course there are some, though, who are still using it in uninformed/exploitative ways.

**KL:** Like rap music, provocative, even controversial cultural appropriation has become an alternative form of awareness and education. A starting point for argument and discussion.

**Ssur:** Many of us use images that we can relate to our own personal struggles on the street and in the industry. This is where this strong association to the outsider—the underdog—comes from.

**Joseph:** Credit is due only when you are educated and aware of your own imagery.

**KL:** So this awareness and responsibility, then, can give justification to certain appropriation and lack of awareness or irresponsibility can discredit others?

**Joseph:** Most definitely.

---

In a society that worships and promotes multimillion-dollar corporate logos and exploits imagery of all sorts, it should come as no surprise that we, who have been denied access to such opportunity, should now turn to those same corporations as a method of rising up and finding a way for ourselves. If nothing else, critics should recognize that, for the most part, we are not using reappropriation as an excuse for design. Instead, we have very specific and well-thought-out reasons behind our work. Reappropriation comes very naturally to us. It has been a necessary step in our development as designers and entrepreneurs. It has been our education, as well as our mode of educating others. In the end, reappropriation has allowed us, at the least, to stake claim to the urban street culture of which we have been both victim and champion.

*Originally published in Volume 14, Number 1, 1996.*

# IS THERE LEGAL PROTECTION FOR CULTURAL IMAGERY?

*Rosemary J. Coombe*

G raphic designers work in an environment shaped by intellectual property laws that commodify, protect, license, and regulate the use of the imagery upon which they draw. The laws of copyright, trademark, and publicity rights (which prohibit the use of celebrity images or likenesses), however, are as routinely violated as they are enforced. Moreover, not all imagery is legally protected from unauthorized use, and this, I will suggest, may be a matter of particular concern for many cultural minorities.

Laws of intellectual property are based upon liberal, individualist principles born of Enlightenment certainties and legitimated by Romantic ideologies. The Eurocentrism of these (purportedly universal or neutral) premises often serves to devalue creative expressive forms produced collectively, intergenerationally, or in unfamiliar media—often produced by those with non-European cultural traditions. As a consequence, although much imagery may be legally available for public use, unauthorized usage may offend the sensibilities and norms of the people who originate the imagery. The ethics and politics of appropriating imagery from other cultures are indeed complex and will increasingly demand the attention of graphic designers as new forms of communications media make imagery from ever-farther corners of the globe readily available for adaptation and inclusion in graphic works.

Laws of copyright protect the creative products of individual authors (in copyright law, all creators are deemed "authors"), pictured as autonomous individuals whose creations are solely the products of the originality of an unfettered imagination. Through the imprint of the authors' unique personalities, expressions that originate with their activity and are fixed by their material form are deemed to be their property. The law assumes that "ideas" are always available for appropriation, but "expressions" are the property of those who inscribe or imprint them. Through their labor, authors make these ideas their own; their possession and control over the "work" is justified by this expressive activity. As long as authors do not copy another's expressive works, they are free to find their inspiration, ideas, themes, motifs, and design elements anywhere they please and to incorporate these into their own work. Any restriction upon their ability to do so is viewed in liberal democracies as an impermissible restriction on freedom of expression. Possessive individualism and liberal democracy are thereby mutually affirmed.

The Romantic individualism that permeates this law has certainly been criticized, especially by those influenced by anthropology, sociology, Marxism, and poststructuralism. Critics argue that all expressive forms are produced in social contexts, that genres, themes, motifs, and design elements are conventionally defined, that art is only recognized as art in certain social conditions. Many forms of expressive activity are not recognized as resulting in "artistic" works, even though they involve significant creativity (certain kinds of food preparation, quilt designs handed down and modified through the generations, ritual tattoo motifs, and collaborative fashionings of ritual costumes are a few examples). All ideas, critics suggest, come to us through the medium of expressions, and it is the circulation of such expressions that provides the very wellspring of creative inspiration. Creativity, these critics assert, must always involve the reworking of those cultural forms available to us.

Copyright laws attempt to preclude artists from reproducing the work of others, making many "arts of appropriation" open to potential lawsuits. On the other hand, the legal emphasis upon individual expression and the requirement of a permanent fixed form leaves many products of artistry unprotected and thus available for incorporation into the work of designers. Although it is tempting to view this aspect of the law as a space of freedom, for many it results in perceived exploitation and expropriation. Creative designs produced by collectives, in ritual contexts, over generations, or not fixed in recognized forms (such as the imagery of the sweat lodge or the sun dance), may be ripped out of sacred, ancestral, and secret contexts to be incorporated into the works of others. A woman in India, for example, may create an elaborately wrought design in the clay in front of her home on a daily basis, using patterns and skills passed down from mother to daughter over the generations. By midday, the design will have disappeared. Should a visiting artist happen upon the creation, sketch or photograph the design, and later use it on the cover of an annual report or as the basis for a textile print, he or she will be deemed its author. Such activities may produce intense feelings of violation in certain communities, where creative forms may serve distinct purposes, may be understood to be appropriately used only in clearly defined contexts, and may be seen as integral to the identity of a lineage or the heritage of a people. The law enables the expressions of some people to become available as ideas for the appropriation of others and may protect the appropriator when the expressions are incorporated into an expressive work that is legally recognized.

Trademark laws pose other dilemmas. A trademark is an image, logo, design, brand name, or any other symbol capable of distinguishing one's goods or services in the market. A trademark cannot simply be descriptive; for example, one could not obtain exclusive rights to use the term *sweet* for pears or candies. Instead, the law requires that a mark be suggestive, arbitrary, or fanciful, like Smarties for candy or Sweet for tires. Such marks are legally deemed "distinctive." Once a manufacturer establishes legal rights to a mark through extensive use in marketing and consumer recognition, it can prevent others from legally using the same or a similar mark, on the basis that it will be confusing to the public or that the distinction of its mark will be "diluted" by the reproduction of the mark in unauthorized contexts.

In their quests for distinction in competitive markets, it is not surprising that designers of trademarks have looked to ever more exotic locales and to other cultures to find signifying forms that are not already in commercial use. This practice may be viewed as an invasive violation by those whose cultural forms become commodified and invested with alien meanings. Imagine the consternation of the Sioux, for example, when a beer manufacturer used the name of their revered ancestor Crazy Horse to market malt liquor. Given the devastation wrought by alcohol in many Indian communities, it was intensely insulting to have a great leader's name used in such a way. Many native people experience great pain when they see the hard-earned, ritually endowed feather headdresses of their ancestors mass-produced as stereotypes to market everything from beer to insurance.

For graphic designers, the trademark field presents two potential sources of ethical dilemma, particularly when design trends move away from abstract symbols to designs derived from vernacular sources. On the one hand, to the extent that trademarks are ubiquitous in the visual culture of commercial societies, they are widely recognized and carry great symbolic weight. It is tempting to incorporate existing marks into new designs because they are so instantly recognizable. Many artists, however, have been threatened with litigation when they have attempted to use trademark forms in new visual contexts (for example, the famous Crayola crayon package used as the basis for a novelty soap presentation). Some artists have deliberately decided to flout the law, using the trademarks of powerful corporations in transgressive works that comment critically upon corporate activities; they take legal risks when doing so.

Another dilemma arises for the designer who is asked to produce graphic trademarks for use in commerce; the legal freedom one has to use motifs, designs, images, and visual signs drawn from other cultures presents the artist with an ethical quandary. Without knowing anything about the traditions, lifeways, and political struggles of those with whom the imagery originates, graphic designers may produce works that are innocuous or merely insensitive. However, these appropriations may also be experienced as insults, if not serious affronts, to people for whom these expressive forms have histories and traditions that serve important continuing social and political needs. Our legal traditions are based upon particular premises that may not do justice to the values, norms, and aspirations of others.

*Originally published in Volume 14, Number 1, 1996.*

# SWASTIKA CHIC

*Steven Heller*

On May 19, 1933, German Minister of Information Joseph Goebbels decreed a "Law for Protection of National Symbols," which prevented the Nazi swastika from unauthorized commercial use and insured its integrity as a national emblem. After the war, the Allies' de-Nazification legislation, which outlawed use of the swastika as being indivisible from the Nazi party, inadvertently increased its symbolic power. Although the swastika originated in antiquity as a symbol of good fortune, the criminal ideology for which it came to stand should forever make it a charged icon that defies legitimacy. Today, use of the swastika as a graphic element is confined primarily to white supremacy groups and commercial publishers of books about Nazi Germany. The same cannot be said of other "Nazi-style" graphics, which have been incorporated into heavy metal, motorcycle gang, and skateboard ephemera—appropriation that may be aware of the genocidal racism that the symbol represents or indifferent to its historic context, a usurpation of the symbol's powerful visual impact.

In the 1970s, the rock group Kiss first introduced aestheticized Nazi iconography to the American youth culture by attaching the emblematic SS lightning bolts to the end of its band logo, thereby inspiring the widespread adoption of demonic German-looking graphic elements by other heavy metal bands. In doing so, Kiss encouraged music fans to accept this otherwise emotion-ally charged image as merely another pop icon. Kiss drew upon the inherent graphic power of this image, as well as its leather costumes and fright makeup, as a means to both shock and entertain its followers. Nonetheless, it seems incon-ceivable that the band members were wholly ignorant of the relationship between its logo and the mark of Hitler's dread *Schutzstaffel*, or defense squad, which administered all aspects of the Final Solution. The visual style of horror and heavy metal rock that Kiss helped pioneer was informed by a trend in gothic superhero and heavy metal comics, which coincidentally appropriated and exaggerated graphic devices from the same Northern European heraldic tradition that inspired much of Hitler's iconography. Nazi-derived graphics also appear on motorcycle gang regalia, a fact known to Kiss and its image makers at the time. Bikers deliberately adopted German-style helmets, Nazi pins, iron crosses, and other medallions to underscore their admittedly racist subcultures. Yet, since nothing else in the Kiss repertoire reveals an anti-Semitic or racist ideology, it appears that the band's fetish for Nazi heraldry was merely a flagrant disregard for the histori-cal significance embodied in these images. Nevertheless, the band must bear responsibility for trivializing the SS logo and helping to neutralize a potent icon.

The subsequent mechandising of heavy metal ephemera, such as death's-head necklaces (another SS symbol) and T-shirts bearing Nazi-derived marks, erodes the meanings of images built upon a legacy of inhuman behavior. Yet, substantive criticism has been all but nil; these images have been matter-of-factly accepted as part of this entertainment genre's overall identity, more or less sloughed off as stagecraft. One of the few critical stabs at the commercial Nazi style is the use of the *S* in the logo for *Spinal Tap*, Rob Reiner's 1985 film parody of a popular heavy metal band on its last, dismal American tour. Although they employ the icons, they are naïfs, not Nazi sympathizers. Moreover, the band's misadventures suggest that even the most tasteless portions of its act were done merely to get a rise out of its fans, often without regard for the ultimate implications of its acts. Such is the case in real life, too.

Although these perverse images have been trivalized, the ramifications are not trivial. In an age when even the crucifix has been reduced to a stylish fashion accessory, images reminiscent of Nazi horror and neo-Nazi racism are becoming more widespread and appealing to an ever-younger market—currently surfacing on skateboards and Pogs (collectible milk bottle caps) sold to boys between the ages of ten and seventeen. In the October 1995 issue of *Thrasher*, a skateboard monthly that dabbles in alternative politics, four advertisements for skateboards exhibit overt and covert Germanic/Nazi visual influences. The iron cross, the traditional German army medallion for valor (indeed, the only medal that Hitler ever wore on his tunic), appears as a component of an Old English logotype for Beer City Skateboards; a Kiss/SS-inspired lightning bolt is the centerpiece in the Germanic spiky Fraktur type for the Real Skateboard logo; a variant of a Flemish SS divisional badge is part of the logo for Vision Street Wear. And the logo for Z Products bears a striking similarity to certain current neo-Nazi iconography. Z Products' logo can be justified as influenced by heavy metal comics and Mortal Kombat video game graphics, but other graphics suggest a more sinister influence. A tear-and-peel promotional sticker with the logo for Follow for Now, a rock group, directly borrows from the logo of the Aryan Nations, a neo-Nazi hate group linked to a variety of political assassinations. And the logo for Focus, a skateboard company, combines two fascistic crosses used by the Ku Klux Klan in the United States and the Afrikaner Resistance Movement in South Africa.

We asked a twenty-two-year-old New York design student who has used Nazi-inspired imagery for a local band's graphics to explain why such imagery has appeal. After requesting that his name not be printed, he said that although he has no racist leanings, the Nazis had the best identity program he'd ever seen. "I don't use the swastika directly in my work, but I have twisted it around and distorted it while keeping the strong graphic look." When told that his imagery resembled some neo-Nazi logos, he responded, "I have never seen them, but I guess it's inevitable that, when working with these graphics, the result would be similar. While I don't want the band to be perceived as skinhead or right wing,

the logo is just so damn strong, and what's more, the war's been over for fifty
years."

Heavy metalists and skateboarders are not the only appropriators of Nazi
imagery. A few years ago, the Meat Producers of America hired a graphic designer
to strengthen its image and, instead, found itself in hot water. The designer
borrowed and slightly transformed a well-known poster by Ludwig Hohlwein, a
German artist and Nazi party propagandist for the Hitler Youth movement. The
original featured a poster boy in Nazi uniform, carrying a swastika flag; the Meat
Producers version substituted a cowboy suit and an American flag. Once in
public, the poster's unmistakable resemblance to the original was recognized and
the poster was quickly recalled from active service. It was also not selected for any
contemporary design shows. This is not the case for the identity and menus for
Lorenzo Ristorante Italiano, which appears in *Creativity 23* and is derived from
another of Hohlwein's posters, this one for Deutsche Lufthansa. Though this
poster did not include a swastika, it originally advertised the 1936 Olympic
Games that Hitler orchestrated to show off his "master race."

While serious "samplers" or "appropriators" of visual imagery argue that
stealing existing logos is a political act that either critiques meaning or empowers
the user, such thinking really shows a disregard for the power of certain key
symbols and the importance of not trivializing the most charged among them. As
eyewitnesses to the Holocaust die off and collective memory fades, a few indelible
images ought to survive intact, unappropriated, as reminders of historical truth.
While photographs certainly attest to Nazi crimes, the magnitude of Nazi geno-
cide demands that every trace of the regime be forever remembered. The various
symbols devised by the Nazi image makers for the most sophisticated visual
identity of any nation are a vivid reminder of the systematic torture and murder
engaged in by this totalitarian state. These pictures, signs, and emblems are not
merely clip art for contemporary designers to toy with as they please, but evidence of crimes against humanity.

*Originally published in Volume 14, Number 1, 1996.*

# BACK IN THE USSR (OR THAT UKRAINE TYPE REALLY KNOCKS ME OUT)

*Paula Scher*

It's funny the way something suddenly looks good. I was recently shocked to find that a couple of terrific El Lissitzky and Rodchenko posters had graced the pages of moldy art history books from my college days. In fact, there were Russian constructivist posters in all the poster collection books that I had accumulated over thirteen years, but, for some reason, I never really studied them until 1979.

I flipped by them when I was looking for Victorian inspiration. I ignored them when I was ripping off art nouveau and art deco designs.

I discovered El Lissitzky when I was heavily into my Cassandre phase. I remember flipping through *The Poster in History* and finding the black-and-white poster of a boy and girl whose heads were merging together. There was a giant red "USSR" running across their foreheads. "That's great!" I said.

At the moment I said "That's great!" I was back in the USSR. I knew I would look for more El Lissitzky posters and that I would incorporate the style into my own work.

I didn't say "That's great!" when I saw the poster in 1974. In 1974, I looked at the giant USSR foreheads and said, "Too weird."

If we want to predict future graphic trends, all we have to do is pick up poster books and tape-record our responses to various genres and periods.

Here's what the responses mean:

"That's Great"—What we are doing now, or will be doing tomorrow, even though every client will reject it.

"Nice"—What we have been doing for the past three years, and what we will resort to when "That's Great" is rejected.

"Tired"—What we have been doing for the past five years.

"Too Weird"—What we will be doing in five years.

"Too Ugly"—What we will be doing in ten years.

It is no coincidence that around the time I said "That's great!" to El Lissitzky, two Rodchenko books were published, followed by a big new Lissitzky book and *The Art of the October Revolution* and *Paris–Moscow* and *The Art of the Russian Avant-Garde,* plus the George Costinokos exhibit at the Guggenheim with the accompanying book, the Malevich book, etc. It was also no coincidence that many of my designer friends had gone "Russian crazy" at the same time. When five hundred unrelated people say "That's great!" at the same time and incorporate the influence into their work, it constitutes a movement.

In analyzing our response to Russian constructivism, I'm convinced that we're responding to our political and economic climate in both emotional and practical terms.

The work of the Russian constructivists represented the optimism of the Revolution and the Marxist utopian dream. But the late seventies and the eighties have been politically depressing times, a period of negativity, conservatism, and a general lowering of our personal and economic expectations. Constructivist work could make us feel we were creating a visual rebellion in inspired times. We could make a graphic statement that was visually strong, although there was no justification for it—another triumph of style over substance.

The practical aspect of constructivism is that it is cheap to do. A vigorous and "important"-looking graphic design can be had for the cost of typesetting and a few photostats.

The drawback to the constructivist design approach is that it is very difficult to sell.

First, the most logical use for it would be on jackets for Russian political books of that period. Unfortunately, publishing editors find type on an angle very difficult to read. This means that a good constructivist design usually is killed in favor of something "less complicated." Another editorial complaint is that it doesn't look "serious" enough. I confess that I don't understand this complaint. They were *dead* serious in 1917.

In four years, and umpteen attempts, I've only had three constructivist designs reach the printing press. Two were posters for a CBS Records promotion of the "Best of Jazz." The problem was to get twenty big names on a poster, not spend any money, and have it look good enough to motivate record-store owners to hang it up.

The wonderful thing about being a designer in the music business is that nothing has to mean anything. That doesn't mean that it's easy being a music business designer. On the contrary.

When I did the "Best of Jazz" posters in early 1980, the CBS Records marketing department didn't understand that I was being influenced by El Lissitzky. They were mostly concerned that the names were big and legible, and that the posters were cheap. The marketing department thought the posters were a little weird stylistically, but that was okay because it made them new wave.

After the "Best of Jazz" posters came out, I began getting calls from the graphics community asking me to submit work to various new wave shows. I would respond that I was not a new wave designer, and then I would be asked specifically for the "Best of Jazz" poster.

How can something blatantly ripped off from 1917 be considered new wave?

Gene Greif, a designer who often displays some constructivist influences in his work, told me recently that when he showed his portfolio two and three years ago, everyone said it was "too new wave." "Now," he tells me, "everyone says it's too postmodern."

I've never liked labels. Constructivism certainly has had an enormous impact on the way I design, but so has nearly every other movement in art history, at different times.

It's 1983. I still think El Lissitzky is "great," though sometimes I think he's merely "nice." I think I only have one year left in the USSR.

*Originally published in Volume 4, Number 1, 1984.*

# DESIGNERS ON A DISK®

*Rhonda Rubinstein*

Some things never change. 1:53:48. Three hours to deadline, and I haven't started the design for this new client. Time to launch a caffe latte on the espresso machine, load some ethnotechnopop on the CD player, and surreptitiously install the upgrade to the hottest designer software program, Designers on a Disk®.

Naturally, some designers were shocked when Designers on a Disk was released in the late 1990s. After all, its ad campaign—"Become the famous designer you've always wanted to be!"—was rather presumptuous. But really, to proclaim that the program would "at best, encourage ubiquitous knockoffs, and, at worst, degrade the entire profession"! How could anyone resist its direct application of the hypermedia formula: technology, infotainment, and financial gain?

With Designers on a Disk, even former typesetters and color separators like me can produce work that looks like it was designed by a brand-name graphic designer. I can be Piet Zwart for a day or Eric Gill for a night. The program characterizes the works of twenty-five graphic innovators and provides a framework in which to use their specific design elements. So now I can create film titles that pay homage to William Caslon or supermall signage à la Neville Brody.

Even back in 1992 there were early versions of automated layout programs for Macs, PCs, and NeXT systems. Their aesthetics were a bit questionable (*jazzy* hadn't really been considered a design term), but the electronic spoon-feeding of the "layout made easy" principles was happily accepted by thousands of consumers. The better programs, like Designer 4.0 and Personal Press for the Macintosh, provided numerous templates that could be tweaked, just like real designs. To cook up a corporate identity, the user simply poured in the essential ingredients: company name, address, and so on, which were then combined into their choice of letterhead templates. Voilà: instant stationery.

Architecture climbed one step higher in template-assisted designer software in 1993, with Possible Palladian Villas. Armed with disk and manual, ordinary people were creating country houses and garages of imposing grandeur and aesthetic harmony. Despite the increase in porticos in Portland, the program produced buildings that went beyond cut-and-paste miniatures of Palladian villas. Some said that they could have been designed by Andrea Palladio himself, had he not met with his death four centuries ago.

2:27:33. Two and a half hours to deadline. I begin by launching the voice-activated program and Select a Designer. Today, I'll pay tribute to the art director of that giddy moment of optimistic elegance in 1993. I ask for <Fabien Baron>, mention a period: <Harper's Bazaar>, and choose a format: <Book cover>. Here's where I get to take advantage of the upgrade, which lets me choose how "designed" I want this to be. Fabien asks, "*Alors*, how much will I have to work?" On a scale from zero (minimal nondesign) to one hundred (maximum overdesign), I venture a suitably illegible eighty-five. The tools have been customized so that I have a choice of two typefaces, Firmin Didot and Stymie Black Condensed. Thanks to facsimile font technology, I can run this program without having to buy all twenty-five designers' favorite fonts. Designers on a Disk caused a rare action of solidarity among the remaining four type suppliers—Monotype, Adobe, FontShop, and FunkyfontFrenzy—who attempted to encode their fonts to prevent them from functioning on any computer on which Designers on a Disk was installed.

Fabien asks, "Point size?" I suggest 60. "*Non, non!*" Fabien tsks. Point sizes in <Fabien Baron> range from 6 to 18 point or 150 to 500 point only. Leading and letterspacing also have their limits: from solid to negative 50 percent. I reconsider: "180 point Didot justified, set solid with negative 10 percent kerning" and receive a Baronesque "bing" to say, okay, he'll allow that. Color families are muted four-color palettes. Images can be any size so long as they're full page. Rules and ornaments do not exist in <Fabien Baron>.

If I had a little more time, I might have given the client the option of something less modern and airy, something more traditional and intricate, such as <William Morris>. I could listen to the Arts and Crafts visionary explain the value of workmanship and utilitarian beauty as I create a unique replica in the style of <Kelmscott Press (1890–96)>. With the choice of Morris's medieval typefaces—Golden, Troy, and Chaucer—and an array of illustrative initial caps and repeatable decorative borders and ornaments, how could I restrain myself from filling every pica of the page?

Although time is finite, the possibilities are endless. I could have selected <Charles S. Anderson> and done something really fresh and new. I could have designed my own late 1990s version of a late 1980s version of a late 1940s ad.

This is much more exciting than screening halftones: it's no wonder designers want to keep it to themselves. But that's no reason for Tibor Kalman to dismiss Designers on a Disk as "a compromising marriage between a design historian with a talent for exploiting the obvious and a software company desperate for content to repackage in order to maintain its market share." At the 1997 AIGA conference, the panel was so busy debating the ethical ramifications of digitizing design heroes that it barely had time to consider the rewards of royalties. Those designers who were not in the computer playroom eagerly trying it out were furious that the program's unveiling at MacWorld had been greeted with such awe. Design professionals didn't want to accept that just anyone with a computer and a slim reference book of design history would be able to mimic the great designers. After all, it was only designers who really had the proper training.

One hour till deadline. 4:02:27. The type is perfect on the cover of *Graphic Design in the 1990s: The Middle of the End.* Now if only I can convince <Fabien Baron> not to use the pricy digital stock photo of Marky Mark's crotch. . . .

*Originally published in Volume 12, Number 1, 1994.*

# UNDERSTANDING MEDIA

# DESIGN FOR THE MASSES

*Julie Lasky*

In 1968, John Leonard, then editor of the *New York Times Book Review*, cata-logued the many virtues of paperbacks: "They can be stuffed in purses, left on buses, dropped in toilets, used as coasters, eaten and thrown away. Their covers can be ripped off! *Their spines can be broken!* To buy a paperback today is to buy the means of revenging oneself on Western culture."

What a nice departure from the sanctity of the printed word, he might have added. What a relief from monumentality and preciousness. Contrary to what snobs believe, mass-market paperbacks aren't always about drugstore ro-mances, although they often are. They aren't about glitzy cover design either, although this often prevails. They are about comfortable informality and the cheerfully infinite potential for abuse. The literary hardcover is the formal living room of the publishing industry: elegantly designed, expensively crafted, some-thing to care for and preserve. You enter this room reverentially. You do not put your feet on the furniture or use it for pizza parties. Mass-market paperbacks, on the other hand, are rec rooms, where people spend most of their time doing the things they like best: watching porn, screening Antonioni movies—no matter, the place accommodates almost every interest. These spaces might be tastefully appointed or stuffed with all the junk that didn't fit into the attic. Either way, if you live in them long enough, the scuffed linoleum will always remind you of floor-hockey games. The teeth marks on the arm of the threadbare sofa may be all that's left of old Rover.

This flight of fancy presumes, of course, that your own mass-market paperbacks (and those belonging to other people) accumulate on your shelves, as mine do. There's an even better chance, however, that you toss out your books after you've finished reading them or pass them along to acquaintances, wonder-ing if you'll ever see them again. The publishing industry expects this of you. Fifty percent of the estimated 20 million mass-market paperbacks published each month fail to survive long enough even to be bought. "If a title doesn't make a splash within two weeks," says George Cornell, vice president and art director at Viking Penguin, "the books are returned to the publisher and destroyed." The other 50 percent have a slightly longer lifespan—perhaps two or three reads before the binding falls apart.

Disposability is not the point here, cost-effectiveness is. "The important factor in a mass-market paperback is price," explains Jackie Merri Meyer, vice president and art director at Warner Books, whose mass-market titles include contemporary bestsellers by Sidney Sheldon, Ruth Rendell, and Janet Dailey, as well as classic fiction, such as *To Kill a Mockingbird.* "As someone once said, we don't want the price of a book to be more than the cost of a chicken."

To maintain cost-efficiency, mass-market books are jammed with small type that leaves little room for margins. According to Steven Brower, vice president and art director at Carol Publishing, who spent two years at the beginning of his career working for George Cornell at New American Library (NAL), paperback reprints of hardcover titles are shot directly from the pages of the trade edition, which have been cut up and pasted onto boards. This crude production technique, combined with the use of newsprint and a web press, yields a degraded look. Generally, however, newsprint quality has improved since the days when the edges of softcovers were stained red, yellow, or green to help hide discoloration of the paper.

"There's no reason to have quality paper in a paperback," adds Meyer. "These books are very much like magazines: they're used up and then usually discarded. Money goes into the cover because it really is an advertising tool, which I think people forget."

The mass-market subculture isn't easy to pin down because it involves everything from bodice rippers to pocket dictionaries. Apart from price and paper, common features are format (roughly 4 × 7 inches), wholesale distribution (supermarkets, newsstands, drugstores, and airports), and design conventions that are intended to catch the eye of an impulse buyer and that vary with the category of paperback being marketed. Romances usually feature the hero and heroine embracing on the cover—an attitude known throughout the industry as "the clinch." True-crime stories tend to employ photos of gangsters and serial killers. Science fiction is an excuse for weird, hyperrealistically rendered illustration. (It also strangely lends itself to the use of Victorian typefaces, says Brower.) Fictional crime stories written by lawyers, a category that took off with the publication of Scott Turow's *Presumed Innocent* and has supplanted espionage novels since the end of the Cold War, favor symbolic illustration ("Got your gavel, got your scales, got your legal thriller," observes Cornell). Tying the different categories together is the "big book look," which emphasizes title and author with large, condensed type, leaving about a third of the cover space for a spot illustration unambiguously keyed to the book's contents.

As Meyer observed, the cover is crucial to mass market because it is the dominant, if not the only, means of advertising a title. Exceptions are made for blockbuster, or "lead," titles pushed through advertising campaigns, but such books represent a small percentage of the industry. Although some of Warner's mass-market paperbacks are distributed in bookstores and purchased by customers who have made a special trip to acquire reading material, books that are sold through wholesale outlets must appeal to people whose first order of business is buying dinner or catching a plane. "This is a glitzy, high-embellishment market," Meyer says, referring to the frequent appearance of foil, embossing, and die cuts on covers. "These are not people who read a review (paperbacks are rarely reviewed) or saw the author on the *Today Show* or always buy mysteries because they happen to love mysteries. We're hitting the person who is going through the supermarket counter and will look at something on the rack and say, 'Gee, I don't have a date Saturday night.'"

Meyer furthermore recognizes that some readers attracted to mass-market titles at a newsstand may be embarrassed to display the books in public, and she routinely matches the demand for high embellishment with a dignified presentation—not always an easy thing to do. Comparing the challenges of mass market to those of trade, Cornell adds, "There's a difference between being able to design a cover that's subtle and pretty and designing one that's going to compete on a rack with hundreds of other titles. Also consider the fact that when I put my product out there, I'm not only competing with other books, I'm also competing with other products."

Given these challenges, it's no surprise that mass-market designers are irritated by the condescension with which the design community treats their work. Invoking popular perceptions, Brower calls mass market the "bastard stepchild" of graphic design, and Meyer uses a similar word, "stepdaughter." "There's a lot of elitism about mass-market anything," she says. "It's made me a little bit bitter over the years because it's unfounded and arrogant, and because I've never had an outlet to say this. I've heard designers absolutely trash any book cover with foil on it, but meanwhile it's okay if they use foil on a corporate annual report. To me, you can use foil tastefully in both cases, and people who say there's a big difference between the two are full of themselves."

"We may not be aware of the cutting edge of graphic design," adds Cornell, "but we're aware of personal taste. I still like to think that underneath all the category material we do there is some social benefit to having the amount of products we put out there."

Bringing the greatest amount of reading material to the widest possible audience has been a goal of book publishers since the early sixteenth century, when Aldus Manutius designed the first small-format ($3\frac{5}{8} \times 6\frac{1}{4}$ inches) editions of classical literature. Even then, Aldus was merely extending the socialist principles introduced by Gutenberg with the invention of movable type. Calligraphic manuscripts were unwieldy because monks found it easier to copy and illuminate large sheets of vellum. And what was the point of portability, anyway? It was hard enough to find a literate person to whom one could lend an expensive manuscript, much less a trustworthy one who could be counted on to return it. Once books proliferated and literacy increased through the invention of movable type, however, it was only a matter of time before someone perfected the movable book.

Paperbacks, as we know them, emerged in the early nineteenth century, with other populist products of the industrial revolution, and organized themselves into the two basic roots of today's mass-market industry: reprints of hardcover literary titles touted for their affordability and convenience, and pulp fiction that evolved out of penny dreadfuls and true-crime magazines. In Oscar

Wilde's play *The Importance of Being Earnest,* Gwendolen Fairfax boasts of carrying her diary wherever she goes, so that she will always have "something sensational to read on the train." Were she not a well-bred Victorian woman, she could have chosen any number of thrillers and romances from a genre known as "railway fiction"—cheap editions whose lurid cover illustrations were designed to capture the attention of train travelers. (These books were also known as "yellowbacks" because of their eye-catching yellow spines or covers.)

When Pocket Books, the first of the American paperback houses, opened its doors in 1939, its list was quite respectable in the manner established several years earlier by Penguin and Pelican Books in England. Among the first titles Pocket published—in print runs of ten thousand—were an Agatha Christie mystery, James Hilton's *Lost Horizon,* and *Five Great Tragedies* by Shakespeare. A 1939 reprint of *Wuthering Heights* coincided with the release of the William Wyler film starring Laurence Olivier and Merle Oberon, and thus was the practice of movie tie-ins begun. As the paperback industry found its market through whole-sale distribution centers, the two branches merged; even high-toned literature was packaged with provocative covers to attract readers who might not appreciate the literary merits of the title or author. For example, a 1951 Signet edition of Paul Bowles's *The Sheltering Sky*—a tense, harsh, and almost clinically unerotic novel—featured a man with chiseled features and rakishly disordered hair caressing a Saharan bombshell beneath the legend: "Strange Romance in the Exotic Desert."

Pocket Books was named for one of the primary virtues of paperbacks—in fact, the company coined the term—and its earliest advertising promoted the ease of carrying around the little volumes. Introducing conventions that have endured in mass market to this day, the books featured typography as the dominant cover element and prominently displayed the publisher's logo and 25¢ price sticker. As an indication of the industry's entrenchment, Brower observes that when HarperCollins removed the price and logo from the front cover of its recently founded paperback line, "It was actually, within the world of mass market, a very bold thing to do."

A quarter remained the standard price for paperbacks until 1950, when Pocket introduced its 35¢ Cardinal Editions imprint and designed the covers with gold foil to make the cost appear justified. Foil has been a cliché of mass market ever since. In *Undercover: An Illustrated History of Mass Market Paperbacks,* Thomas L. Bonn points to the influence of greeting cards, which use foil, die cuts, embossing, gatefolds, and rack displays—all common features of mass-market design and retailing. Cornell notes that foil is common on perfume packaging, one of the many products that compete with paperbacks in drugstores.

Constrained by practical requirements of distribution and sales, and wedded to traditions that may no longer even make marketing sense, paperback design is sheltered from the fads that besiege other sectors of the design community. "We're still in the tight-not-touch world," explains Meyer, referring to the heavily kerned cover typography of popular books. Brower recalls being handed the assignment of designing Regency romance covers ("I learned more about swashes than I thought I'd ever know"). Whenever he was given the chance to work with a new author, he vowed to clean the slate and do something that would set his covers apart from all the examples that had been handed to him as models—something that would convey a unique sensibility behind the clichés or at least have a certain typographical elegance. About a year after he left NAL, however, he returned for a visit and saw a display of romance novels the company had published. "I couldn't tell which ones I'd done," he admits.

And yet, the industry is not so formulaic that Brower can't distinguish the work of different mass-market art directors. "NAL covers usually have dramatic imagery and strong type treatments," he observes. "George does not use a lot of foil; he fights it. On the other hand, the covers designed by Jim Plumeri at Bantam, which are very stark for mass market, are dramatic because of their starkness, not because of their imagery. And then I can always tell Jackie's covers because they look like small-trade covers a lot of times, and she uses trade illustrators."

Meyer is, in fact, adamant about crossing the boundary between mass market and trade. The illustrators Brower referred to include Paul Davis, Bascove, Wendell Minor, and Mel Odom. And Meyer is as enthusiastic about packaging a hardcover with a touch of glitz as she is about bringing a sense of refinement to a paperback title. Although her peers insist that she has achieved rare license within the industry, she believes that her efforts to cross over represent a larger trend. Pointing out that Knopf, among the most prestigious publishers in the country, designed a trade book with an acetate jacket ("If that's not a mass-market idea, I don't know what is.") and issued its paperback version of the novel *Damage* with small, elegant type, she says, "One of the reasons the lines have become blurred is because art directors like myself have been pushing to let publishers know that we believe the taste level of the audience is higher than they think it is."

Certainly, few can dispute Meyer's observation that, as cable and video infringe on the book-buying market, only really dedicated readers seem to be left. This portends interesting developments for designers, she suggests—if the high and low ends of the industry are forced to compete for the same audience, trade publishers will more freely adopt the aggressive design strategies of paperback lines, while mass marketeers will be able to appeal to more elevated tastes.

The image of the book publishing industry under siege does not portend well, however, for those who enjoy an S&M relationship with their library. If Meyer is right, John Leonard will have to revise his assessment. To buy a paperback will not be the means of revenging oneself on Western culture, but of preserving one of its remnants. In short, we will all have to be very careful not to drop our books in the toilet.

*Originally published in Volume 11, Number 2, 1993.*

# MAGAZINE DESIGN: THE RATIONALIST'S DREAM?

*a symposium edited by Steven Heller*

Leo Lionni said there is nothing like designing a magazine: "It's a rationalist's dream—in which the elements of architecture, sculpture, and film come into play." Once, a handful of magnetic magazines influenced our thoughts and perceptions; now, the newsstand is awash with more varied magazines than ever before. Though publishers admit that business has never been better, is it as euphoric for designers and art directors? Is the magazine still a fount of visual innovation or a well of conservatism? What, indeed, remains of the "great behemoth" tradition, when oversized magazines were springs of serendipity?

For a discussion of this issue, nine designers, whose bloodlines go deep into magazines of the past and present, were asked to comment on the role of magazines and their art directors in the eighties. The participants were: Cipe Pineles, director of Publication Design at Parsons School of Design and former art director of British *Vogue, Seventeen, Charm,* and *Mademoiselle*; Henry Wolf, president, Henry Wolf Productions, Design & Photography and former art director of *Harper's Bazaar, Esquire,* and *Show*; Leo Lionni, current AIGA medalist, former art director of *Fortune* and editor/art director of *Panorama* and *Print*; Sam Antupit, vice president and director of design of Harry N. Abrams and former art director of *New York Review of Books, Art in America,* and *Esquire*; Milton Glaser, partner in WBMG and former design director of *New York* magazine; Will Hopkins, of the Will Hopkins Group, art director of *American Health* and former art director of *Look* and *American Photographer*; Walter Bernard, partner, WBMG, former art director of *New York* magazine, *Time,* and design director of *Fortune*; Ronn Campisi, design director of the *Boston Globe,* former art director of *Fusion, Boston* magazine, and the *Real Paper*; and Paul Davis, designer, painter, and art director for the New York Shakespeare Festival.

*How have magazines changed in the eighties?*

**Pineles:** Magazines today are timid. They have no self-confidence. There aren't many magazines that are so certain of their mission that they don't put the whole ball of wax on the cover. The entire contents are given away. The decline of the magazine rests on the need to outdo the competition on the newsstand.

When I started, this business was a free-for-all for inventive layouts and ideas. The editors frequently turned with great eagerness to the art department to solve their problems—ideas were needed and wanted. More important, it was a time when advertising looked to editorial for inspiration, not the other way around.

Now the well (the uninterrupted section of editorial content) has been relinquished to the advertisers, which underscores the problem because the well defines the magazine. It's how the magazine fulfills its promise to the reader. It's hard today to find more than four spreads in sequence in any magazine.

**Wolf:** The art director can only be as good as his or her bosses, the editor and the publisher, and I think there aren't any editors like *Esquire*'s Arnold Gingrich around anymore. Today the advertising departments run magazines, but once there was a kind of congressional immunity for editors. None of the editors I knew in the fifties and sixties would have stood still for today's page breakup. How can you build a feature layout in the women's magazines, for example, when so many pages have a quarter-page ad for salad dressing in the left-hand corner? It's like going to a museum where every other room is a bathroom. You can't develop the pace. And the pace depends on having a stretch of pages where you can have points and counterpoints, features and bridges. The decreased size of magazines is only a symptom, rather than a cause. I don't even mind the new sizes. Magazine design is essentially the relationship between the full page and the smaller elements. Of course, it's not fair to accuse magazines of becoming advertising devices. They always were, only in better days, the editorial department had priority.

**Glaser:** Something happened to the magazine in the sixties; it was the loss of potency. There was a moment when magazines were instrumental in American life, in terms of shaping opinion and shaping perception. What happened was that television basically replaced the magazine in its dominance.

Professionalism also took its toll. With the earlier magazines, it was as much the mistakes and the misunderstandings that created vitality as it was the professionalism. In fact, I would say that the greatest handicap for vitality today is too much professionalism. The risks are diminished because everybody knows what sells, everybody knows about editorial balance, everybody knows that you have to use a lot of cover lines. But this kind of methodology basically yields predictable results. In those days, it was the lack of understanding that protected art directors and editors, by creating things that sometimes didn't work and that other times were extraordinary. What we've done in professionalizing the activity is protect the possibility of failure at the bottom and also cut the top off the imagination.

**Antupit:** I think that art directors today have too much impact. It's increased astronomically in recent years, and most of the magazines are overly art-directed, resulting in a lopsided ratio between what should assault the eyes versus what must be assimilated by the mind. Editors are relying on design to sell lame ideas. They are bamboozled by the mystique of graphics, thinking it can do more than it can. A good editor should collaborate with graphics. Instead, today's editors seem to have rolled over dead, allowing graphics to swarm like the marabunta, those man-eating red ants.

**Bernard:** Magazines are forever changed. Now that's an awful statement to make because I don't mean that they have stopped changing. But people do not get their primary source of visual information from magazines anymore. Magazines no longer say: "We're going to show you something for the first time that will knock your socks off." Since their primacy is diminished, magazines are changing in terms of the way they apportion space. Now they dress for success. Advertorials (independent advertising supplements enveloped by soft editorial features) have taken over. With them, the quirkiness and serendipity of design is lost so that the Calvin Klein ads are more inventive than the editorial.

**Hopkins:** The proliferation of specialized magazines has contributed to the problem, and many art directors don't have any particular interest in the subject matter; therefore, there is a lack of passion and concern for their content. The kids today, because they have no connection with the past, are out there reinventing the wheel, and I wish they would move on and get the hell out of this ornamental stuff, which most of the time has nothing to do with the content of what they're dealing with.

Magazines are also suffering from demographics. It seems like many magazines are developed for media buyers, who don't read anything, and can look at a design and say, "That's a good environment for me to be in." That's not what design is all about.

**Campisi:** In the past, magazines relied less on a formula and more on the instincts of the art director. The art director's impact has changed. Magazines are products in a crowded marketplace. Marketing has become more important than ever. Along with that, consistency has become a necessity, and the role of the art director at most magazines is to *maintain* that identity. The question is: Who determines the identity? More and more, it's not the art director, but the publisher, editor, and circulation director.

Much of the reason why magazines are no longer an exciting medium has to do with specialists designing engineered messages that get produced in a factory-like manner. Hence, magazines tend to have standardized content.

*How has the qualitative standard of magazine design changed today, for better or worse?*

**Hopkins:** I feel like an old fuddy-duddy talking this way, but, nevertheless, there were once basic aesthetic standards for magazine design that do not exist today. There was also a lineage that was broken at the beginning of the seventies. Major magazine art departments were like farm clubs. It was a training ground. And these clubs put many talented people, with design standards and a knowledge of history, into the marketplace.

It burns me up that art directors have no notion of structure. You see, the well scares the hell out of advertising departments who don't know what it can do for them. They've all but obliterated it. And now that the precedent is set, it gets continued by the young art directors who just follow the herd. They don't know any better, they don't know there's another way.

**Pineles:** There is currently a middle-of-the-road kind of work without any real peaks of brilliance. We don't look at a new magazine with the idea of seeing exciting graphics. That mantle has been inherited by the coffee-table book.

**Antupit:** The reason for generic, look-alike magazines is that most art directors make use of the same contributors, so it makes magazines look homogeneous. The seminal magazines fostered new illustrators and photographers to help establish an identity for themselves.

**Glaser:** There are many standards and principles of magazine design. The fashion magazines, using a cut-and-paste look, figured out a way to make their product look casual, sprightly, and lively. That means that since the spirit is more important than the words, they became increasingly devoted to that principle— and people responded to it. Part of the new professionalism is an unabashed catering to the responsive market. But what you don't get now, which you used to get (or maybe it was just an illusion), was the sense that somebody was doing something out of passion and out of his or her own obsessive need to invent some kind of form, or to say things in a particular way, and simply let the audience make a judgment about whether it liked it or not. Now there's endless second-guessing and preconceived ideas of what the audience wants in an attempt to accommodate all those things before the publication even gets started.

Design, like any vernacular language, depends so much on the moment as well as its own history—the balance between what is current and what is classic is an issue that all individuals decide, in their minds, how they want to address. Some people really want to be on the fashion-turn and some people want to be behind it. Some people have loyalty to ideas that are forty years old.

There is a tribal allegiance too. That's why a lot of the stuff that doesn't make any sense in terms of conveying information nevertheless creates a certain kind of atmosphere that people want to identify with.

*Do you feel that there was a golden age of magazines?*

**Bernard:** Maybe the Magazine Publishers Association would tell you this is the golden age of magazines, but it's not a visual one; it's simply a profitable age in which there are now a lot of magazines making money.

**Antupit:** There were a lot of golden ages, with seminal magazines at each stage. Though *Vanity Fair, Harper's Bazaar,* and *Vogue* were terrific in themselves, I would not call them seminal because their influence was on other things, such as advertising. The first was *Harper's Illustrated* magazine during the mid-nineteenth century. That was a perfect example of classic magazine design. There were no demographic studies to see who liked what kind of illustration and no eye-motion measurements studies to see whether the illustration should be on the right- or left-hand page. Next, in the early 1900s, there was an interest in magazines for children, such as *St. Nicholas* and *Chatterbox.* Those designs were sensitive to frivolity. In the thirties came the French *Verve.* It embodied the jazz age look and featured original lithographs bound into the magazine. In the fifties, it was *Twen.* Nobody could do photographic spreads as well. The most recent seminal magazine was *Ramparts,* which is what *New York, Time,* and even *Newsweek* merely adapted, consciously or not.

**Davis:** I don't like the phrase *golden age* because it suggests that there isn't a chance of anything as interesting happening again. But looking back, it seems that such an age existed from the mid-fifties to the mid-seventies. There was a revolution in design, illustration, and photography. There were strong art directors who were willing to take risks and, hence, gave opportunities to innovative illustrators.

The difference between then and now is that these art directors saw illustrators as artists with something of their own to say, rather than as renderers of other people's ideas. I don't know why this changed, but it has. Today, the roles of the art director vis-à-vis the editor seem diminished. Illustration is mostly eclectic rehash. That may be, in part, because there is no single place to look for what's happening or for young illustrators to get the kind of exposure to make them stretch.

*Art directors used to shepherd magazines for long periods of time. Under the tutelage of Agha, Brodovitch, and Hurlburt, to name a few, many others came up through the ranks. Now the turnover from one magazine to another is pronounced. Where does the talent come from these days?*

**Glaser:** The talent to lack-of-talent ratio is always pretty much the same historically. The engine of will is what really produces results. I think that what happens is that you have to be really obsessive about wanting to do something, and then you use your talent.

**Pineles:** I perceive a lack of talent now. At the time I was working on magazines, there was the *Vogue* studio where photographers were given space in which to experiment. There was a great deal of interest in finding new talent on the part of the editors.

**Wolf:** Magazines once offered the opportunity for new talent and, moreover, encouraged their contributors. Artists and photographers would bring in something, and, if it was good, it would get used. There was really a point to seeing an art director because work was used, even if it was useless for selling anything.

*How do the magazines fare aesthetically?*

**Campisi:** Specialized magazines have had a bad effect on the quality of art and design. They look the same and use the same formulas.

**Wolf:** Magazines today spend a lot of money. I've done covers for some of these. Many commission four covers per issue on the same subject, then they make a big decision about which to run. It is almost an axiom that the ones with least artistic merit will get printed—the ones with the least change from the usual.

**Glaser:** There's always a lot of bad work around because excellence is a rare quality. There's also a lot of camp following, copying, and plagiarism. It makes magazines tribally unified. Each generation, to some extent, wants to invent the forms that it feels represent it and reject the history of what's preceded it. It's a kind of narcissistic self-display.

**Antupit:** Except that new wave styles have added a sprightly clutter to a few recent magazines.

*How can an art director function effectively and meaningfully within the constraints of publishing today?*

**Lionni:** An art director should be an aestheticist and should work within a span of personal taste because that's the only way to do a good job. Taste is the specialization, but, within that, the art director is a problem solver. First of all, one should know what kind of magazine it is and for whom, and then determine the highest level of performance that can do justice to that subject. Then, the art director should give it an identifiable form and, within that identifiable form, as much variety as possible. And always within that limited taste, one must be continuously innovative, since that is the nature of the beast. The real challenge is to have unity with freedom.

A magazine is not simply a *mise-en-page* of type. It is a *mise-en-page* of meanings—expressed in type, photographs, illustration, or all together.

**Antupit:** The ideal working relationship between art director and editor is yin and yang. A respect for each other's intelligence and abilities, not just authority, has to be the rule.

**Bernard:** Something good can happen if the art director doesn't make believe he or she is living in a nonexistent world. That doesn't mean compromise as much as it means understanding the purpose of the magazine. You cannot pretend, if you're working for a small boat journal, that you're working for *GQ,* or if you're working for *GQ,* that you're working for *Life.* The worst working relationship between an editor and an art director is like the husband-whose-wife-does-not-understand-him syndrome. I hear too often things like: "My art director is weak or cantankerous." But usually these are euphemisms for a lack of communication in which the art director refuses to understand what the magazine is all about.

*What are some of the other problems affecting this era of magazine publishing?*

**Glaser:** One of the main reasons for the decline of the magazine is a strange sort of social and professional change. Before, there was more of a true dialectic among editors, art directors, and contributors—in a sense. Magazines are now done internally. They are no longer communal activities, wherein the people who contribute to a magazine also define what it is. The procedure now is for the editors and the art directors to create the product totally, and then find people to execute it.

**Bernard:** In the magazine classes that I've observed, I am surprised at the usual exercises. The students are given the easiest, most superficial visual problems in the world and allowed to use pickup material. They end up believing that magazines are made that way. They are rarely taught to deal with anything demanding or difficult.

**Hopkins:** Not since the early sixties have I heard an art director say: "You write the words, and I'll design my page." But I hear that now. If that is the case, then a magazine is no different from an annual report.

**Antupit:** Clay Felker once said that there are cycles to magazines; they come, and they go, and they should be allowed to die. The problem with many magazines is that something has been pumped into them to keep them artificially alive. And a lot of what's being pumped in is an ersatz chicken soup called design.

If the magazine content is good and the design isn't exemplary, people will accept it, I'm certain. When the content is irrelevant, the magazine is irrelevant. But once people are aware of only the design, it's all over. There is still a terrible sour taste caused by the demise of the *Saturday Evening Post,* when it had more design per square inch than anything produced in the country. It wasn't the design that killed it. It was already dead. The design was just the elaborate wreath on the casket.

*Is there a future for magazine designers?*

**Glaser:** It's sad when you have any vehicle that has imaginative or creative potential and it's not utilized. A beautiful glass can be used to convey champagne or muddy water to your lips. Likewise, the magazine is still a wonderful vehicle for ideas. There's nothing that can move you like a beautiful drawing or a beautifully told story. But there is not enough demand for that level of excellence. In all these cases, if a single person does something extraordinary with some consistency, everything changes. The great encouraging factor is that individuals make a difference.

*If asked, would you redesign an institution—the* New Yorker?

**Wolf:** I would try. But I would make a clause that if I didn't think it was successful, I could abandon it. I was at McCann when it redid the Coca-Cola trademark. I said, "Why touch it? It's got a hundred years and a hundred million dollars behind it. Why change it when you're not really going to change it anyway?" And that's what happened. It was hardly changed.

**Glaser:** First, I'd have to determine for what purpose. I certainly wouldn't redesign it to improve its visual content. But if the *New Yorker* came to me and said: "Our average reader is fifty-seven and dying, we're losing 5 percent of our circulation to old age alone, and we're not getting enough interest from the college kids," then maybe the form of address would have to change. But, in the Platonic sense, in terms of pure form, upgrading the graphics is not the answer. No one can really answer that question out of context. There are, however, a few things I always said I'd like to do at the *New Yorker.* I would like to know how long a story is before I begin—so thank heavens it put in a table of contents. Also, I would like to know who the author is before I start.

**Bernard:** I think it doesn't have to be redesigned. If the *New Yorker* changed dramatically in its visual presentation, it would be an entirely different magazine. What interests me about the *New Yorker* is that if it did not exist, it could not be invented today. And if invented, it could not survive. One could never get investors to support a cartoon/literary magazine today.

**Antupit:** Absolutely. I'd probably wreck it. But, the *New Yorker's* design no longer reflects the editorial content of the magazine. It was originally designed as a frothy fiction magazine. Now the analysis pieces are some of the best writing in the world. I think that the *New Yorker's* design is a disservice to its current material.

**Campisi:** Sure. It's only a magazine.

*Originally published in Volume 3, Number 3, 1985.*

# DESIGNER 'ZINES

*Paul Lukas*

Thanks to desktop publishing, editorial entrepreneurs all over America are cranking out more self-published fanzines, chapbooks, and newsletters than ever before. These amateur publications, usually just called *'zines,* run the gamut from awful to brilliant and back again, but most have one thing in common: the person designing them is usually not a trained designer.

Sometimes this means the 'zine is pretty much unreadable; often it means the best the reader can hope for is a design that doesn't get in the way. Occasionally, however, oddball concept and inspired execution combine to become more than the sum of their parts. Here are five excellent 'zines whose designs, whether by accident or intent, fuse nicely with their editorial thrust:

*Crap Hound*: The downfall of most 'zines is bad writing, but *Crap Hound* avoids this trap by featuring almost no writing. The 'zine consists primarily of clip art, which editor Sean Tejaratchi arranges according to a different bizarre theme for each issue ("Clowns, Devils, and Bait," for example, or "Sex and Kitchen Gadgets," which have more common ground than you might think). Tejaratchi, who carries a little pair of scissors on his key chain for on-the-spot clipping and has amassed a line-art archive numbering in the tens of thousands, is something of a 'zine rarity: he actually is a trained graphic designer. It's his biting sense of the absurd, however, that makes *Crap Hound* the best 'zine in America today. (Send $6 cash (or check payable to S. Tejaratchi) to P.O. Box 40373, Portland, OR 97240.)

*Other People's Mail*: Whereas *Crap Hound* reproduces found graphics and thereby sidesteps any chance for bad writing, *Other People's Mail* simply reproduces bad writing. The 'zine is exactly what its title says: straight repros of found letters, notes, love poems, and similar hand-scrawled ephemera, complete with bad handwriting, bad spelling, bad grammar, bad emotions on display, and all the rest. The material is assembled by editor Abby B., who combines her considerable snooping skills with the efforts of a small army of contributors (including at least one sticky-fingered copy-shop employee) to come up with a sensational read that should please cultural documentarians and cheap voyeurs alike. Designwise, it's nothing special, which is precisely the point—when you're printing a bunch of other folks' discarded communiqués, the best thing to do is to just stand back and let them speak for themselves. (Send $2 cash to *Other People's Mail,* 106 Morningside Drive #92, New York, NY 10027.)

*Fuck Everything*: Another 'zine that lives up to its title, *Fuck Everything* describes itself as an "equal-opportunity despiser," and that turns out to be pretty accurate. But it's not just nastiness—it's articulated nastiness, with a cleverness that belies its sociopathic agenda. This 'zine is essentially an extended inside joke aimed at every sacred cow on the postpunk, indie-rock scene, with venom and savagely funny vitriol in hilariously ample supply. The best part of the joke is that anyone laughing at it is likely to be skewered as the next target. As for the "design," pseudonymous editor Tokin' Dylan sticks mainly to a primitive cut-and-paste collage approach that makes you wonder if he has opposable thumbs. But it never quite turns into the mess you expect it to become, mainly because he appears to know exactly what he's doing. The result is a publication that looks and reads the way good punk rock sounds, which was once the whole idea behind this 'zine thing in the first place. (Send $1 cash to P.O. Box 40521, Redfern, MI 48239.)

*(Sic) Teen*: The crudity of *Fuck Everything*'s nondesign raises an interesting question: What happens when troglodytes learn how to use computers? The answer can be found in *(Sic) Teen,* another 'zine that leans toward the visceral. Originally published in the 1980s as the venerable *Sick Teen,* with a brilliant Xerox-collage approach sort of like *Fuck Everything* raised to a higher power, this 'zine disappeared for six or seven years, and then resurfaced with a slightly ad-justed title to reflect editor Norb's passage into, uh, adulthood. It's unclear what Norb did with all that downtime, but he definitely spent some of it learning Quark, as *(Sic) Teen* now features a slew of desktop tricks that would have been unimaginable in the 'zine's initial incarnation. While the overall feel is clearly slicker and never approaches the chaotic levels of information overload that characterized the original *Sick Teen,* for the most part Norb has been successful in using his newfound technological prowess to further the basic feel of his very entertaining writing and to evoke the aura, if not the precise look, of his nondesktop days. In short: a gimmick-heavy design that actually works, and from the last guy I would have expected. (Officially available for 53¢, but just send $1 cash to P.O. Box 1173, Green Bay, WI 54305.)

*Dishwasher*: One way to avoid employing bad typography is to dispense with it altogether. *Dishwasher* is one of several 'zines that are completely hand-lettered, and it's easily the best of the lot. *Dishwasher* works sort of like a diary, charting the nomadic movements of editor Dishwasher Pete, who's well on his way toward realizing his dream of washing dishes in all fifty states. In between ruminations on the metaphysics of dishwashing culture, Pete manages to fill out the 'zine with dishwashing-related comics, interviews, and historical features. His genuine enthusiasm for a task most of us would consider utter drudgery is part of *Dishwasher*'s considerable charm, which makes his painstaking hand-lettering all the more inviting. And don't worry—it's completely legible. (Send $1 cash to P.O. Box 8213, Portland, OR 97207.)

*Originally published in Volume 14, Number 3, 1996.*

# SKATEBOARD GRAPHICS: NOT READY FOR PRIME TIME

*Jennifer Kabat*

**Y**ou hear the wheels on the pavement before you see anything. Then he skates right past you and *ollies,* which is skater lingo for jumping. There's a flash of color off the bottom of the board, a hint of an image, nothing really—certainly nothing that registers as art. Most people just dismiss skateboard graphics as skulls and crossbones anyway.

Skateboarding's such a closed world, outsiders have no way of really knowing it. It's like an obscure fraternal order with secret handshakes. Or a soap opera, as one artist, Alyasha Owerka-Moore, described it. Then again, the company he co-owned, American Dream, Inc., just got dumped by Deluxe, its parent company, and its other co-owner in a three-way split. The ensuing storm of accusations and counteraccusations is too difficult to follow. Obscure, as I said.

None of that's too surprising, not when you've got companies run by guys, pro skaters who by twenty-four are at the end of their career and need to diversify, so they're given these companies, divisions of larger conglomerates, to head. The big companies usually manufacture a few lines of skateboards, clothes, shoes, wheels, trucks, and magazines, and are owned by guys (also ex-skaters) who are just slightly older than the pros. Business is done with a handshake, oral contracts, trust. If the subdivision isn't doing that well, the owner can end up in a compromised position. But, "it's all good," "it's all about fun," and "you can do anything you want." That's what people say about this laid-back corporate culture.

"I would skate the things I skate and the way I skate even if I didn't have this company. It's not like I'm putting on a clown suit and doing back flips hoping some kid will buy a piece of me," Chris Pastras tells me as we walk up the stairs to his house, a big warehouse space on the edge of San Francisco's Mission District. Outside, someone is shooting an old fifties-style radio for a graphic. Chris heads up Stereo, a division of Deluxe he started when he "got sick of riding for other companies." He's responsible for just about everything at Stereo—the company's team, ads, look, graphics, and image. Its look is so unapologetically nostalgic, borrowing so heavily from fifties and sixties jazz album covers, that it would never fly in the straight design world. But Chris doesn't worry about how kids see the graphics.

Skaters are pretty traditional consumers, though. They buy based on brand image, which currently depends on how punk rock, hip-hop, East Coast, or bad-assed a company is, as well as which pros ride for the company. There are so many companies with similar images that they all blur together; it all comes down to graphics. That's why Ed Templeton, the owner/pro/artist of Toy Machine, "thinks about what would make me look at the board and notice it, or what would be funny on that board, what I'd laugh at if I walked into a shop. The whole purpose of a graphic is for that five minutes when a person comes into a shop and looks at it. Once a kid buys it, it gets wrecked anyway."

Boards get trashed really quickly. The top graphic is covered with grip tape before the skater ever takes the board out, then the bottom gets ruined in action. Depending on how one skates, the board is broken and destroyed in a couple of weeks. So there's a constant need for new graphics. People won't buy the same board twice, particularly in the current market. New boards are released in editions of a thousand or fewer every month. Once that series is sold out, that's it for that graphic. "This started about five years ago when skateboarding slowed down after the eighties and World Industries [one of the big conglomerates] started flipping boards over all the time, so the shops would want to buy new ones and started forcing this mentality of new, new, new," Templeton adds. People in the industry describe the market as hopeful that kids will buy just to get something new and different, even when they don't need a new board. They criticize the way things are done, but still accept that standard.

World has really set the tone for how the industry looks and works. Shortly after he started flipping boards over more quickly, Steve Rocco, World's owner, got in a big dispute with store owners. They refused to sell his boards, saying their look was too explicit. He then got skaters to boycott the stores, breaking their hold on him. Now companies and artists can get away with just about anything, giving skate graphics their gnarly rep.

World established the T&A, cartoony, violent, misogynist look of board graphics. It's easy to dismiss them, as a couple of artists do, as just "spread-eagle chicks" or the "bright neon colors and bad-assed, sex-and-violence-oriented images that would stir a kid's mind, make him run home, grab his mom's pocket-book, and steal forty or fifty bucks." Yeah, they are juvenile and shock for shock's sake because sex and violence is an easy formula to sell, particularly with kids. But skating's a "fuck with you" industry targeting adult standards, the status quo, and traditional mores of good taste.

"That's what we love to do. We really live to fuck with people, particu-larly adults," Cleon Peterson says. He's the artist for Foundation Skateboards. Cleon's not just some juvenile, though, he's a "serious" artist whose paintings have been influenced by the artist David Wojnarowicz. We also talked about the issues and problems with the last Whitney Biennial—you know, grown-up high culture. He sees his boards on another level than his art. With skateboards, he tries to give people something to think about, "a story involved in the picture for people to figure out, not just something that looks cool, that's just a design." He calls his Barbie board "cynical and real." It has "Bondage Barbie packaged with a dildo and Straight-from-the-Pen Ken equipped with action arm, yelling 'Get me a beer, kids.'" It's a pretty wicked commentary on contemporary culture—funny, too. Surprisingly enough, Mattel never noticed.

Cease and desist orders are pretty common in skateboarding—so many boards rip off corporate logos. Using trademarked material for graphics started as a cool way to do a bit of guerrilla warfare aimed at the big mac daddy corporations. A board like Jason Lee's, where his name is sandwiched between the trademarked Burger King bun halves, garnered a letter from Burger King's lawyers telling his company to cease and desist production and send the rest of the boards to Burger King. Of course, by that time, the boards were long gone. After a few years of these kinds of boards, it's getting old and easy. Now they and the World-type graphics are falling out of fashion.

Five years is a long time for something to be around in skating. Styles change frequently, and now simpler graphics are in. People are buying "logo" boards that sport a company's logo. According to Cleon, "Kids like logos. They're not into graphics; they like generic things. Everyone wants to wear a big Nike logo and Adidas." There's a lot more consistency in graphics and ads now, which is pretty amazing considering at one point World used to change their graphics every week.

Another company, Girl Skateboards, is even making ad campaigns. They're a bit like a miniseries that will run for few months tying together the boards, ads, and catalogs and repeating graphic elements and themes. You never used to be able to repeat anything. Kids reading the magazines are always looking for something new, checking out the tricks, the latest thing. Ads are traditionally really formulaic, too. They have to be different each month and show an action shot. You "can never repeat an ad or else you'll get slapped down," Girl's art director, Andy Jenkins, says; so he'll run a series in a few issues until he gets bored with it or thinks kids will.

Artists are taking board graphics more seriously. They're looking at them as a powerful tool to communicate their ideas and philosophies like Chris Johanson's graphics for Antihero this past year. He's sick of the "ambiguous messages" on most boards—the "clichéd images of sexy chicks and violence." He tries to present a more real image of the world, thinking carefully about the art's impact on the kids looking at it. American Dream—not even a year old when it dissolved this winter—used its boards to explore issues of race and culture. For one board, Alyasha Owerka-Moore, ADI's artist and co-owner, took a photo he found of a black man shackled to a tree and ran it with "Emancipation: 1865–1995?" written underneath. The bold graphics and stark image couldn't help but cause controversy and discussion. Ed Templeton drops some commentary into his boards, too, slipping fake subliminal messages from "the consumer control center" and "the toy machine blood-sucking corporation" into his ads along with bits of philosophy to get kids to think about what they're seeing and buying.

The next wave of trends in skateboarding probably won't be clear for a while, not at least until 1998, when skateboarding hits its next boom. Right now, the questions are just forming. The industry is shifting from its old model partly because fashions change, and the people creating them, building the industry, are getting older. Now, too, skateboard graphics are being taken seriously as "art." That changes the terms. Is it art, is it fun? What? It certainly is more than skulls and crossbones.

*Author's note: I'd like to thank Aaron Rose and Alleged Gallery, Tobin Yelland, Dave Carnie, Mike Mills, Neil Feineman, Ron Allen, and Ed Templeton for sharing their insights and resources.*

*Originally published in Volume 14, Number 2, 1996.*

# THE MYTHOLOGY OF ADVERTISING
*Randall Rothenberg*

How does advertising work?

Mr. Whipple, Coca-Cola's polar bear, and the Bud Bowl—how do they make us, Mr. and Ms. Consumer, buy things?

Most Americans believe advertising works by subliminal manipulation. Old-timers in the advertising industry claim it works via persuasion, while their younger colleagues say it works by entertaining us. Sociologists think it works by creating a cultural context favoring the acquisition of goods.

But if you spend time burrowed deeply inside the belly of the ad industry, you discover that advertising works—when it works at all—by a different means altogether. It succeeds by creating mythology—a mythology often so subtle and private that it can be understood only by a small fraction of the audience for which it is ostensibly intended.

It's no small issue for American business and for our overtaxed, overwhelmed, media-drenched minds. Companies in the United States will spend $120 billion on television and radio commercials, newspaper and magazine ads, billboards, and myriad other forms of marketing communications this year, according to Robert Coen, a respected forecaster at the giant advertising agency McCann-Erickson.

And, lord, will we watch! By one count, Americans are exposed to some 3,500 ads each day. By our watching—and the product purchases that presumably follow—we help advertisers pay for *ER* and *GQ*, Rush Limbaugh and Larry King, *Nightline* and the *New York Times*.

How does it affect us? Three-quarters of all Americans believe that images, words, and sounds are secretly embedded in the media to sell products subconsciously, according to the *Journal of Advertising Research*. So convinced are we that such hidden messages work that we spend $50 million a year on subliminal self-help products.

Belief in the power of subliminal advertising dates to the late 1950s and an experiment allegedly conducted by an ersatz marketing researcher named James M. Vicary. Vicary claimed he had used a tachistoscope, a device that could flash images on a screen at speeds of 1/60,000th of a second, to transmit the messages "Eat popcorn" and "Drink Coca-Cola" to patrons of a movie theater in Fort Lee, New Jersey. Although the images could not be perceived consciously, moviegoers exposed to them increased their purchases from the concession stand, buying 57.5 percent more popcorn and 18.1 percent more Coke, Vicary said.

Later, Vicary admitted that he had faked the data: indeed, a subsequent investigation indicated that the ballyhooed "Popcorn Experiment" never took place at all. But the publicity surrounding the test-that-never-was made an impression on the public—subliminally, as it were. The near-simultaneous publication of Vance Packard's bestseller *The Hidden Persuaders* (which was not about subliminal manipulation but the ham-handed efforts of Madison Avenue to use Jungian archetypes in advertising design) only served to reinforce the widespread conviction that we are but pawns of the evil geniuses of "Adland."

The continuing popularity of Wilson Bryan Key, the former journalism professor whose books, notably *Subliminal Seduction*, have sold more than 1 million copies since 1972, attests to the power of the thesis. (In his most famous example, Key claimed to have found—embedded in a single magazine ad for Gilbey's gin—the word *sex*, a leering face, three naked women, two men, partially erect male genitals, and semen.)

The problems with the subliminal thesis are twofold: nobody does it, and it doesn't work. A recent study published in the *Journal of Advertising Research* and using a projectible "probability sample" showed that almost no advertising or media professionals surveyed had created or used subliminal messages in ads. "Evidence suggests that the few positive responses were due to a misunderstanding of the term *subliminal advertising*," the study's authors concluded. For good reason: at least five other studies conducted between 1979 and 1992, according to the journal, have "refuted the possibility of eliciting predictable responses" to subliminal ads "that could be useful to marketers."

To advertising professionals, this is no surprise. Their job, they say, is *to persuade*, a process that takes place at a supremely conscious level. "If advertisers tell people to do something over and over, people will do it," Chris Weir, a market research expert at the BBDO agency, told an interviewer from the Smithsonian Institution who was conducting an oral history of the agency's Pepsi-Cola campaign.

Certainly ads can persuade. Who among us has not been moved by notice of a fabulous sale at Macy's, or by the announcement of a great new product from

IBM or Chrysler? But the contention that the persuasiveness of advertising is a testable fact—that is a different story altogether.

For decades, advertisers have relied largely on recall tests to prove the effectiveness of their advertising. And time and again, they have proved virtually no connection between the memorability of an advertisement and its ability to induce us to buy. Even Leo Bogart, a longtime official of the Newspaper Advertising Bureau and one of the preeminent researchers in the business, has said, "From the evidence, it appears that while there is more than a random relationship between recall and persuasion, it is not all that better than chance."

Most advertising "creatives," as the writers and designers call themselves, agree with Bogart that "measurement can only distort and falsify" the true power of advertising, which lies in its ability to arrest the eyeballs, to touch the emotions—in short, to entertain.

The ad industry's entertainment impulse dates to the 1950s. With a populace grown more sophisticated and acquisitive because of the G.I. Bill, suburbanization, and the baby boom, marketers had to work harder to differentiate their products. Then, when congressional investigations into sponsors' rigging of television quiz shows, fictionalized in the recent Robert Redford film *Quiz Show*, led the fledgling television networks to separate the advertisers from the programming, the agencies had to make advertising as appealing as the shows themselves.

By the late 1950s, two of advertising's more enduring innovations had been developed. David Ogilvy connected the concept of "brand image" to words and pictures that, while divorced from the product, told a story that conveyed an impression about that product and the people who used it. It was Ogilvy who invented both "the Man in the Hathaway Shirt" and "the Man from Schweppes." And, under the leadership of Bill Bernbach, agency copywriters and art directors began working together, in teams, to create something that had, by and large, been absent from the advertising that had gone before: the Idea.

The Idea was more than just a fact about a product or service. It was something—a story line, a theme, a tone, a look—that somehow gave the advertising an aesthetic appeal. For Volkswagen, Doyle Dane Bernbach's Idea was "honesty." The execution—a forlorn little car set again a stark white background, with the startling headline "Lemon" identifying a flaw perceptible only to the auto's demanding engineers—was funny, and very, very real.

Advertising's entertainments have been largely Rockwellian or vaudevillian. Consider McCann-Erickson's grand 1980 paean to Coca-Cola, a spot entitled "Mean Joe Greene." In it, the massive football player staggers off the field, only to encounter a little boy who has sneaked his way past the guards. The boy offers a bottle of Coke to the distracted jock, who at first refuses, but then accepts it. Ignored, the kid turns away. The gridiron great calls to him, and when the boy turns, the smiling player tosses him his towel. "Wow!" exclaims the child. "Thanks, Mean Joe!" "Have a Coke and a smile," concludes this *Saturday Evening Post* cover come to life.

For vaudevillian advertising—with a bit of postmodern self-referencing thrown in—try the recent BBDO spot for Pepsi, featuring a fierce Shaquille O'Neal of basketball's Orlando Magic. In it, Shaq tears up a playground, demolishes a backboard, and turns opposing players to toast. Sweating and thirsty, he sees a tiny boy holding a can of Pepsi. The music turns romantic. The lad stares at O'Neal adoringly. In slow motion, the ballplayer, his heart melting, moves to claim the beverage from his fan. As he is about to grab it, the kid, without missing a beat, says, "Don't even think about it."

Away from prying clients, advertising creatives rarely talk about whether these entertainments "work." For them, such ads are a chance to play Hollywood. One of the crisis points I witnessed during a two-year observation of Subaru of America's effort to retool its image was the breakdown between the ad agency and the commercial director it hired to film its ideas. At the peak of their dispute, the director, a veteran of *Interview* magazine and Talking Heads music videos, blurted out: "This is not commerce. It's—I hate to say it—art."

Such people consciously model their efforts on the work of film directors. The fact that Hollywood filmmakers Ridley Scott, Adrian Lyne, Hugh Hudson, and David Puttnam all got their start at the same London advertising agency hasn't gone unnoticed on and around Madison Avenue. One copywriter at Fallon McElligott told Smithsonian historians that the agency's ads for Federal Express were consciously modeled on the movies *Brazil, Metropolis, Modern Times,* and *Blade Runner.*

But do their efforts work? Here, again, the jury is out. While some studies show that consumers' aesthetic appreciation of an ad—a factor the pros call "likeability"—will predict whether people will buy a product more accurately than recall or other traditional measures, others refute the conclusion. A 1993 study by Research Systems, a company in Evansville, Indiana, for example, found out that humorous ads wear out as rapidly as do other forms of advertising.

Maybe sociology holds the key to understanding advertising's impact. In his influential book *Advertising, the Uneasy Persuasion,* University of California sociologist Michael Schudson posited that advertising's power derives from its ever-present but unacknowledged articulation of the values of American capitalism.

Through the acquisition and ownership of goods, our private satisfactions—of family, friendship, and kinship—are enhanced, advertising informs us. It doesn't persuade or manipulate us so much as alter our perceptions over time. Advertising, in Schudson's formulation, is a form of "capitalist realist art." Like the socialist realist art of the Soviet Union, which idealized workers and their public lives, American advertising "subordinate[s] everything to a message that romanticizes the present or the potential of the present."

Of course, this scholarly construct, while eminently reasonable, only purports to describe the influence of advertising—all advertising—over time. It can't even begin to fathom why we might go "koo-koo for Cocoa Puffs" or "come to Marlboro Country."

For that, we have to turn elsewhere. For "the great Idea in advertising," Leo Bogart has written, "is far more than the sum of the recognition scores, the ratings, and all other superficial indicators of its success; it is in the realm of myth, to which measurements cannot apply."

That consumption can be a religious experience, with advertising its hymnal, were once considered laughable notions. Marketing researchers preferred to describe human behavior via the safer, more denatured concepts of brand "loyalty" to and consumer "involvement" with goods. Then, in the summer of 1986, an itinerant group of university professors, experts in marketing theory with special interests in psychology, literary theory, and anthropology, hopped in a van and crisscrossed America to observe consumer behavior in sites their traditionalist peers conventionally ignored.

In swap meets and flea markets, community festivals and museums, gas stations, bookstores, supermarkets, restaurants, and homes, they took out their tape machines, cameras, and notepads to record the ways men, women, and children transacted business and sheltered their wares.

The researchers (who referred to themselves and their venture as the Consumer Behavior Odyssey) observed a middle-aged seller of homemade dolls, which she began making only after a car accident rendered her unable to bear children, who kissed each of her fabric creations on its forehead before releasing it, with a blessing, to an equally reverential paying customer. The Odyssey scholars interviewed an elderly couple who purchased a home, built a lake on the property, and gave their children pieces of furniture hewn from the walnut trees they'd removed from the lake site. From such surveillance, these marketing experts reached a conclusion that has altered the course of consumer research.

"Consumption," the Odyssey affirmed, "involves more than the means by which people meet their everyday needs. Consumption can become a vehicle of transcendent experience; that is, consumer behavior exhibits certain aspects of the sacred."

The Odyssey scholars found in the shopping experience and the treatment of goods the very properties of sacredness people exhibit toward religious items and inside houses of worship. Ritual and mystery, a belief that sacredness manifests itself, a willingness to sacrifice, community and ecstasy—all were present when men and women beheld their favored wares.

Certainly, the religious basis of consumption and the mythological dimensions of marketing are no secret to advertising experts. Advertising has even appropriated the language of myth: in commercial production, the gorgeously rendered, beautifully lit product shot that closes a spot or sits centered in a print ad is called, simply, "the hero." Like the hero of myth, the advertising hero is, to use Joseph Campbell's words, "perfect, unspecified, universal," a teacher of the "lesson . . . learned of life renewed."

But the American advertising industry has routinely assumed that the only object of its heroic narratives was the consumer—the hapless outsider, easily conquered by the siren songs of Madison Avenue. It too often fails to consider that its myths must be relevant not only to the consuming public, but also must ring true to the men and women inside their companies. For if the tribes do not believe, how can they proselytize effectively?

The most inventive American marketers have long understood that marketing must look inward. When General Motors was trying to rebound from the financial crisis that nearly bankrupted the corporation in the early 1920s, it turned to Bruce Barton, the co-founder of the Batten, Barton, Durstine & Osborn agency.

At the time, General Motors was little more than a financial holding company sewn together from the bits and pieces of small, independent automobile companies and suppliers. As the historian Roland Marchand recounts, the company was the embodiment of the "soulless corporation" social critics loved to attack. Worse, the managers were still far more loyal to their once independent divisions than to the meaningless construct known as G.M. It required what its visionary leader, Alfred P. Sloan, Jr., called "a working-together spirit."

Bruce Barton came back with the recommendation that G.M. undertake its first corporate advertising campaign—advertising that was separate and apart in intent and content from the campaigns of its automotive divisions. And Barton counseled that the new campaign promote the idea of the General Motors "family"—a word that served simultaneously as a description of the company's lineup of products as well as a humanizing agent for the corporation itself.

In guiding the campaign, Barton made clear that its target included not only the public, but the corporation's own managers, employees, dealers, and sales personnel. The "famous family" advertisements were posted inside factories and auto dealerships. The adman told G.M.'s senior executives that spurring new sales had to be a secondary goal of the campaign: its primary purpose was to spread goodwill inside and outside the company, a prerequisite for sales.

At a time when his competitors on Madison Avenue were claiming that advertising was a science with predictable results manifested in consumer response, Bruce Barton affirmed that advertising's influence was more internal and spiritual. "I like to think of advertising as something big, something splendid, something which goes deep down into an institution and gets hold of the soul of it," Barton wrote. "Institutions have souls, just as men have souls."

Subaru of America—the maker of quirky, decidedly unfashionable four-wheel-drive cars, and a company I followed for two years in an attempt to come to grips with the power of advertising—knew all about souls. When it began its search for a new advertising agency in the spring of 1991, like a pilgrim wandering from ashram to ashram, the car company was self-conscious in its affirmation that it was seeking "the soul of Subaru."

The company also knew it needed to express that institutional soul with a mythological tale of heroic dimensions. The ad agencies competing for its account, in their bardic role, presented the car company with a full range of heroes, drawn from the chrestomathy of ancient myth, from which to make the choice.

One agency positioned Subarus as "cars that can," the four-wheel-drive vehicles by which families could be brought together despite impassable mountains, muddy riverbeds, tropical rainstorms, and frigid snowdrifts. This was Subaru as Odysseus, "the man of many ways, who was driven far journeys . . . yet straining to get sight of the very smoke uprising from his own country."

Another agency called Subaru "the perfect car for an imperfect world." This was the auto as Jesus, the "master of two worlds," the "guide, the way, the vision and the companion of the return" from God in heaven to the fallen on earth.

A third agency commanded consumers to drive Subarus "for all the right reasons." To this ad shop, the car was the Nietzschean *Übermensch,* a "higher form of being," which combined "spiritual superiority with well-being and an excess of strength."

A fourth agency said Subaru was "the car that will change your mind." That slogan referred to the auto as Buddha; it did not reveal the Truth, but in ads that recounted a supposedly typical consumer's sales experience, Subaru, like Buddha, could illuminate the path to ultimate Truth.

None of these alternative mythologies persuaded the corporate executives themselves. In their hearts, they knew their cars were physically unappealing. They had great transmissions, to be sure, and they lasted forever, true, but, well, they were dowdy. They weren't outwardly heroic. This is the way Subaru's designers and engineers had built the cars for decades, and these were the cars the dealers knew how to sell.

For Subaru, an advertising agency crafted a special campaign. Its ad conceded that a car was "just a car," whose "sole reason for existence is to get you from point A to point B." Despite its hidden, internal powers, "it won't make you handsome, or prettier, or younger." Subaru, in this agency's formulation, was a funny-looking, manic-depressive, whiny but nonetheless superstrong automobile that could still run rings around every other vehicle on the road. This was no hero; this was an antihero. This was not Odysseus or Christ or the *Übermensch* or Buddha. This was the car as Spiderman, by night the web-spinning, sixth-sense-possessed crime fighter, by day nerdy Peter Parker, overwhelmed by life.

It was the perfect evocation of what Subaru was—the underdog, ugly but superior, fighting against long odds. It matched what the company's own insiders knew it to be. "As soon as I learned of their pitch, I knew they won," said Kunihiro Sakurai, an executive at Kentsu, the agency that has handled Subaru in Japan for some twenty years.

When this campaign was introduced, an auditorium full of dealers erupted in thunderous applause. "That," said one dealer, who had seen years of declining sales, "was as good as an orgasm."

To succeed, advertising must reinforce and redirect the existing image— the soul—of an organization. It must serve as a form of mythology, giving the corporation's various and often competing constituencies—of which consumers are only one of many—the heroes, villains, principles, rules of conduct, and stories with which they can rally the faithful to remain true to the cause. Only then, with luck and effort, can they win new converts. If consumption is the religion of advanced capitalistic societies, then advertising is its bard—the singer of tales composed to remind believers of their past triumphs and their rendezvous with destiny.

Is Pepsi "the choice of a new generation" because young people prefer it—or because Pepsico is, forever, the upstart out to topple stodgy Coca-Cola? Is Chevrolet "the heartbeat of America" because patriotism sells cars—or because its dealers, who in earlier times trilled "see the U.S.A. in your Chevrolet" and "baseball, hot dogs, apple pie, and Chevrolet," see themselves as the nation's muscle and life?

Think about it the next time you're wondering what lies behind the thirty seconds.

*Originally published in Volume 13, Number 2, 1995.*

# A DECADENT IMAGE OF GLORY

*Michael Anderson*

The iconography of athleticism, paradoxically enough, is less concerned with action than with attitude. Sports photographers face eternal frustration in the effort to record the defining moment; hence the proliferation of visual clichés: the slide in baseball, the dunk in basketball, the collision in football, the nose-to-nose finish of horse racing. All form a sort of shorthand to suggest the fluid grace of motion.

As documentarians, sports photographers depend uncommonly upon luck: that they are in the right position at the right moment where angle and perspective converge and the story can be told within the frame. For example, in Manny Millan's breathtaking image of Magic Johnson's winning shot in game four of the 1987 National Basketball Association championship series, one can see Johnson's leap, just above the outstretched lunges of three Boston Celtic defenders, with the eyes of Celtics coach K. C. Jones joining those of 13,909 anxious fans to watch the ball in midflight. But take the case of the most celebrated sports photograph in history, which depicts Willie Mays making his over-the-shoulder catch of Vic Wertz's fly ball in the 1954 World Series. As a spot news shot, it is remarkable. However, less famous, unjustly, is the series of photographs that shows Mays making an abrupt stop, then throwing from the deepest center field in baseball to hold the Cleveland Indian runners on base. Even viewed in sequence, these photos do not elicit the gasp provoked by watching the play on film, when Mays seems to sense exactly when to extend his glove while running at full speed with his back to the ball. Or again: the characteristic image of Babe Ruth, so familiar that it is the basis for a postage stamp, shows him holding his bat upright, gazing into the air, tracing the arc of a home run. The action is outside of the frame.

The frozen moment of the sports photograph must not only summarize accomplishment—the triumph of will over physical limitation, the concentration of skill, the determination to surmount pain unto agony—it must also contain meaning; perhaps, in collaboration with the viewer, the sports photograph creates meaning. Two standard shots of boxing matches illustrate the difference. Outlined against the light, face distorted by the impact of the opponent's blow, sweat exploding from the fighter's head—thus, the bout as shown in the tabloids, time and time again, the approximation of the action. But more memorable, even if the names of the fighters are forgotten, is the winner standing over his fallen foe, as in the great photograph from 1965 showing Muhammad Ali snarling over a prostrate Sonny Liston. There we have the essential tableau of victory and defeat.

Indeed, the evocation of the atavistic is the secret appeal of sports: in place of the civilized table of values, good and evil, is a brutal standard, winning and losing. The frisson of confrontation is raw, elemental; and confrontation is the essence of every sports photograph, even in Robert Riger's shots of Warren Spahn winding up or Sandy Koufax staring at his catcher for a sign—the invisible opponent asserts his presence. (The most chilling evocation of the invisible opponent is in Riger's haunting photograph of a thoroughbred, Lake Erie, galloping riderless after a collision during the 1959 Belmont Stakes.) The confrontation can be with gravity, as in the sculptural shots of Michael Jordan dunking or of Marjorie Gestring suspended in midair in the stills from Leni Riefenstahl's *Olympia*. It can be with time, as in Riger's shots of Seattle Slew winning the 1977 Kentucky Derby and Wilma Rudolph finishing the 400-meter relay in the 1960 Olympics.

Bill Russell, the philosophical center of the Boston Celtics, once remarked that sports fans respond only to the rawest of emotions. Primitive indeed is the suspense of the athletic contest, which is why its thrills are so vehement: the sensation of victory is narcotic in its intensity and brevity, the shatter of defeat is as devastating as it is trivial—the pain can linger because it essentially is unimportant. What remains are the athletes, each the focus of hope and fear, and perhaps that is why sports photographs become a study of faces. Riefenstahl's film *Olympia* is an unfolding ballet of flowing forms and striking poses. The book of stills is most memorable for its portraits: Glenn Morris preparing to launch a javelin, the Japanese marathoner Kitei Son in victory, a concentrated Jesse Owens preparing to outdistance his competing runners. The pioneering Charles M. Conlon snapped the much-reproduced photo of Ty Cobb sliding into third base in 1909. More than the cloud of dirt, what is memorable is Cobb's clenched-teeth grit. However, most of the photographs Conlon took from 1904 to 1942 are posed studies of individual players, their faces a marvelous panorama of early twentieth-century Americana. Walter Iooss has continued this tradition of baseball iconography, as in his portrait of Yogi Berra: the pinstriped back bearing the number eight hunched over on a baseball diamond.

The images of athletes' faces almost inevitably become studies in suffering. Nothing is so banal as the winners' locker room, with its hackneyed rituals of spraying champagne and boisterous cheering; the onlooker feels excluded and covertly resentful. (Perhaps one reason Magic Johnson became an icon was the sheer incandescence of his joy. His smile overflows to the brink of caricature, yet is so powerfully contagious that the spectator happily surrenders.) What has proved most memorable are images of loss. No image of Babe Ruth's homers can rival the devastating beauty of the photo showing his bowed figure acknowledging teammates and fans at his farewell to Yankee Stadium. The archetypal image of Mickey Mantle does not illustrate that sweet powerful swing; rather it is Robert Riger's shot from the 1961 World Series: Mantle has swung and missed, his body twisted but his face more so, a horrifying mask of physical agony. The athlete in decline—the lion in winter—gives the most poignant image for Conlon, whose yearly portraits illustrate the slow deterioration of a generation. Riger's shot of Forrest Gregg, the offensive tackle for the Green Bay Packers, shows sports iconography in all its tensions: the white teeth startle in contrast to the mud-caked helmet, face and uniform; is it an image of joy, sorrow, exhaustion, triumph?

As with the best of illustration, the sports photograph at its summit depicts a decadent image of glory—decadent because the confrontation with fate is as ancient and familiar as humankind. Yet, in depicting the anxious encounter with complacency, the expectation of defeat, the quick snatch of success against an implacable destiny, the sports photograph reminds us that there is indeed a glory to be found in the human condition.

*Originally published in Volume 14, Number 2, 1996.*

# IDENTITY AND ICON

# THE TYRANNY OF THE SWOOSH

*Phil Patton*

## 1. AT THE MALL

**A**t the mall, we walk into the athletic shoe stores, marveling at how many there are—Athlete's Foot, Foot Locker, Take Me Out to the Ball Game, Herman's—and how many new models appear between visits. My kids and I check out the latest arrivals rack: new carbon composite Nike Air basketball shoes, the new white patent leather Jordan. We regular mall marchers have noticed something else: how the Nike swoosh has more and more and more come to decorate products in the vast Nike line—floating all by itself, an icon, without the company name.

The swoosh has become one of the most powerful logos of our era. It ornaments—and here an epic catalog is required—not just shoes but caps, running suits, socks, scarves, headbands, and water bottles. It is set on ovals at the end of wire racks and embossed in leather jackets, printed in trompe l'oeil embroidery patterns on hang tags, upholstered in shiny white patent leather, marked out in mesh on warmup suits, cut out of neoprene and raised in suede. Part of the effect is to produce flocks, schools, swarms of swooshes floating across displays of caps, of socks, of shirts.

At Niketowns, the company's showcase stores-cum-museums in Portland and Chicago, the swoosh becomes a three-dimensional form, rendered in chromed steel as part of the stair and balcony rails designed by in-house architect and design whiz Gordon Thompson. Now, it marks a construction elevator on the site of the Niketown building on Fifty-seventh Street in Manhattan. In one of Nike's television ads, featuring Dennis Hopper, the swoosh in the oval morphs into a bone in a steak, a clever video pun in the tradition of MTV and the Disney Channel on-air logos. And *Swoosh* is the title of a book recounting an insider's view of the rise of Nike.

The swoosh's liberation from letter and word began about three years ago, when Andre Agassi won the men's championship at Wimbledon. It happened like this, according to Ron Dumas of Nike. Nike had signed up Jim Courier and designed a line of clothes that emphasized his Americanness by taking cues from baseball uniforms—stripes and a cap that displayed just the Nike swoosh, like a Cleveland Indian or a Florida Marlin. But Agassi donned the same cap; when he won, his picture decorated, among other media venues, the front page of the *New York Times*. The swoosh caps became popular, and Nike designers and marketers saw the usefulness—as they tried to expand sales outside the U.S.—of a logo that transcended language. So the swoosh began to break free.

The swoosh-marked products that mall walkers encountered during the fall of 1995 became part of a wider design transformation. Beginning with a top-level meeting in September, Dumas and other designers persuaded top Nike management to use the swoosh logo, sans the more familiar lettered name, as the keynote of a whole corporate image rehaul—a change in everything from hang tags to boxes to stationery and business cards. The old logo, with the Nike letters, says Dumas, seemed very eighties. It had a big, corporate feel to it. The swoosh, by contrast, has something pure to it. And, Dumas reports, recognition of the swoosh alone as Nike's symbol ranged above the ninetieth percentile in consumer surveys.

The swoosh may be the most widely visible icon in sports, and in a world of global marketing, it joins a list of very few trademarks completely free of association with names or letters. Think for a moment and you will note how short the list is: McDonald's Golden Arches, although even here there is a visual pun on the *M* of McDonald's; the Shell scallop, perhaps; the bold Texaco star; the three-pointed Mercedes star; the Chevrolet bowtie; the tortured hieroglyph associated with the artist formerly known as Prince; and, to smaller audiences, Apple's apple and Greyhound's dog (cleaned up by Raymond Loewy).

Evoking a checkmark and a boomerang, the swoosh may be unique in suggesting movement and sound. As one Nike ad reads, "Swoosh is the sound you make blowing by somebody." Abstract and rather graceful, it is also an extremely versatile graphic element. But, ironically, one of the advantages of the swoosh by itself is that it goes well with other images. The swoosh appears in cross-licensing deals almost as an imprimatur, like the Olympic rings. Nike's growth from running shoe company to basketball shoe company to sports giant has seen the swoosh come to cohabit with professional team logos, college mascots, and even Warner Brothers characters on sweatshirts and in ads. Like the checkmark it resembles—the swoosh, by the way, seems to come from a right hand, not a southpaw's, except when it rides the right side of a shoe—it serves as a stamp of approval from the organization *Sports Illustrated* once called the most powerful force in sports.

"I work for Nike," said center Alonzo Mourning, also of the National Basketball Association, demonstrating a loyalty not evident toward his employer, the Charlotte Hornets, who were forced by his salary demands to trade him this season. But the power of the swoosh lies in the fact that Nike is bigger than athletes, bigger than teams, bigger than whole leagues. It has been criticized for its deals with college coaches such as UNC's Dean Smith and, most recently, for its deal with Dallas Cowboy owner Jerry Jones for bypassing NFL Properties, the league's official licensing and marketing arm. Such deals invest the swoosh with the powerful equity (as the marketing types put it) of the Cowboys or of Carolina.

Nike's iconography coexists easily, like software. It attaches, like a gene or grammatical prefix, to college team logos on hats and shirts. Another part of Nike's power lies in an ability to transcend individual sports, yet be associated with all of them. That may be why it latches on to the rare multisport athlete such as Bo Jackson or Deion Sanders and is able to make what they do lack any hint of gimmickry.

## 2. ON BROADWAY

In a shoe store on Broadway in 1974, I bought my first pair of Nikes, and my friends laughed. They were light, comfortable, and cheap. They were blue and already bore a white swoosh along their sides. At that time, Nike was seen as a low-cost Asian shoemaker, and, indeed, the company was established in its current form only in 1972. Through repetition, the swoosh came to seem almost the fact of nature it is today.

In 1973, an art grad student named Carolyn Davidson designed the swoosh for Phil Knight, a former runner who founded the company with Oregon track coach Bill Bowerman. Bowerman is the man who famously set a strip of rubber on a waffle iron to create the first waffle training shoe. The original waffle iron is on display at Portland's Niketown. Knight didn't much like the swoosh, as it soon came to be called, but wanted an identifying mark for his shoes that was functional as well as decorative, like the three supporting stripes on Adidas, then the market leader. But, over time, the swoosh became the master mark of a series of subbrands: Nike Air, Air Jordan, All Conditions Gear, and so on, each with its own logotype. For Air Jordan, for instance, whose original basketball with wings logo is almost forgotten, the logo remains a silhouetted figure of Jordan stretched out against the sky. Taken from a photograph used in one of the ad campaigns for the shoe, it seems a mock evocation of the silhouetted polo pony and rider on a Ralph Lauren shirt. But simple repetition has made the swoosh almost ubiquitous.

Walking along Broadway today, I conduct an informal test: how many "exposures" (as the ad execs say) to the swoosh will I experience in a given time period—say half an hour? The streets teem with caps and jackets. Descending into the subway, I see more. A cap, there by the standee pole. A jacket. An ad above the window. A black-and-white photo of Michael Jordan, in midair, on the back of a *Daily News* a seated passenger is reading. There are so many carriers of the swoosh that a cynic might see a leech shape in it, and the way it attaches itself to objects and images. I total twenty-eight, conservatively counted, in the thirty minutes.

## 3. AT NIKE

Inside "the berm," as they call Nike's Oregon campus, surrounded with a grassy bank raised like a fortified Roman road to support a running track, the analogy between shoes and automobiles is a ruling metaphor: running shoe as sports car, hiking boot as off-roader. Shoes are vehicles for the brand, Nike's Phil Knight once said, carrying that metaphor to a new level. Nike products are counters, chips, icons for values and associations, the soft emotional attachment called brand equity, some swirling compound of Jordan's aura and Deion's neon glow. All this is most intensely compounded in the swoosh. These products change, as the stars change in the eyes of fans, year by year, and technologies advance, together producing their own form of fashion. But the swoosh offers persistence amid change. So is it entirely perverse to think of the swoosh as a selfish *meme*, like the selfish gene of Richard Dawkins's theories, driving all of Nike design and marketing? Dawkins reminds us of the real basis of biological evolution: its basic units are not shapes or spots, not even species and certainly not specimens. With complexity theory postulating an analogy between genes and the *memes* of culture, it is fun to entertain the theory that the constant evolution of Nike's products—from the first waffle trainers to the latest Air Jordan, a whole line renewed four seasons a year—is actually driven by the tyranny of the swoosh itself.

*Originally published in Volume 14, Number 2, 1996.*

# THE CRASH OF THE NASA LOGO

*Philip B. Meggs*

Last week our spirits were lifted by the triumphs of the Endeavor mission," proclaimed Daniel S. Goldin, administrator of the National Aeronautics and Space Administration (NASA), in an address to NASA employees on May 22, 1992.

"The magic is back at NASA," he continued. "The can-do spirit of the past is alive and well. In honor of this spirit, it seems only fitting that the original NASA insignia, affectionately known as the "Meatball," be a part of our future. I know you feel this way too, because large numbers of you have told me so in my visits."

In an instant, Goldin jettisoned NASA's sleek 1974 logo (nicknamed the "Worm" by NASA employees) and reverted to a dated relic. This event raises several important issues about design and visual identification. How valuable is the equity in the graphic standards manual and logo recognition value of the Worm after almost two decades of use? Should it be discarded so cavalierly? What processes should be used to make decisions about visual identification? When the Meatball was replaced by the Worm, an evaluation by communications professionals was followed by a complex design process to develop a unique and highly recognizable visual identifier; but, apparently, the decision to revert to the Meatball was a unilateral knee-jerk decision by an administrator.

NASA gave me the bureaucratic shuffle when I tried to get information about the logo change. Few NASA employees would discuss it with me, and the ones who did insisted that their names not be used. One said that the decision to return to the Meatball was initially conceived when Goldin visited Langley Field, where one longtime employee complained about being unable to get the Meatball on his business card and called this a horrible injustice. One version circulating among NASA employees says the director of Langley Field told Goldin, at a cocktail party welcoming him as new administrator, that revival of the Meatball and going back to the 1950s would be a great way to hype morale.

"Without consultation or research," another employee said, "Goldin decided to revert to the old logo. It's not the most popular decision, and only a minority of NASA employees agreed."

Designer Bruce Blackburn, who created the Worm, thinks NASA's decision to revert to the Meatball is "ill informed, regressive, and without foundation."

The Worm was birthed by the now-defunct 1970s Federal Design Improvement Program, which sought to rescue governmental architecture, interiors, and graphics from numbing mediocrity. It also worked to attract outstanding design talent to federal service. Federal bureaucrats are often ignorant when it comes to matters of design and communication; therefore, the Federal Design Improvement Program used professional consultants to hire designers by portfolio review; evaluate existing publications and environmental design; and develop improved visual-identification systems, graphic standards, interior space design, buildings, and landscaping.

A panel of communication and design consultants evaluated the Meatball and found it to be inadequate. It lacked the extreme-distance legibility required for distance reading on spacecraft, primarily because the wishbone shape and oval line interfered with the clarity of the letterforms. The primary deficiency of the Meatball was its very poor legibility on television. NASA, dependent on public and congressional support for billions of tax dollars, was, and is, very conscious of publicity and image.

The Meatball's fussy details are overly complex for many printing and copying processes, where these fine elements will blur or simply become lost, while its funky Buck Rogers appearance is inappropriate for the advanced-technology space agency that put people on the moon. Another pressing issue was the lack of graphic standards and a unified identity for NASA: the agency lacked a clear, consistent graphic image.

In 1974, the design firm of Danne and Blackburn was retained to design a new logo to replace the Meatball and develop a NASA graphic standards manual. Danne and Blackburn developed the acronym *NASA* into a typographic logo. By dropping the crossbars on the *A*'s, the designers turned these triangular letters into an upward thrust. This provided a subtle symbol of the agency's mission and created a unique word-image. In the process, they created one of our great name logos. As do the logos for Coca-Cola and Exxon, a coined word combines with an unusual visual form to provide a singular and distinctive identification. This logo has excellent legibility from great distances, which is a decided asset for an organization whose space shuttle launches and landings are watched by millions of people around the world.

Blackburn remembers how directors of NASA centers absolutely rebelled when the Worm was introduced. He and Danne flew to several NASA centers to explain the rationale for the logo and the need for communicating in a systematic and coordinated way. NASA officials were extremely hostile; many of them wanted their own logo for their center. "The closer we came to the manned flight program," Blackburn recalls, "the greater the pressure to do things their way."

As NASA retires this logo, which has achieved familiarity around the globe, it is discarding two decades of recognition value. Mr. Goldin probably never stopped to consider that everyone under twenty-five—a majority of the people on the planet—does not remember the old Meatball, beloved though it may be by NASA's old guard. The Meatball can never hope to achieve the Worm's success in recognition value because the Meatball is too similar to hundreds of other logos in circles, and its fussy complexity makes it difficult to decipher. The retro design sensibilities of the 1980s, when designers were reviving old clip art and eccentric typefaces of the 1930s and 1940s, may render the Meatball less offensive than it was in the 1970s; nevertheless, its odd pointed-serif letters and stylized wishbone are inappropriate, for they convey nostalgia rather than cutting-edge technology. The Worm was designed as pure form, timeless and undated, but the Meatball was designed in the style of its time and remains locked there.

While the shift from the Worm to the Meatball has dismayed many professional designers and communicators, it could have been worse. NASA might have even reverted to the Meatball's father, a consummate example of the bureaucratic design stereotype. In keeping with NASA's tradition of nicknaming logos, I'll call it the "Cornball." One can interpret the Cornball as a giant Meatball flying between the spread prongs of a chicken's wishbone, or read the Meatball as earth while the wishbone symbolizes a zooming space craft. By any rational measure of design *and* communication, it was *and is* a failure.

Designing a Cornball requires three easy steps: (1) Draw two concentric circles with a compass. (2) Take the long bureaucratic name of your agency or department, set it in a condensed bold sans-serif type, and let it run within the circle. While type set in a circle certainly has its place, a long name set this way is hard to read from a distance, causing major legibility problems if, for example, you want people to read it on the tail of a Space Shuttle traveling at high speeds. (3) Put a complex line drawing inside the circle—either a pictorial allegory or a collection of symbols—to signify your institution. Hire the cheapest possible artist to draw the allegorical picture. Professional artists and designers charge too much, even demanding more than a minimum wage for their services; therefore, a high school art competition with a $25 prize will garner positive publicity while achieving an appropriately unschooled image. Make the picture as trite as possible.

So pervasive is this bureaucratic cliché that anyone can find federal, state, and local examples readily at hand. The logo for Virginia depicts a bare-breasted Virtus, the genius of the Commonwealth, dressed as an Amazon holding a sword over a slain Roman centurion to symbolize the triumph of justice over tyranny. Henrico County, Virginia, has the Native American Pocahontas whose interracial marriage "brought peace between the Indians and the colonists." The barely recognizable weeds behind her are tobacco and corn. (It is amazing that the state that produced ultraconservative televangelists Jerry Falwell and Pat Robertson uses a topless lady on its logo, and how Native Americans are used as emblems after their dislocation and massacre by the European settlers of North America.)

At a time when the federal deficit exceeds a billion dollars a day, thousands of dollars of taxpayers' money could be wasted to change a far-flung agency's vehicle and aircraft identification, signage, and printed materials in a dubious program to replace a fine logo with an ugly, outmoded bureaucratic relic. Changing logos is very expensive; for example, the newly formed NationsBank is spending $40–50 million replacing signs, etc. NASA preempted the inevitable howl about spending tax dollars on a visual-identity change by declaring that no budget would be allocated for reverting to its quaint old logo; supposedly, the changeover is occurring as supplies are depleted. Signs, vehicle and aircraft insignia, and other permanent applications will be changed as they are refurbished or replaced. One NASA employee says enormous expenditures are unavoidable, but NASA spokespersons pleaded ignorance on this issue.

Until now, the NASA logo and graphics program were considered—along with a handful of programs including the National Park Service publications and the Department of Agriculture design office—to be one of the federal government's few success stories in the area of design. This bizarre design regression affirms the truth of H. L. Mencken's observation that no one ever went broke underestimating the American taste.

*Originally published in Volume 10, Number 4, 1992.*

# THE MISSION IS THE MESSAGE

*Larry Keeley*

Imagine you were in an army going off to war. Imagine that your country was behind you, the enemy was clear, everyone agreed the enemy was heinous, all diplomatic efforts were pointless, and there was no alternative but to fight. However much you abhor war in general, try to conjure up this situation. Black and white, no grays.

For such an army, creating great insignias, uniforms, songs, posters, films would be no trouble; they'd be popular and, if matched with great leadership, eventually legendary. Such an army would have a clear purpose. This is because the mission outlined is clear and compelling.

Now let's talk about corporate identity (CI). Where missions make sense, corporate identity works. It can stir men's souls and make a difference. The problem is that not too many corporate missions currently make sense. Most are mere pabulum, the kinds of statements written by corporate flacks, which few people would bother to read and with which no one would disagree.

Which ushers in the bad news: corporate identity doesn't matter much now and will matter less as time goes on. Unfortunately, the reasons are structural: we have entered a new era where individuals are important and institutions aren't. In a nutshell, it is getting harder and harder to create missions that matter, and when they don't, it is both impossible and undesirable to motivate people.

Coming to grips with this big change will test the integrity of the design field because many large design firms need to sell large-scale conventional CI programs to survive. This amounts to a classic ethical dilemma where what's right for the consultants is harmful to the clients.

It may be hard to buy this theory, especially since you may well be one of the thousands of designers just itching to develop the next logo to end all logos. Before you rush to send me hate mail, stay with the argument as it develops a little further.

First, the historic arguments for corporate identification are almost never relevant today. There are two such classic arguments, based on the now-quaint notions of investor or employee loyalty.

The idea that the company needed to be positioned for and understandable to investors, au courant in the 1960s and 1970s, is a joke today. Wall Street finance experts have long since learned to track corporate finance at the speed of light and ruthlessly shift investments to those that deliver returns. Naturally, this is much more a function of weird events (takeover rumors, oil spills, acquisitions,

The Donald's divorce[s], Leona's conviction) than anything as old-fashioned as company performance or product quality.

Similarly, doing up a bright, shiny CI system so that employees will love the institution and give it their loyalty is senseless. Large companies routinely downsize. (Wall Street firms have dumped 40,000 employees since 1986, and agencies have dumped 30,000.) Superstar employees get raided and willingly jump to the competition. The rest know that they can be sacrificial lambs whenever a division needs selling or some other shenanigans are necessary to boost the quarterly numbers.

Second, there is a new emergence of brands over companies as the entities that matter. Designers think they love Apple. In fact, what they love is their Macintosh, and even that is a bit tenuous. Apple Computer is increasingly run by marketers, most of them imported from places like Pepsi and IBM. The Apple II computer is a totally different beast than the Macintosh; it's sold differently, and it has different goals. Few people care deeply about both sides of Apple.

Most companies are like this. Few people who like Godiva chocolates think they're good because of Campbell's Soup, the company that makes them. Same with Häagen-Dazs (brand) and Pillsbury (parent company), or even *thirtysomething* (program) versus NBC (broadcast network.) Closer to home, it is possible to have great respect for the work of Siegel & Gale (operating unit) while harboring great doubts about Saatchi and Saatchi (parent company, a.k.a. "Snatchit and Snatchit").

It isn't accidental that Honda, Toyota, and Nissan all created new pseudocompanies when they introduced their high-end cars (Acura, Lexus, and Infiniti). Much of the impetus comes from their realization, probably subconscious, that people cannot care about institutions anymore—unless the mission matters.

Naturally, the CI field has been slow to get the point. As a result, we have lived through a time of insipid, silly, expensive, and irrelevant corporate identity programs. Proof of this wild-eyed assertion can be found in the hyperbolic launch campaigns that typically accompany new CI programs. These usually take one of the following hackneyed forms: *Our name has changed but we haven't. . . . , A bold new look for a new era. . . . , A new face but a familiar smile. . . . , Two great companies now even better together. . . .*

The announcement then builds on these banal thoughts with a name change and/or graphics with all the warmth and charm of an airport washroom. Examples abound. There's the Allegis program, which introduced a name that has the force of a clenched sneeze. Or Unisys, which developed its name through an employee contest. Other recent triumphs include Navistar and Primerica.

Most recently, we've seen the emergence of smarmy pseudowarmth in CI campaigns. This trend, designed to be compensatory for chilly names, has seen the rechristening of Consolidated Foods as Sara Lee Corporation and IC Industries as Whitman Corporation. Both have been reviewed positively; neither deserved it.

By elevating one brand name to act as the parent company name over many other brands (L'eggs Hosiery from Sara Lee Corporation?), the essential silliness of this direction becomes apparent.

In all these cases, it is easy (and appropriate) to attack the corporate identity program. But, invariably, CI is not the cause of the problem. These identities are a mess because the corporate missions are unenlightened. Indeed, the big CI firms—like AGP, Landor, and Wolff/Olins—are absolutely dependent on such screwed-up companies for survival. Usually, this has just bought a bit of time until a hostile takeover or some other crisis flushes management out.

With corporate identity in eclipse, the agile CI firms have moved on to other arenas. Some, like Siegel & Gale or the Chicago-based Meta-4, have moved on to the next generation of corporate identity management. This largely entails searching for ways to tame laser printers, which are out of control within very large organizations. This is an important way to help clients manage visual appearance programs, but it should not be mistaken for management of identity. Most CI firms have gone blithely on, selling programs that have no proven value and may well harm the clients they purport to serve.

There is a pathway out of these woods. In concept, it's simple: create missions that are clear, missions that matter. There are companies that have their act together. Ben & Jerry's, however nutty, has a sense of itself; Starbucks Coffee Company is one of the best examples around. Of course, both these companies are small and easy to dismiss. But before doing so, consider the degree to which the vitality in our economy has come from small companies over the past ten years, while large companies have boosted profits principally by cutting their employee counts dramatically.

Very few larger companies provide encouraging examples. Until recently, Apple seemed to have a clear sense of itself, and perhaps it may get it back. Herman Miller, recently retrenched from some confused forays, may again become a shining example. Corning and Nike both offer some vitality. Compaq Computer, despite having some of the most pathetic product and graphic design efforts around, continues to progress. This is evidence that a clear mission, even without great design, is a powerful force. Creating meaningful missions for large corporations is nearly impossible in practice, particularly if you try to do so as a designer pleading with unenlightened managers. When you get a good top manager to take you seriously, tell him or her this: Do not be content merely trying to put the best face on a bunch of activities that don't hang together. Don't pick a theme or a name for the things that exist today. Pursue a bigger idea: Pick a mission that isn't true now, but could be if everyone in the organization worked toward it. This should be a stretch, this should require great leadership. It should be a war worth fighting.

*Originally published in Volume 8, Number 1, 1990.*

# ANNUAL REPORT: 84-POINT ERROR BOLD

*Mike Hicks*

While many designers may lie awake nights in a frothy sweat over details, I never lose much sleep worrying about such things. Because, when the spectacle of utter failure looms large on the horizon, it is seldom (make that *never*) really anticipated. These things come from the blind side. From the dark, myopic periphery of never considered, never discussed, never pondered possibility. And that's what makes this ilk of catastrophe so frightening: the idea that an entire project (or worse, your entire financial well-being) could be wiped out so suddenly, by sheer stupidity, in a totally spontaneous manner. *Surprise! You're homeless and detested by all.* This is the fear that keeps me from peaceful slumbers.

The lessons one can learn from this type of failure (assuming one survives) are: (1) you should be very careful to avoid a giant disaster, and (2) you can never be careful enough to avoid small disasters.

When I first began my career, I was lucky enough to witness a monster disaster secondhand. I've changed the name of the company involved, primarily because I don't want to be sued by the survivors.

I was hired as part of a team to design and produce the Colonial General annual report. This was a very detail-oriented insurance company, whose annual reports were (and probably still are) filled with minutiae presented in a dull and unexciting manner. The entire senior vice president management group was vested with the responsibility of making certain that not even the most insignificant error or omission occurred in the report. Our team labored weeks over rewritten copy and recalculated financials, eventually setting the entire report seven times. We stopped even talking about design around the third or fourth reset.

On the occasion of each final reset, all boards were trotted across town, where each page was read and signed by six different senior executives. Toward the end, I doubt if there were any bowel movements occurring at all within that group. These six men, probably normal-enough guys most of the year, were in the grips of High Anxiety. Each was seeing his life, family, and luxurious River Oaks home disappear instantly as the result of a momentary lapse of attention on this project. Each lived in abject terror of the Chairman, who was due to be choppered in to sign off on the final, *final* blueline immediately prior to the printing of several hundred thousand copies.

At last, every decimal point was in its correct place, and every word had been checked and rechecked. Not a man among us was willing to concede that there was even the remote possibility of an error. Imagine our pride and general guffawing when the Chairman himself, after an excruciating three-minute review, agreed and signed off each and every one of the sixty-odd pages right above the names of his soon-to-be-extinct senior managers. It was a heady moment, standing there twenty stories above the city in the prop wash of his Jet Ranger as it left the roof of the corporate headquarters. Today, such a moment would fill me with unspecified dread. Then, I was simply making a mental note of my total hours on the entire project and thinking of buying a new Corvette. Our general euphoria lasted almost two weeks until that fateful moment when a $4.25-an-hour floorman at the press warehouse asked his supervisor where he should put the remaining two pallets of those "General Colonial" annual reports.

I imagine there was a puzzled expression on the supervisor's face as he said, "You mean those Colonial General reports?"

"No, I mean those General Colonial muthers I got left over from the mail dump." I imagine the supervisor's expression turned to horror just about then.

Sure enough, right there on the cover, bigger than Dallas, in 84-point bold type was the only error that had escaped our many razor sharp, microfine inspections. As word quickly spread, there was a nanosecond or two of chuckling and forehead slapping by everyone just before the absolute gravity of the error set in and the mind's eye focused on a giant tsunami racing toward our various fiscal sandcastles. I had just returned from a beach test of my new Alfa convertible when I learned in rapid succession that: (1) the name was reversed on the cover, (2) there was indeed a large competing firm named General Colonial, (3) the postal service wouldn't return the 150,000 already in the mail, (4) 5,000 corrected versions had already been printed and were in the hands of 5,000 couriers who had fanned out across the U.S. with instructions to wait for the mail to be delivered to the 5,000 largest stockholders and switch the dyslexic original with the correct version, (5) the entire run would be reprinted in the near future at an unspecified entity's expense, (6) the new report would be proofed by six new vice presidents and a special envoy from the Chairman's office, (7) payment of any monies due was being suspended pending a full audit of fees and an assessment of responsibility, and, finally, (8) everyone associated even remotely with the gaffe would have the status of a cockroach in perpetuity with the client and anyone the client could influence.

The news almost ruined my day. But not quite. My fee, most of which was now parked out front, had already been paid. My bill was considered both inconsequential and commissionable by the poor devils who were now about to bite a bullet bigger than a boxcar.

Needless to say, their life insurance policies were not renewed, and I'll bet they still have trouble getting their cars insured. There were, of course, ugly consequences all around, mostly of the financial variety. Two of the three partners of the design firm are now involved in other lines of work. The Chairman, I was told, adopted the persona of a wounded pit bull throughout the proceedings,

drawn equally by an instinct to survive by dissociation and an insane desire to
wreak bloody vengeance on all those responsible for his plight. At any rate, he
didn't get me. I was simply too small a target at too great a distance. However, to
this day, I always read the big words and never *assume* anything I can possibly *get
explained* (preferably in writing). That, in a nutshell, is why I still have all my
fingers two decades later. I managed to keep the Alfa, which rests under a tarp in
my driveway as a constant reminder.

*Originally published in Volume 10, Number 4, 1990.*

# SAUL BASS ON CORPORATE IDENTITY

*interview by Philip B. Meggs*

On October 11, 1990, Philip Meggs interviewed Saul Bass. They discussed
corporate identity, which some observers feel is in a state of crisis today.
Saul Bass talked about the design process, plagiarism, clichés, and the effect
of negative publicity upon a company's identity system.

**Meggs:** Let's start by discussing the design process. I've heard many
graphic designers say that they avoid designing trademarks and symbols like the
plague because it's so difficult. The designer has to invent a new form from
scratch that has never before existed in the world. Over the years, you have
invented trademarks that have become real icons, celebrated for their originality.
How do you approach the problem of designing a new trademark?

**Bass:** Trademarks are usually metaphors of one kind or another. The
enterprise that you are communicating about has to explain itself in some way,
the nature of what it is or does, what its areas of activity are. Communicating that
is usually the starting point for developing imagery. Trademarks are, in a certain
sense, thinking made visible. The process of defining what it is that you wish to
communicate inevitably defines the objectives of the design process. Then, the
search is for imagery or form that will adequately—and, one hopes, interestingly—express this. Where one goes from this starting point can be unexpected
and may not follow a totally rational methodology, but it is helpful to frame the
problem in rational terms as a beginning point. From there, the design will
evolve on intuitive levels, and it may take peculiar turns.

**Meggs:** As you go through the process of searching for a solution and alternative designs are generated, how do you select the appropriate solution?

**Bass:** It usually turns out to be something that satisfies the objectives as originally defined and, at the same time, is sufficiently interesting and provocative to separate itself from the cacophony of messages and visual phenomena that we wade through every day. In this respect, metaphor and ambiguity are useful in enhancing levels of interest and attention. However, accessibility must be maintained when you are communicating with popular audiences—as is the case with many larger corporations. It's much more possible to employ richer metaphors and greater ambiguity when dealing with more defined activity and more specialized audiences and businesses.

**Meggs:** Much has been said and written lately about the impact of computers upon design and visual communications. When designing a trademark, does the computer play a role in your design process?

**Bass:** Not in relation to the fundamental concept, the idea of what it is. Computers can respond quickly and efficiently to questions like, "How will it look if it's turned this way or that, made heavier or lighter, squeezed or expanded?" But these are secondary issues—modifying factors. The basic notion still has to come out of someone's head.

**Meggs:** We have this old adage, "Imitation is the sincerest form of flattery." You have designed some very original trademarks, which have spawned many imitations. Original thinking seems to turn into a cliché as a result of plagiarism, which is rampant in design. What is your reaction when you see trademarks that look so very much like other trademarks, and what does this do to the original?

**Bass:** This happens in all pop-cultural areas. Hitchcock made a film a long time ago called *The Lady Vanishes*. In it, he juxtaposed two cuts: a close-up of a lady opening her mouth to scream and then a shock-cut to a close-up of a train whistle screeching. This device has been used in subsequent films, I don't know how many times. A student of mine once referred to this moment as a cliché when discussing it with me after he caught *The Lady Vanishes* on late-night television, not understanding that this is where it all began. Ironic! As we know, clichés become clichés because they do what they do extremely well. Then someone comes along and does something similar. And, of course, it works well again and again and again. And voilà! A cliché! Clichés deserve study. There's something there working very well. If you understand what it is, then it may be possible to take the cliché and turn or refresh it in some way, express it in new terms. I'm not terribly disturbed by seeing things pop up again and again, as long as they are not boring and something is being added or changed in a significant way.

**Meggs:** What is the value of visual identity to the client and culture?

**Bass:** It may be useful to look at the issue historically. Corporate identity as a clear discipline is a post–World War II phenomenon. It's only thirty or forty years old. During this period, it's grown from a cottage industry to an institutionalized form, has become an acknowledged component of business activity. Now—to whatever extent corporate managers believe in the value of design as affecting the so-called bottom line—I think it exists where visual style has essential marketing values in relation to product or service. There's great commitment to the function of design, for example, in cosmetics, fashion, and high-tech products. Contrast this to the notion of design commitment in areas involving commodity products. Even those corporations that are willing to commit design resources to specific areas like product design or packaging don't necessarily commit to other areas across the board. We've been inundated with books on corporate excellence. What they don't say is that excellence is not selective. If it's not set as a standard everywhere, it's not going to happen appropriately anywhere.

Corporate identity has, over the years, taken an interesting form. Historically, its original expression involved the total image. In the original exemplars we admired—Olivetti, IBM, Container Corporation, and others—every manifestation of the company was aimed at excellence. Somewhere down the line, this got translated into corporate identity as consisting of a trademark, which is attached then to communications, which may or may not be excellent. So, despite loss of market and foreign competition, business hasn't really totally embraced the value of design. It seems that we've not really done as good a job as we ought to have in explaining the value of good design. Often, I think it exists by default. From time to time, we see corporations embrace design where the chief executive officer sees it as a fashionable cultural phenomenon, neither a link to the efficacy of the business nor a life-enhancing cultural activity ... in a crunch, it's discarded precisely because it's neither.

**Meggs:** How does one measure the economic value of a trademark and corporate identity program? Can its value be measured?

**Bass:** It's quite feasible to measure quantitatively—that is, measure recognizability and association. What is difficult to measure is what it may add to people's understanding and feelings about the company. We've measured recognizability and association with many marks we've designed for corporations. For instance, when I redesigned the old bell for the Bell System, the recognition level two years after the new redesigned bell was introduced rose from 71 percent to

over 90 percent. That is, people saw the bell and understood that it represented
the phone company.

The economic value of a trademark is elusive. I don't know of any
systematic means of arriving at a figure. I do know of cases where the use of a
new trademark was accompanied by a significant increase in sales. But it's
difficult, if not impossible, to separate the contribution of the trademark from
the rest of the marketing mix: advertising, sales promotion, packaging, distribution, pricing, etc.

I did hear a rumor a while ago that Coca-Cola once was involved in
trademark infringement litigation and was asked to value its trademark. This is
just gossip, of course, but the figure I heard the company used back then was $3
billion. It doesn't seem unreasonable.

**Meggs:** Let me ask if you have any thoughts on another process. When a
company gets negative publicity, how does this relate to the reading of the mark
and identity program? To take a recent example, I know many people who refuse
to fly Eastern Airlines because they are sympathetic to the strike by mechanics
and pilots. Do you know what happens, or has there been any research on what
happens, when a mark becomes a symbol—not of positive impressions, but of
negative reactions?

**Bass:** The trademark has to be understood as simply one element in the
communication mix. In and of itself, it doesn't change anything. Bill Bernbach
once observed that an effective advertising campaign will kill a lousy product
faster than no advertising at all. If a promise is made that can't be fulfilled, it's
worse than making no promise at all. Whatever the manipulative power of
design, the fact is that if you aren't basically accurate in what you say about
products and companies, you will fail, simply because—in the end—the performance of the product or the company is the basic determinate of how the product
or company will be viewed. With Eastern Airlines, the identifier will take on the
coloration of what is happening. When Eastern straightens out, gets organized,
and does a good job, the emblem will have another meaning. Certainly, changing
it is not going to accomplish anything. We have to understand the limitations of
what we do as well as the potentials.

**Meggs:** Are these limitations and potentials of visual identification
constant, or do they change?

**Bass:** Historically, identification was specific, literal, illustrative. The fire
insurance company spouted fire or flames; the refrigerator company showed
icicles. Then, along came the highly reductive, abstract, formal visual work. It
was startling, effective.

**Meggs:** Which marks achieved this?

**Bass:** I'm thinking of the CBS eye, the Alcoa mark, the Chase Manhattan Bank mark. These appeared in a world of illustrative literal marks. They were quite powerful in this context and had tremendous impact. Reductive became fashionable. And designers created a flood of reductive, abstract trademarks. Slowly the visual uniqueness of the reductive mark diminished. And those expressions that are more specific, even illustrative, then become contextually more interesting.

**Meggs:** Why do we have this herd instinct?

**Bass:** The moment something "works," the pressure is on to play off it. Because the economic stakes are so great, everybody is looking for certainty. And things that have worked in the past are more likely to work in the future. And it happens very fast. The process used to take longer. Now, the new grows old without ever having had a childhood. What we have is a herd of independent minds.

We seem to be in a cyclical process in which context is significant and drives the situation. The form continues to change as the context evolves. This is an interesting contradiction in view of the logical definition of the trademark as fulfilling long-range strategic communication objectives.

**Meggs:** And, yet, we have some pictorial logos, such as the RCA dog, as well as reductive marks, such as the CBS eye, which are very potent and stand the test of time over several decades. What makes a mark powerful enough to sustain itself in a cyclical situation where context is shifting?

**Bass:** I might add the Mercedes trademark to this group, in terms of staying power. I'm a little dubious about the RCA dog. It's a lovely piece of nostalgia, but it doesn't tell you a lot about the firm. It certainly doesn't signal the technology. The theoretically ideal trademark is one that is ultimately reductive, but is still accessible, and yet is ambiguous in a formal sense. Ambiguity and metaphor add tension and interest to a form or expression. It keeps the mark alive. Ambiguity is even more significant in film and in some graphic forms, such as the poster.

**Meggs:** Let's talk about these properties in some specific marks. For example, the mark you designed for Minolta. It has strong recognition value and has been widely influential upon the genre.

**Bass:** The intent was to suggest a lens. All of Minolta's products— cameras, copiers, etc.—use lenses in some way. The center lines running through the blue oval were intended to do so, in as reductive a form as I could develop.

**Meggs:** Your design of a reductive mark for Quaker Oats—starting with a very literal mark used for decades and expressing it in a contemporary manner—was a completely different problem.

**Bass:** The old Quaker man is a wonderful figure that we all grew up with. It sat on our breakfast table every day, and we learned to live with it in a very comfortable and friendly way. The impetus for this new mark was based on the fact that the Quaker Oats Company had diversified into chemicals, agricultural food products, restaurants, etc. The objective was to find a way to differentiate Quaker, the company, from Quaker, the cereal product, without giving up the values associated with that great American icon. At one point, before we came into the picture, it was proposed that the Quaker Oats Company should adopt a stylized *Q* as its corporate signature. This was judged to be an inappropriate thing to do, and I believe it would have been.

**Meggs:** The AT&T globe is another mark that has a powerful identification. Could you comment on the metaphor and symbolism of this mark?

**Bass:** Here we were in a transition from the Bell System to a new company, from a system that could be described as "the national telephone company," to one that we wanted to suggest was "an international telecommunications company," with information bits circling the globe. An important component of the program is the tag we developed for television, where the information bits are gathered up by the globe. It's useful in the "seating" of this mark.

**Meggs:** What do you perceive as the current dilemmas in corporate identification?

**Bass:** One of them has to do with the "generalization" of corporate logos, involving a loss of individuality and interest. A number of factors have contributed to this condition. The pressure of corporate development in the last forty years, I think, has changed the game. Large companies are no longer in a single business. They are involved with diverse products and diverse services. That differentiation makes it very difficult to be specific in the identity metaphor you create for a company.

Also, many large corporations have become cross-cultural, multinational. This further defies specificity in the trademark. There is also the frequent desire to project stability, trust, good solid management, and so forth, further pushing toward generalization. Other factors affecting this issue have to do with the vast proliferation of trademarks, which simply have "used up" the generalized metaphors and are making it more and more difficult to find original forms and ideas.

All of this pushes toward the homogenization of corporate identity. We're getting slowly to the point where we're talking about General Amalgamated International. I think that's a problem. Now the challenge as I look ahead is to, in a sense, push the clock back—how to do the communication job well and simultaneously maintain emotional components, individuality, and accessibility.

*Originally published in Volume 8, Number 1, 1990.*

# HISTORIC PRESERVATION IN CORPORATE IDENTITY
*Michael Bierut*

**M**odernism once had a very clear mandate: down with the old and up with the new. In architecture, this meant keeping the wrecking balls swinging as one ornate behemoth after another fell in the name of urban renewal, to be replaced by buildings that were shinier, taller, newer, and generally better suited to life in the atomic age. It took the demolition of New York's sumptuous Pennsylvania Station in 1964 (designed by McKim, Mead and White to resemble the Baths of Caracalla) to make way for the loathsome Madison Square Garden complex before people began to realize how much history was being lost in the rubble. Historic preservation became a popular cause rather than a hobby of the odd curmudgeon.

A parallel shift in attitude is occurring twenty years later in the field of corporate identity. For years, an unquestioned cornerstone of corporate identity practice was the unceremonious dumping of the client's quaint but irrelevant existing trademark. But, if the field had to name its own Penn Station, it might be Lee & Young's 1984 recasting of Prudential's craggy engraving of the Rock of Gibraltar. The outcry from members of the public who saw the new characterless mark as symptomatic of the continuing dehumanization of corporate America was especially disconcerting to designers, many of whom still consider the logo a skillful, dynamic piece of work.

As we enter the nineties, the tide has turned. Today we see the rebirth of icons like Mobil's Pegasus, RCA's Nipper, and NBC's peacock, all of which were once thought safely vanquished in favor of typographic and geometric solutions by responsible firms like Chermayeff & Geismar and Lippincott & Margulies.

Perhaps the time is right for a historic preservation movement in graphic design. Paul Rand once said, "Taking a trademark and replacing it with something worse is a terrible sin." Should the following logos be designated as landmarks? Until they are, maybe firms asked to redesign them should just say no.

The General Electric monogram, attributed to New York advertising executive A. L. Rich (who sketched it in 1899 as a decorative emblem for fan motors) appears to be safe at last. When Landor Associates was asked to undertake a new corporate identity for GE in 1986, rumors flew that the graceful, art nouveauish logo was on the way out, especially in light of Landor's reputation for bulldozing first and asking questions later. Instead, the firm devised an ingenious system which preserves the existing logo and prescribes dynamic layout strategies that dramatically revitalize it.

The Ford Motor Company logo was designed in 1904 by Ford chief engineer Childe Harold Wills, based on the signature of Henry Ford himself. The company toyed with eliminating the script logo in the mid-sixties and entertained a proposal from Paul Rand that would do just that. Ultimately, the brand-new design conglomerate Unimark International won the CID in competition, in part because it promised going in not to rename the company or touch the logo. Instead, as Landor would do twenty years later, it created a system to place the mark in a modern environment, using what was then the most contemporary of all typefaces, Helvetica.

Editor Bennett Cerf, describing his plans to publish books "at random," decided to name his company Random House. Rockwell Kent, who had been hired to illustrate a luxury edition of Voltaire's *Candide*, was present and sketched the logo for the new publishing house on the spot. The imprint first appeared on books in 1927 and, in a slightly cleaned-up form, continues to serve as the primary corporate symbol.

A more streamlined version of the mark, which now usually appears on the books' jackets, was introduced in 1968. Random House's book designers can use this mark, the older mark, or any number of variations depending on their needs.

A logo doesn't have to be old, quaint, or even pictorial to be part of the cultural landscape. Chermayeff & Geismar's 1960 mark for the Chase Manhattan Bank was the first truly abstract logo, referred to, at first derisively, then affectionately, as the "Beveled Bagel," the Chase octagon.

Does it seem unlikely that a mark as timeless as Chase's is due for an overhaul? The same might have been said for Chermayeff & Geismar's classic 1961 monogram for Manufacturer's Hanover Trust, which nonetheless received an utterly pointless makeover at the hands of Murtha, DeSola, Finsilver, Fiore in 1987.

Finally, we turn to the logo of the AIGA itself. With irregular thicks and thins, verticals, and horizontals, and particularly nasty-looking serifs, the logotype of America's leading national graphic design organization is problematic, to say the least. It doesn't work well in small sizes, yet doesn't work well when overscale either. Because it doesn't combine well with other letterforms, it's rather ill suited to function in combination with chapter names, a considerable handicap for an organization that communicates with its members primarily through a chapter structure. In short, the AIGA logo, nearly thirty years old, desperately needs to be redesigned. That is, if there's anyone out there ready to throw out a logo designed by—you guessed it—Paul Rand.

*Originally published in Volume 8, Number 1, 1990.*

# EYE/EAR TODAY — GONE TOMORROW

*Steff Geissbuhler*

I was as surprised as anyone when I read the following press release of May 20, 1993:

> Time Warner Inc. today unveiled a new logo at its annual shareholders meeting in New York City. Chairman and CEO Gerald M. Levin said, "Time Warner's powerful product brands and divisional identities are the best known and most effective emblems of Time Warner's vitality and strength. We felt that simplifying the corporate logo would make for a more harmonious overall identity system and would grant our brands the prominence they deserve."

The vice president of corporate communications said in her letter to me (which arrived at my office on the same day as the press release): "The symbol you designed is so strong that it's hard to make it work with other divisional symbols." (It was never meant to do that.) "Time Warner Cable will continue to use your design, while the corporate parent will assume a new logo that consists of the name framed by two lines. . . . The eye/ear logo continues to be much admired by the design community." Thanks, I do appreciate that. It's unfortunate that the client doesn't anymore.

*Identity* magazine wrote recently: "A piece of the past was replaced recently at Time Warner. The old logo was replaced with a new. . . ." Come on, guys—barely three years is not old and a piece of the past. Or is this a backhanded compliment because it seemed the symbol had been around for much longer?

So much for the facts, though I still have more questions than answers. Can a logo be too strong? Can it be too appropriate?

Aren't we creating identities to endure the test of time? Or are we lucky nowadays if a trademark or logo survives a couple of years in this corporate world of hostile takeovers, mergers, acquisitions, and management changes?

Is a change of identity a way for new management to signal its arrival and make its mark? Steven J. Ross, Time Warner's former chairman and CEO, who accepted the symbol and loved it, died about a year ago. Maybe contemporary identities should no longer reflect the company but the person who runs it.

Okay, so what do I think of the new logo? As one insider put it: "Yes, it's true that Time Warner has dumped your excellent eye/ear logo in favor of a plain vanilla Times Roman logo that looks as if it were torn from the side of a moving van." (He said it, not me.)

It's uneventful, not memorable, and, in my biased opinion, a strategic mistake. Why wasn't at least the typographic part of the identity retained, which clearly combined Time Inc. with Warner Communications into a single strong name? And how is the new type solution going to work better as a corporate tagline with, for example, the HBO and Warner Brothers identities or, for that matter, with Time Warner Cable now featuring the eye/ear symbol?

One thing I do know. Not just the design community but the public— including New York City taxi drivers, European businesspeople, media executives, and my neighbors—related to the symbol and found it meaningful and appropriate. Even the *New York Times*, for example, keeps using the "old" eye/ear symbol to identify the corporation.

As they say in the commercial, we thank you for your support.

*Originally published in Volume 12, Number 1, 1994.*

# ARTS AND CRAFTS

# GRAPHIC DESIGN IS NOT A PROFESSION

*Gordon Salchow*

I was recently interviewed on the topics of ethics, criteria for professional practice, and so on by *Designer* magazine. My questioner was challenging our "professional" claims, since any novice can do graphic design and may legally advertise this expertise.

During the interview, I was intrigued by the refreshing revelation that this writer could redirect the identical provocations toward his own profession. The tools and rules of writing can also be employed or dared by amateurs or by professionals for reportage or for artistry.

Graphic design is a fundamental humanist communications discipline. This makes it even more heroic than we have generally claimed. Its peers are the liberal arts, such as music and literature, rather than architecture or industrial design.

Everyone respects writers and musicians despite the fact that they can develop eloquent abilities with or without a concentrated degree or a license. The realization that today's TV celebrity may write a bestseller does not diminish the might of great literature. In fact, that same teen idol, who studied grammar beginning with his first Twinkie, is likely to respect the written word enough to involve a ghostwriter. The public is inspired by literary majesty because of, not despite, our heady schooling in reading and writing. Executing an occasional backhand winner does not make me a professional athlete, but it certainly helps me comprehend the beauty of Stefan Edberg's mastery. Our own firsthand experiences cause us to admire the knowledge basis, originality, skill, and personal discipline required to produce superior work, whether literature, music, or tennis.

Scribes are engaged in a fundamental cultural discipline that uses the written word for analysis, expression, documentation, and communication. We manipulate visual elements for the same purposes. Since language, whether written, oral, or visual, is fundamental to the public domain, we cannot claim exclusive proprietorship. In any discipline, however, a great deal of training, dedication, education, and practice are required of anyone who hopes to excel. The doers who get paid for such activities are professionals, even when their turf may not constitute a discrete dictionary-defined occupation.

Graphic design should be recognized as an innately precious and useful sociocultural field that directly parallels other communication/expression disciplines. It is not only a job path. Like journalists, the more informed, motivated, experienced, and creative we are, the better our chances to poeticize and add to the human legacy, while attending to everyday issues.

One problem is that formal and informal education concerning the written word is so much more valued and integral to our Western upbringing than is the case for visual articulation. Visual illiteracy raises various poky imperatives concerning graphic design education at the primary, secondary, and college levels. For instance, all college students ought to encounter some muscular graphic/visual design education, with masters' programs housing the career-oriented professional programs. Graphic design should become a required general education component so that visual skills might fall into place alongside written and verbal abilities. All baccalaureates should be able to speak, write, and visualize with clarity and grace. This charge is becoming particularly urgent now that computer literacy is being dangerously equated with visual literacy.

One stumbling block may be that the term *graphic design* is still being misinterpreted and does not have the categorical twang that *visual design* or *communication design* may have. Whatever it is called, our field will become dramatically more elegant and spirited if our vision of and for it emulates that of our linguistic kinfolk.

*Originally published in Volume 11, Number 4, 1993.*

# IF IT'S NOT IN THE DICTIONARY, IT'S NOT A REAL WORD
*Alina Wheeler*

Over 315,000 entries. . . . Over 50,000 new words. . . . Over 75,000 new meanings," claimed the ad for *The Random House Dictionary of the English Language.* Surely this new, greatly enlarged, completely revised and updated, unabridged edition of this monument to American wordsmithing would have a definition of *graphic design.* And yet, despite its claims, this dictionary supported my findings that no American dictionaries include a definition of our art and profession.

If graphic design isn't defined, what words are? I found: *desktop publishing, art director, interior design, advertising, computer graphics, environmental design,* and *marketing.*

I called Random House and spoke to an editorial assistant. She didn't believe me and looked it up in her own dictionary. "You're right," she admitted and told me to write to the editor to defend my position. ("He doesn't take phone calls," I was told.) I asked how a word gets into the dictionary, and she revealed that there are hundreds of subject experts who are constantly reading periodicals for new words; if one recurs frequently, it becomes a contender.

Next, I called Houghton Mifflin about its *New American Dictionary* (which includes such words as *break dancing, designated hitter,* and even *Woody Allen*). An editor there claimed that he had heard of graphic design and was quite surprised that it was not in their dictionary. "There are universities with departments of graphic design," he exclaimed in support of my position, and encouraged me to write a letter to the editor including a definition for inclusion into its database.

I was curious about whether this oversight was a Western phenomenon, so I called up a Japanese interpreter. Ironically, the American term *graphic design* is in Japanese dictionaries. As I have since found out, the term is very much in the mainstream of Japanese life, and, as my interpreter explained, even teenagers know what it is. It was defined as design that is expressed through the print media, like a poster, catalog, calendar, wrapping paper, and so on. Currently, it refers to every form of visual expression, such as video and computer animation. Having the word in the dictionary is an indication of the importance that the culture has assigned to graphic design.

Finally, I called American designers to learn how they felt about graphic design's omission from American dictionaries. Historian Philip Meggs encouraged me to continue my mission to get the word included. "American encyclopedias do not feature graphic design history, either," he said. Designer and author Richard Saul Wurman said he would like to see *graphic design* in the dictionary, "but I'd prefer the term *information architecture*," he said. And what does my six-year-old daughter Tess say? "Mom, if it's not in the dictionary, it's not a real word."

*Originally published in Volume 11, Number 1, 1993.*

# ELITIST DESIGN: HOW HIGH IS HIGH?

*Chuck Byrne*

In the Bay Area, where I live, there is a TV ad that refers to "designer luxuries." It seems to portray the public's current view of design. Design isn't supposed to be a luxury, it's supposed to be a necessity.

In its post–World War II incarnation, graphic design was seen as the means to more effective visual communications. When stated, that goal had the ring of truth about it—not unlike "freedom for all." It had a primal quality about it. The understanding, expression, and practice of that mission served graphic design well for some time. In fact, it made the profession in this country.

With the gradual acceptance of graphic design, those of us who had been involved in the profession for a few decades had to explain less and less what a graphic designer was. It was a relief not to have to explain that graphic design meant "good design" and commercial art meant "bad design." Never mind the obvious flaws in the argument—it worked. And, if occasionally you did have to explain further, it was just a matter of declaring, with great authority and smugness, that commercial art had been eviscerated by mindless advertising executives and MBAs, and that it produced only an endless stream of visual clutter that no one could read, much less understand.

By the 1980s, the profession had seduced itself into believing that it had established itself securely in the world, and why not? Many firms and designers were making more money and enjoying a popularity, particularly in the corporate world, that had never before been seen. At times it appeared that at any moment some graphic designers might even break through the final frontier of success and enter the realm of popular culture, heretofore visited only by fashion designers and a few interior designers and architects. With the occasional graphic designer beginning to appear on early morning TV, coverage on "Lifestyles of the Rich and Shallow" would surely follow.

For a variety of reasons ranging from changing personalities and the desire for personal distinction to anti-intellectualism, during this period there was a philosophical and aesthetic shift away from that rather rigid, collective, professional mission of effective communications toward a softer, less analytical, more decorative and personal kind of design. With that change, both in the minds of designers and the public, the perception of good design as a necessity shifted more and more toward design as a luxury.

During this transition, the efforts to enlighten the world to what constitutes our professional values began to be limited to publications and exhibitions that implied a holier-than-thou, take-it-or-leave-it attitude. In retrospect, these were more examples of professional aggrandizement than sincere attempts to enlighten the world to the value of good graphic design. The profession began to court art museums and shun business schools. And why not? Business was great and we began to believe we were the elite of visual communications.

This elitism extended to our relationships with others whose work is not so unlike our own. If they happen to have had the bad luck to have gone to the wrong school, where the words *commercial art* were used rather than *graphic design,* or—God forbid—found themselves working in advertising after they got out of school, or (worst sin of all) working for a marketing firm, or (the newest sin) taking a job in desktop publishing, they were and are, for the most part, considered not to be of the *true* brotherhood.

Sadly and slowly, in something akin to self-destruction, this elitism extended to clients—who soon had to meet an acceptable profile. It became a matter of course at many a design talk for the esteemed speaker to lecture those assembled not only about the evils of certain "outlawed occupations," like advertising, but then to regale the audience with at least one example of the ultimate in design machismo—the hasty dispatch of an unworthy client.

Taking this to heart, in some quarters it became common practice to reject clients for having too little budget or the wrong type of project to produce a publishable, award-winning piece. The profession's reputation for being difficult to deal with began to evolve.

This narrow set of values and attitude became known as "high design"— not necessarily a compliment.

A few years ago, in a report about the AIGA conference in San Antonio, which I wrote for *Print* magazine, I stated that graphic design appeared to be entering a period of "self-analysis." In great part, that self-analysis was prompted by the fallibility of the values of high design. That same questioning has trickled down to the interesting phenomenon of small groups of designers coming together for a kind of group therapy. In this recovery-like atmosphere the self-conscious designer rises at the prompting of the group leader, and in a quivering voice says, "My name is Chuck Byrne, and I'm a . . . a . . . graphic designer!" And the others present smile and nod in a gentle, knowing way.

Comradeship in one's confusion always seems to make one feel better. But the reasons for this awkward questioning and puzzlement seem to me to be, in part, obvious. Here the young and middle-aged together try to deal with the discrepancies between what they are told to believe about high design and the reality of their professional lives.

This chasm is nowhere better demonstrated than in the now fashionable use of the word *passion.* The simplistic use of the word has become high design's way of differentiating between the good guys and the bad guys. You're good if you have passion—or at least talk about it a lot—bad if you don't. This wonderful word has become symptomatic of the aloofness and remoteness of high design from the day-to-day facts of life for most designers.

It's easy to pontificate about "design passion" from high on a pulpit at a weekend design conference. Monday morning comes and the speakers are all back in their pristine studios, glancing over the work that their talented, hard-working helpers have done for the studio's suitably humble, but wealthy, clients in the master's absence. Meanwhile, most of the conference congregation, and the vast majority of other designers, have to face the often hard reality of their jobs, which, incidentally, they and their families would like them to keep. These are often designers with plenty of fire in their bellies, but who have to deal with a world of brand managers, art directors, marketing directors, department heads, and clients who have their own passions, few of which involve design.

*Passion* is a great word and a great feeling, and high design has no doubt produced some astoundingly beautiful work, but both have come to represent intolerance. Those who are quiet about their commitment, or who hold their clients' interests in at least as high esteem as their own, or lack access to rich clients, or lack certain powers of persuasion, can be committed to good design. They may simply be prevented from practicing it.

A stirring sermon delivered to them on design passion is not what they need. What they need is information. Detailed information on the primal values of design and, just as important, how to convince others to let it be the great contribution that it can be. They need the president of their local AIGA chapter to speak passionately to the Rotary or Jaycees about the value of effective communication through good design. They need the charismatic design leaders of this country to preach to the students in the leading business schools about "the necessity of design to the bottom line" rather than selling design students the "luxury design" line.

*Originally published in Volume 10, Number 3, 1992.*

# MAGICALLY DELICIOUS PACKAGING

*Forrest Richardson*

Imagine the almost-perfect consumer graphic design assignment: you create the package, get involved in the actual industrial design of the product, drive the positioning statement, and give birth to a mythical spokesperson. Do you stop there? Of course not, design buckaroo, you soar even higher by designing animated sequences, original music, and unforgettable jingles that help drive sales. Millions of people will fall in love with what you do. What you write on the package will be treated as a pseudoperiodical. On several occasions you will create games and design toys that serve as special promotions. You not only create something good for sales, you create something good in the eye of the consumer.

Anyone who's ever been four years old, had a four-year-old, or has been watching television at a time when only four-year-olds are supposed to be watching television knows what I'm talking about. Yes, Lucky Charms™—the single greatest example of total food packaging ever created and brought to market. The key here, of course, is the fact that it *was* brought to market. One ponders how (or if) something this on-target and this pointed could possibly make it through the jungle of nineties corporations, middle managers, business school mentalities, and product brand dweebs.

A few facts. Lucky Charms was introduced in 1964 by General Mills. The spokesman is L. C. Leprechaun. The critical concept here was well before its time:

oat-based cold cereal with tiny marshmallow surprises, referred to as "marbits" (feel free to sing along): "pink hearts, yellow moons, green clovers, and orange stars." The introductory campaign cost General Mills $2.5 million (amazing for 1964), but resulted in sales far exceeding any previous cereal launch by the company. In the mid-seventies, someone got bored and tried to force a new character, Waldo the Wizard, onto the box; all hell broke loose in Rainbowland, and L. C. was hired back. At the end of 1975, the "blue diamond" marbit made its debut, and sales went up 31 percent. Yes, 31 percent. In 1984, "purple horse-shoes" were extruded, and sales "only" increased by 25 percent. Recently, the world was introduced to a seventh marshmallow surprise, the "red balloon." Sales figures aren't in yet.

In a recently introduced limited-edition box you will find "dark green tree" marbits. With two proofs of purchase, General Mills will send you an actual tree, which I suspect will come with the message, "Kids! Don't attempt to eat this tree, it's a real live tree! Plant it, and do your part to make the world a greener and better place for laddies, lassies, and leprechauns of all ages."

So what's wrong? Well, hear me out. The problem here is that we fail, millions of times daily, to recognize that, as graphic designers, we can have influence on not just the decoration of packages, but the actual heart and soul of products.

I find most cereal packaging hideous and unimaginative. Until recently, this wasn't serious stuff. In my childhood, I was taught to get up, use the toilet, find the kitchen, reach for a box, smell the milk, pour the cereal, pour the milk, and spend the next ten minutes intently reading the back of the box regardless of how many times I'd read it before. It could have been written in Chinese. If there was an interesting toy inside, I'd empty the box into a broiler pan and take the prize to school. If there was an interesting toy offer to mail away for, I'd mutilate the box and eat an extra bowl to force another purchase, thereby moving toward the goal of obtaining the specified number of box tops required to get said toy.

Nowadays, we have serious-looking cereal packages where I believe there's a place for an alternative. What on earth is Product 19? Special K? These are high-fiber cereals that have been designed to look like medicine. No charm. No character. No marbits! Certainly marbits could be made in the shape of vintage Porsches. Certainly Ralph Lauren could come up with tasteful, preppy marbits in soft renaissance colors or fly-fishing motifs. Certainly we do not need to live our lives with Nut 'n Honey commercials.

It wouldn't be fair (or entertaining) to not mention Teenage Mutant Ninja Turtle cereal. There are marshmallow bits, but this cereal hasn't been built from the ground up. It's riding on the back of Turtle toys and Turtle motion pictures. Where's the glory in this? Nothing makes sense here, including the decision to make pizza-shaped marshmallow bits (because everyone knows these Turtles love pizza) that taste like hotel shampoo, not pizza. There is very little story line. The boxes may as well be used for target practice because everyone knows these

Turtles also like violence. This cereal, by the way, is made by Ralston Purina, which hides its name in black ink on a saturated red background. If you're listening, Ralston Purina, please consider enlarging your "checkerboard" trademark and putting a massive banner on the box that reads, "From the Makers of Monkey Chow." What better way to sell to young consumers than by letting them know their cereal is made by the same company that makes cereal for monkeys?

Well, I suppose it's time to get back to the *AIGA Journal*; after all, that is what you expected to be reading. Just indulge me one further step as I demonstrate the detail to which I refer. Do you know what shape Lucky Charms cereal is made to resemble? Not the marbits, the cereal.

Perhaps now you'll believe the value of packaging well beyond boxboard and laminated wrappings, beyond inks and typography, beyond trademarks and UPC codes. I believe in designers being a party to the design of the product, the design of the reason for the product, and the design of the story of the product—including all the subtle designs that come with that story. Somewhere in all this, I believe there is a value to the client.

And I believe several of you will go buy a box.

*Originally published in Volume 10, Number 3, 1992.*

# THE LIMITING IMPERATIVE
*Ralph Caplan*

There are a million things you can do, you know that there are.
—*Yusef Islaam (formerly Cat Stevens)*

Sure we know that there are. The problem is choosing among them. That's why the creative process is likely to begin with the recognition of limits, the acceptance of constraints, the search for a wall against which to beat one's head. Freedom can imprison you with choices.

Once, at a design management conference, I was preceded on the program by the creative director of a greeting card company, a charming speaker who said he had a staff of several hundred "creatives." He showed slides of their work. I don't know how many creatives there were in the audience, but there seemed to be a number of inquisitives, and perhaps an aggressive or two, for some of the greeting card copy was itself greeted harshly. "Just remember," the speaker said defensively, "My writers have tight restrictions. They aren't writing sonnets."

I was stunned. I tried to imagine the rules his writers must have had to follow. Maybe a few lines of humorous, patriotic Father's Day copy to accompany a line drawing of a paterfamiliar bear and aimed at a target market of adult children of either gender who still live at home. Even so, compared to the requirements of a sonnet, those were not so much tight restrictions as a mandate for permissiveness, a license to play.

When my turn came, I could not resist pointing out that a sonnet consists of fourteen lines. And that the meter must be iambic: *da dum, da dum,* not *dum da, dum da.* And that each line needs five iambs, the last of which has to rhyme with another line. And not just any other line, but with the line decreed by a rigid rhyme scheme, like *a b b a, a b b a, c d c d e e.* In other words, the first, fourth, fifth, and eighth lines have to rhyme with each other, as do the second, third, sixth, and seventh lines. Of the last six lines, the ninth has to rhyme with the eleventh, the tenth with the twelfth, and the thirteenth and fourteenth with each other. Half the lines, in other words, are in a sense dictated by the other half. Talk about constraints. . . .

Well, prompted by the flagrant defamation of sonnet form, I did talk about constraints; and I have been doing it ever since. As an introduction to design constraints, I have sometimes asked design students to write a sonnet in one half hour. That takes a little longer, but not much. It really isn't hard to do, and every designer understands why it isn't: the constraints are so tight that there are virtually no formal decisions to make. To be sure, that's no way to write good poetry. It's not even a good way to write bad poetry. But it is a very good way to make a point about design, and about creative work in general, whether performed by artists, writers, composers, designers, or creatives. The very process of producing a sonnet that, however awful, meets all the technical requirements of the form, usually also yields a line or two that can be read without cringing. In fact, the best lines are often those that come into existence only because they are required to rhyme with weaker ones.

The literature of the creative process is studded with examples of the limiting imperative. "My liberty," Stravinsky said, "consists in moving outside the narrow bounds which I set myself. . . . I experience a sort of terror if I set down to work and find an infinity of possibilities open to me." All creative people must feel this. By circumventing that terror, the formal limits seduce you into decisions, just as such standard design constraints as cost, tooling, time, and materials do.

Charles Eames, all of whose work was rooted in a fierce embrace of constraint, observed that it was easy to do something bad in plasticene, but hard to do anything bad in granite. It was not, he conceded, easy to do anything good in granite, and that, in a way, was the point. The hardness, the resistance of the material, meant that even the worst sculptor was inhibited from excess.

Not all constraints encourage good work, however. The constraints of fashion are an example. A grid can be liberating, but the grid-as-fashion became a device for strangling any impulse toward originality or even communication. Helvetica was meant to be liberating, but, as fashion, it became the typographic equivalent of leg irons.

An experienced designer knows that some constraints must be rejected out of hand, but no genuine designer objects to constraints as such. The aim is to eschew the constraints that militate against excellence, while embracing those that, like any other aspect of truth, will at last make us free.

*Originally published in Volume 8, Number 4, 1991.*


# ART AND DESIGN: LOVERS OR JUST GOOD FRIENDS?

*Lorraine Wild*


It may well be that only graphic design students worry over whether design is an art or a craft, particularly those studying design in the cradle of an art school. The student's desire to inject self-expression into design is abetted by envy of the fellow art student's apparent self-determination and freedom from headlines. Of course, the paycheck and lack of personal thinking time that accompany an entry-level design job help push questions about art versus function back into the murk. These questions are dormant until one is successful enough to afford that ultimate luxury, time to muse. This occurred to me upon the observation that Paul Rand's latest book is titled *The Designer's Art*, and its first, impeccably reasoned but ultimately inconclusive, essay is titled "Art for Art's Sake." The fact that Mr. Rand teaches design, and therefore is still struggling with students and their uncomfortable questions, may explain his ongoing attempt to situate design between expressive art and obedience to function, once and for all.

But there is a historical dimension to all of this. Mr. Rand is certainly one of our leading modernists, a designer whose ideas bear witness to the great influence of modernism on the development of the graphic design profession. The generation of designers producing work just before and after World War II (besides Rand, this would include Herbert Bayer, Lester Beall, Will Burtin, William Golden, Alvin Lustig, Herbert Matter, and Ladislav Sutnar, among others) believed that form *did* follow function and that the content of a problem would dictate the terms of a stylistic solution. This is basic modern rhetoric, inherited from the philosophers of the Bauhaus, constructivism, and so on. But a significant mutation of the ideas and forms of European modernism occurred during the transatlantic crossing. Ideals of functionalism were accompanied by formal experiments of cubism, the typographic excesses of futurism, or the images of all the other isms, without regard to the fact that the movements themselves were often at cross-purposes to one another. American designers (native or émigré) did not organize themselves into a coherent movement; they accepted modernism as a buffet from which one could pick and choose favorite dishes. This freedom of individual interpretation was exacerbated by the rise of abstract expressionism in the late forties—another modern art movement that could be used as a style. Abstract expressionism elevated the artists' gestures as evidence of the mind (conscious and subconscious) and the artists' processes. This got mixed in with the modern principle of design empowered by concept, and the result was work that did not look like anything that proceeded it.

This confusion of art and function can be seen in an essay titled "Eleven Painters Influencing Graphic Arts" by the art historian Thomas Hess, published in the *Ninth Graphic Arts Production Yearbook* (1950). In the article, Hess reproduces images by De Chirico, Mondrian, and others to analyze the effect that the arts might have on graphic design. Talking about abstract painting and using a de Kooning painting for an illustration, Hess says, "The new style, with its rich textures, its ambiguous forms that seem abstract but still retain human associations, exists; it may well have an effect on how the magazines of the next generation will look." Abstract expressionism is subjectivity taken to an extreme, yet here Hess seems to be saying that it has a place in the functional design of modernism. Hess also says, "The art of today has two common characteristics: emphasis on the beauty of order and of the materials themselves, and absorption in the drama of the individual creator whose ultimate expression commands an equally intimate response from the spectator. Are not these two characteristics also relevant in describing most of the best graphic art?" Of those two characteristics, the former is more obviously connected to what graphic design is supposed to be; the latter, less so. On the other hand, an "intimate response" is exactly what the most persuasive graphic design is supposed to solicit—immediate comprehension. Whether this could be accomplished subjectively or objectively was not determined.

So there, right at the beginning, the line between art and function in design was comfortingly confused. And if we look at the work of designers who produced such compelling images at that time, we see just as wide a range of views on the subject as designers assume now. For instance, Herbert Bayer always claimed that he was primarily an artist (actually, he was more specific than that—he said he was a painter), and that the only difference he could detect between art and design was that function was internal to art and external to design. If you look at Bayer's painting and compare it to a work such as his *World Geographic Atlas* of 1954, the differences in subjectivity allowed in his highly rationalized painting and the absence of it in the atlas attest to a different attitude taken by Bayer in his art than in his design. But then you have some of his idiosyncratic

designs for the "Great Ideas of Western Man" ad campaign for Container Corporation; they are hybrids in which the function of personal expression in the service
of a concept seems quite obscure.

Paul Rand takes almost exactly the same stance in refusing to draw a
strong line between art and design in his work, stating that the real difference lies
in need (the fact that there is usually a real problem that initiates and is addressed
by the work of design). Despite this liberal stance, one has to search for any work
by Rand (this writer has not found any) that does not fall solidly into the category
of functional design. There are some pieces—particularly those where Rand had
to invent a symbol—that are more imaginative and therefore more personal than
others, but it is almost impossible by the most objective standards to find one
that doesn't work, first and foremost, as a piece of public visual communication.

In 1949, *American Artist* described Lester Beall's working method (with
jazz on the turntable in his studio): "The insistent beat works into his subconscious mind and stimulates creation. The emotion that initiates his design is
subjected to cool scrutiny as the project advances." It is impossible to tell if this
description parallels Beall's idea of what his own process was, but there is no
doubt, looking at much of Beall's work, that intuition was the engine for many of
his design solutions. Many of Beall's projects show direct evidence of his hand,
either in the forms themselves or in their spontaneous quality. The influence of
abstract art and the value it placed on individual expression was very useful for
Beall, for the presence of his own subjective artfulness is visible, to a greater or
lesser degree, in every piece that he produced.

At the other end of the art-function spectrum stands the work of William
Golden. Golden was quite disdainful of the infiltration of art into design, particularly the personal references made acceptable by abstract expressionism. He
claimed that clients accepted design solutions based on modern art because it
provided socially acceptable camouflage for the fact that they really had nothing
to say (or worse, something to hide) and that the designer who looked for deep
meaning beyond the function of a piece would be better off at the psychiatrist's
office. Although the work that Golden art-directed at CBS was actually done by a
changing staff of illustrators, photographers, and designers, there is no doubt that
it is animated by a singular vision of appropriateness and quality, the same values
that one could attribute to any well-crafted object. Objectivity, function, and
craft are elevated above the personal statement, and the work still functions as
valid modern design.

One gets the feeling when faced with the question of art versus function
that it is a conundrum not worth trying to solve. But we are now working in an
era when even the most self-indulgent designers refer to themselves as "problem
solvers," while appropriating imagery from art, pop culture, or anywhere without
thought as to what this might mean. The earlier generation of designers could not
avoid redefining design in the face of art versus function because they had no
immediate models to follow. Perhaps the fact that they had to deliberately posi-

tion themselves on the spectrum is what gives so much of their work a sense of coherence, commitment, and vitality that we so desperately seek today.

*Originally published in Volume 5, Number 2, 1987.*

# SIDESHOWS IN THE EVOLUTION OF THE ALPHABET
*Jerry Kelly*

In the history of literacy, an extremely significant development (credited to the Phoenicians) was the use of a visual mark to represent a sound of spoken language, rather than a complete idea. Earlier systems had relied upon pictographs or ideograms to represent complete ideas or objects. While the new system required far more written strokes to represent a thought than the earlier systems did, since most words would require many characters, it also meant that far fewer characters would need to be learned. For example, Chinese—a modern pictographic alphabet—requires well over two thousand characters to be memorized, while English has only twenty-six characters to be learned, which in an almost infinite number of combinations can represent the most complex ideas. Pictograms were adapted to form the early phonetic alphabets (as in "alpha/betas," or ABCs). The letter *A* began as a stylized ox, but became the symbol for the first sound in the Phoenician word meaning "ox"; *B* was a stylized floor plan representing "house," *M* was a stylized symbol representing "water," and so on. All these letterforms were originally pictograms representing entire words, but were adapted to phonetic use to stand for sounds instead. In many cultures, both ancient and contemporary, these symbols do a remarkable job of representing all possible sounds in a language, and thereby all possible words. For example, today, the Roman alphabet of twenty-six characters is almost perfect in its ability to represent the spoken Italian or German languages.

However, some languages have not developed as neatly as Italian or German. In these other instances, spelling has evolved in such a way that the twenty-six symbols for sounds do not consistently represent a unique sound, but instead can represent several sounds. The most notorious example of this is in English, where a single character (such as *y*) can represent totally different sounds (as in *try* or *you*). In this troublesome language, there are also many sounds that are represented by more than one letter (*th* forms a unique sound). Some sounds have just the opposite problem, where different alphabetic symbols can represent the exact same sound: the *y* in *try* represents exactly the same sound as *ie* in *lie*.

English has a far from precise system of using symbols to represent sounds. It can get very confusing to the uninitiated. This certainly adds to the difficulty of learning the system, and for this reason and others (perhaps even just a sense of tidiness?), several attempts have been made to develop a system of symbols that accurately represents all the spoken sounds in English. (Reformers have conducted similar experiments in other languages as well.) These systems take two basic forms. Most commonly there have been attempts—for centuries—to modify the Roman alphabet to represent the forty or so sound units upon which all words in English are built, or to otherwise change the accepted alphabetic arrangement. The other method would be to develop a new, distinct set of symbols—perhaps not even based on any previous alphabet—to depict each of these sounds.

Throughout the history of printing, numerous attempts have been made by spelling reformers, often in collaboration with type designers, to adapt type-faces to phonetic requirements. The earliest attempt in English was probably the thirty-four-character Alphabetum Anglicum. Another early experiment, and certainly one of the best known attempts at changing letterforms, is the alphabet Sir Thomas More appended to his most famous work, *Utopia,* in 1516. However, More's reform was totally imaginary and somewhat facetious, concerning itself solely with changing the forms of the letters, not the sounds they represent, and is therefore out of the scope of the reading/phonetic proposals we are considering. A fascinating experiment in phonetic alphabetical reform from earlier in this century (and, in my opinion, the most aesthetically successful since the Arrighi/Trissino collaboration of the sixteenth century) was the modified alphabet used by Robert Bridges, Britain's poet laureate, in the volumes of his essays published by the Oxford University Press. Bridges had the good fortune to be assisted in the development of his new font by Stanley Morison, one of the giants of typography in this century. As a typographical adviser to the British Monotype Corporation, Morison was in an extremely advantageous position to work with Bridges on his alphabet. His program of typeface development at Monotype, based mainly on well chosen and carefully manufactured revivals of historical types, but also a sprinkling of original modern designs such as Eric Gill's Perpetua and Joseph Blumenthal's Emerson, was well established by the time he began working with Bridges on his font in 1927. Morison, an expert in typographic history and an admirer of Arrighi's italic types, chose his own adaptation of Arrighi's third type, made by Monotype in 1923 and christened Blado (after Arrighi's printer), as the basis for the Bridges phonetic alphabet.

It is a sound premise to use an italic rather than a roman design for adaptation to a phonetic usage. Roman letterforms are ultraconservative to the extent that variants common in the early years of printing, such as *h* with a round right stroke or *p* with a line through the descender, are now considered jarring. However, we still readily accept alternate forms, such as g or ɡ and *a* or a. Morison exploited these acceptable alternate forms in creating the additional symbols Bridges needed for his phonetic alphabet. The result is one of the most successful experiments in this direction. The Bridges alphabet can be read fairly easily in the normal manner, while still delineating a wider range of sounds required in English through the use of alternate forms. Morison himself, often a severe critic of his own work, thought well enough of the type to include a reproduction of it as plate 345 in his monumental survey *The Typographic Book 1450–1935.*

There has also been much experimentation in this century, much of it avant-garde in nature, with combining the standard roman font of twenty-six lowercase and twenty-six uppercase letters. Lucian Bernhard, Herbert Bayer, Paul Renner, Bradbury Thompson, Charles Peignot, and others have all designed alternative types based on our Roman letters, but with changes radical enough to be deemed a variant alphabet. Bradbury Thompson's alphabet consisted of basically combining upper- and lowercase forms (totaling fifty-two characters) into one alphabet of twenty-six letters, which he called the Monalphabet. In 1944, inspired by Bayer's work in a similar vein, Thompson set an entire issue (no. 145) of *Westvaco Inspiration for Printers* in a Monalphabet based on Futura. Four decades later, in 1988, Thompson acknowledged that "critics today may view the Monalphabet experiment as a futile waste of time," but, nonetheless, he believed it to be "an idea that remains to be tested and played with" (*The Art of Graphic Design,* Yale University Press, 1988, page 37).

William Addison Dwiggins, the famous American type designer, also experimented with combining a mixture of upper- and lowercase letters with unusual characters in an alternative version of his Winchester typeface. He began dabbling with this new alphabet, which avoided ascenders and descenders, in 1942. By 1946, the type was ready. It was used only in a few unusual pieces designed by Dwiggins himself and in some promotional materials for Mergenthaler Linotype (which produced the font). An interesting essay in what Thompson called Monalphabet design, and one of the few that sees any use at all today, is A. M. Cassandre's Peignot type of 1937. This font, which is serifless but has stressed weight to the strokes like Lydian or Optima, was produced by the Deberny and Peignot foundry in Paris. Occasionally, one sees it used today for very specialized typography, although almost never for running text. (Readers may remember it as the typeface used in the title captions for the *Mary Tyler Moore Show.*)

There have also been more radical attempts at modifying the symbols used to represent sounds in English. Surely the most revolutionary in modern times was the Shaw Phonetic Alphabet competition. In his will, George Bernard Shaw instructed his executors to offer a reward of £500 for a totally new set of characters, not based on any previous alphabets, to represent all the sounds in the English language. Some thought this to be Shaw's last sarcastic joke, and, indeed, this aspect of his will was contested. However, in 1958, a committee selected a compromise submission, incorporating a system developed by Kingsley Road to which it appended aspects of three other entries. In 1962, Penguin Books published an edition of Shaw's *Androcles and the Lion* with English text in Roman letters and the Shaw phonetic alphabet on facing pages. This was the only book ever printed in the type.

The most thorough and serious attempt to reform the phonetic aspects of the marriage of the Roman alphabet with the English language was made by Sir Isaac Pitman. At its height, it was claimed that the Pitman alphabet (called ITA, or International Teaching Alphabet) was used in over ten thousand schools. Monotype Ehrhardt with special ITA characters added was a particularly handsome example of this alphabet and appeared in many of Monotype's specimen books.

Surely no one would want to stand in the way of anything that would make reading (and, by extension, learning) easier. However, the forms of our letters are so well established that any attempt to modify them results in a deterioration, not enhancement, of comprehension. One can rightfully question whether there is any need for reform. To my knowledge, no studies have been done comparing the difficulty of learning English, whose system of spelling is woefully inadequate from a phonetic viewpoint, to learning a language with a totally phonetic alphabet, such as Italian. I would guess that to the facile mind of a young child there is negligible difference between totally phonetic and semiphonetic languages, even if older, less receptive minds find English more difficult. The attempts at alphabet reform throughout the centuries make interesting sideshows in the evolution of our alphabet and language, but I think it is fairly safe to say that the current forms of our twenty-six letters will be around long after the already rusting fonts of Pitman, Shaw, Thompson, and others have disappeared.

*Originally published in Volume 15, Number 2, 1997.*

# PLACING AN ORDER WITH THE AAA SIGN PAINTING COMPANY
*Steven Heller*

Last June, I called the AAA Sign Company for three placards; the following is a transcript of that conversation.

*AAA, this is Joey, can I help you?*
I need some signs made. Do you do limited quantities?

*You mean more than one and less than three? How many you want?*
Three should do it.

*Yeah, we can do three. How big?*
Well, about four by four feet each. They're for my kid's day camp.

*Four by four! Sure, we can do four by four. For when?*
I need them in two weeks; you see, they're having a father and son
carnival—

*Two weeks. We're real busy now. It depends on what you want to say.*
Well, not a lot. One should read "Dunking Dad," another is "Simon Sez
Who?" and the last is "Ring of Fire." They're some of the events.

*Sure, sure, I know. Well, I can do it in two weeks at the regular price, but only
if you go for the plain lettering.*
Plain? What's plain? Do you have a sample book or something?

*You want to come by the shop and see some of our old signs, be my guest. But
plain is plain! You know, straight letters, like on the sanitation trucks—
nothing fancy, no flourishes, no shadows, no feet. You want feet, it costs extra.*
Feet? Oh, you mean serifs.

*Huh? We call the bars on letters feet. In any case, for a rush it's extra.*
Extra's OK. But I'd like them to be festive, maybe country fair-like, not
like the average supermarket sign—

*You know we're well known for our supermarket signs. But, never mind, I know
what you mean. You want it to look like a cartoon splash panel—or a pinball
machine, right?*
Yeah, I guess a comic book motif would be nice. Can you do it in two
weeks?

*If Vinnie's free. He's great with that stuff—he draws superheros in his spare
time. But it'll cost you.*
But, listen, just because it's in comic book style, I don't want it to look
scrawled or graffiti-like. I need to have big bold letters, with drop
shadows, and a striking in-line color so you can see it from a distance.

*Shadow, color, and feet too, right?*
Yes, but can I see a rough before you do it?

*You mean a sketch? If you want to come down to the shop you can see it on the*

*board before Vinnie paints it, be my guest. But we ain't got much time. Listen, it'll be fine. The kids will love it. Vinnie's been doing this stuff for a long time—he's even gone to art school. Trust me.*
But if I don't like it, I'm not going to pay for it!

*Sure, sure. But we need half of the money in advance. I can take Visa and BankAmericard over the phone.*
Okay, how much will it cost?

*Three four by fours: Vinnie's time and labor. Plus rush service. That comes to $165 plus tax. Give me 80 bucks on deposit. By the way, how'd you hear about us?*
You were the first sign painter listed in the Yellow Pages.

*Yeah, it pays to advertise.*

*Originally published in Volume 10, Number 3, 1992.*

# A MASTERPIECE!

*Massimo Vignelli*

**A**mazing but true: there is a masterpiece of information architecture printed on every food package sold in the United States. The first time I saw the Nutrition Facts label, it earned my unlimited enthusiasm. The label is perfectly structured, with a bold rule at the top to draw attention and support the height of the text that hangs from it. Following the bar, a bold line of type, *Nutrition Facts,* boldly states the content line by line, separated by a light rule. Every nutrition component is entered in a clear manner. There are no highlights, no balloons, no flashes; in short, none of the marketing devices normally associated with the junkyard of packaging design. The label is a clean testimonial of civilization, a statement of social responsibility, and a masterpiece of graphic design. Not a small achievement in today's graphic landscape.

You can imagine my joy in seeing it exhibited at the AIGA *Information Graphics* show. Beyond the aesthetics of the design solution, what strikes me more than anything else is the built-in mechanism to control the implementation. I have seen the label on all kinds of packages: round, square, rectangular, vertical, horizontal. On some packages, its orientation is "portrait" and on others "landscape"; sometimes it is extremely landscaped (as on Hershey's chocolate bars, for example). In all the variations, the label maintains its visual integrity, even if basically distorted by such different sizes and shapes. This is one of the most difficult things to obtain in a graphic design program and they have done it. For this accomplishment alone they deserve the Presidential Design Award.

The only thing that strikes me as strange is the anonymity of its authorship. In the wall caption for the *Information Graphics* show, the AIGA credits the office responsible for enforcing the application of the label, but will the real designer step forward and receive our unlimited gratitude for having spared us another visual humiliation and for having given us a sign that civilization still lives?

This little label is indeed the best piece of graphic information—or better yet, information architecture—that has surfaced in this country in the last twenty years. It reaches us at a time when graphic design has almost disintegrated and, perhaps for this very reason, it seems to have greater value.

This responsible little label comes at a time when I feel a schism is rocking our profession. On one side are information architects, rooted in history, typography, semiotics; on the other side are graphic designers, rooted in advertising, pictorial arts, and trends. It seems to me that the development of our profession, as we have seen in countless annuals, awards, and magazines, is clearly pointing out that this dichotomy is in action. Personally, I feel I no longer have anything to share with the so-called graphic design of today: not the concept, not the typefaces, not the layout—nothing.

But I do have a lot to share with many of the designers in the *Information Graphics* show. Therefore, I conclude that I am no longer a graphic designer, but an information architect, and from now on that is how I will describe the meaning of my work and the scope of my activity.

For me, to be an information architect means to organize information in a way that is essentially retrievable, understandable, visually captivating, emotionally involving, and easily identifiable. Information should be semantically rooted, syntactically correct, pragmatically efficient: it doesn't work otherwise.

I am sure there is room for two sides of the schism, ours and theirs. Finally accepting this reality, I feel much more relaxed now than I have ever been. All of a sudden everything is clear, each of us with our Nutrition Facts label, revealing our content to the world, where, indeed, there is room for all of us designers.

*Originally published in Volume 14, Number 2, 1996.*

# DESIGN FOR UNDERSTANDING

*Richard Saul Wurman*

Twenty-six years ago, I produced a book called *Cities: A Comparison of Form and Scale,* a very simple, single-idea publication. Out of white plasticene, my students and I modeled cities and towns of the world—contemporary and historic—on the same scale. We photographed them from above and put them into a big book so that one could see relationships between scale and size. The clarity and strength that came from this exercise far exceeded my expectations. This visual comparison of the cities of the world taught me that you only understand something relative to what you already understand.

In the next few years, there will be a transition from beauty-driven to information-driven graphics. It is a mistake to think that every graph or chart, such as those in the many redesigned American newspapers, represents information, because they don't. We are surrounded by all these things that look like information is supposed to look, but which do not inform—nor are they expressed in the appropriate form.

It is easy to look at information, but information is frequently not so easy to understand. The prime task of graphic designers, and, indeed, of writers too, is to communicate understandably. Even a simple idea made clear has tremendous power.

As designers, our task is difficult because of the prevailing idea that information graphics is anything that looks like information, rather than that which truly informs. Take the word *information* and see that the word *inform* is its root. And take the word *inform* and see that the word *form* is its root. If things don't inform, I would say that they are not information—although they may look like information.

*USA Today*'s weather map meets all the popular criteria of informational graphics, and, yet, it is a bad map. It looks the way we were taught that information should look. It has three dimensions and multicolors (where they are not needed), and it is full of numbers (redundant information). What it wants to be is a comparative map that informs, and, to be so, it must represent not only temperature, but comparative human comfort.

Ninety degrees in New York City is not ninety degrees in Phoenix and therefore cannot be on the same contour. Taking other factors into account—wind chill or humidity, as well as temperatures—a weather map could reflect relative levels of comfort around the country. But we have been conditioned to accept faulty and inadequate information because nothing better is at hand.

Information made understandable and allowed to perform becomes handsome, particularly when its primary purpose is not beauty. I have a great belief in the value of graphics that perform well—not only function, but perform.

It is really silly to have the job of making things understandable as a specialty. It should be the rule, not the option. But many designers who do not specialize are seduced only by aesthetic beauty. So, a number of otherwise workable maps have been gussied up with clifflike shorelines (making them three-dimensional), shadowed roads, and misused color. By floating them in space, putting them on angles, and using other conventional devices, they say, "I don't inform, but I am so friendly and stylish that it is okay to look at me." This gets in the way of understanding.

Two years ago, the AIGA held a competition called *Functional Graphics*, a misleading title at best. Judgments were based not on performance but on appearance; entries were okay if they looked the part. I am not faulting the jury because I do not know how we would evaluate the performance of "functional" graphics in the given time, but if that show couldn't set the standard, what can we expect from others?

My interest in function comes from my background as an architect. In the past, an antiseptic way of describing architecture was "form follows function." To me, function is something basic, like digestion, but performance is like the interpretation of Shakespeare; it is the art of satisfying a need. Function is a basic requirement, and it doesn't require artfulness. It is a word that has to do with something being adequate; it is a basic term. That is why I take exception to the title of the show. To appreciate it, one must elevate it to an art form, and then it becomes the art of information, not the function of information. The term *functional graphics* is a put-down.

The end result of functionalism as an aesthetic from the 1920s wound up in the architecture of the Centre Georges Pompidou in Paris. It expresses the way one would fantasize a building to function. It is like a Hollywood model of the way a Donald Duck building would perform. But a building doesn't function that way, and the architecture is patently dishonest. I can understand the seduction of doing that. I can see in my own work the error of trying to make things look more informative than they are: in making presentations so that some piece of information will be taken more seriously.

What interests me is more elusive than theories and rules. It is trying to figure out the morphology, the structure, of a body of data; trying to discover the organizing principles so that I can navigate my path through it; so that I can allow others to find their own paths; so that the relationships within it are not prescribed, but occur in the mind of the person using it. It all sounds a bit mystical, but it is really no more than following personal interests rather than the rule book. I am particularly interested in the idea of indexes and tables of contents, and how they work as an outline that invites readers to put the contents and connections together in their own head and draw their own conclusions. This might be called a Tinkertoy approach: the little pieces fit together. That was my approach in the various *Access* books and in the Yellow Pages for Pacific Bell Directory; to apply the guiding principles of time, the fundamental issues of proximity, or spatial relationships as a focus on subject matter driven by interest, location, connections, tasks, and time of day. The result is accessibility to information.

We all seem to suffer from the phenomenon I call *information anxiety*. It springs from several false notions, such as it is better to say "I know" than "I don't know," answering a question is better than asking one, or you learn from success.

Good questions lead to good answers. In asking the question, you learn. When you answer the question and have already found the answer, there is no growth. One learns by examining what doesn't work. One learns from failure.

Learning is remembering what you are interested in. My father told me, "Don't learn what is in the *Encyclopedia Britannica*, learn how to use it." The idea that the fashioning of an educated person can be accomplished by knowing one thousand or ten thousand facts is absurd.

The following story is therefore apropos: let's say I contact Avanti, a company that makes lifelike stuffed animals, and ask it to make a set of 260 life-sized stuffed dogs. I ask Avanti to make a male and a female of each breed accepted into the American Kennel Club. When they arrive, I have this extraordinary bevy of stuffed dogs. I stand them on a large floor facing every which way, and I say to the people standing there, "You organize them smallest to largest, the tallest to shortest; by popularity in the U.S., by actual population, by when they were accepted into the American Kennel Club, by length of tail," etc. At the same time, we tie ribbons around their necks, colored according to which of the six major categories the dog belongs—sporting dogs, hounds, work dogs, terriers, toys, and nonsporting—so that as they are arranged in various groups, I can also see what classification of dog they are. We add ribbons made of flags from the countries of origin.

Why is this such a revealing story? Because every time the dogs are arranged in a different way, I start seeing new information created by relationships independent of the subject of the arrangement. I can see that the most popular dogs are perhaps big dogs, or which dogs came most recently into the club, or how few of the little dogs have ever been champions. I am able to see relationships that are independent of each of the rather arbitrary organizations of those 260 animals.

The creative organization of information creates new information. *The dogs never change.*

There are only three businesses that have to do with communication: the transmission business (telephone, television, and the delivery of data), the storage business (which is experiencing an exploding technology of data compression such as laser disk technology, CD-ROM, CDI, and CD video), and the understanding business. The transmission business represents a river of data, and the storage business is like a reservoir into which the river flows. Yet this reservoir is held back by a huge dam, and very little understanding is getting through. Enter the understanding business. There's no corporation in the understanding business. Writers, even good writers, serve the twin gods of accuracy and style—not understanding; graphic designers serve the single god of looking good.

We are drowning in data. This has resulted from the combination of slightly better transmission and enormously better storage, and is exacerbated by the lack of attention from any profession, field, corporation, business, government, organization, or institution on understanding that data. So, while we have data being transmitted slightly more efficiently and being stored enormously more efficiently, there is not an increased level of understanding coming out of that mix.

The understanding business, brought about by this extreme situation, is going to be born out of necessity, out of the black hole of American corporations and businesses. Until now, it hasn't existed, but in the next five to ten years it will exist in a big way. And there are just two reasons why. First, people have finally started to recognize this incredible backed-up volume of stuff, in incomprehensible form, that has to be dealt with somehow, and, second, there is a lot of money to be made in understanding.

*Originally published in Volume 6, Number 2, 1988.*

# GENERIC DESIGNERS
*Dugald Stermer*

Among many graphic designers, it has long been an article of faith, if not propaganda, that we are, above all else, problem solvers. It is indoctrinated into us like a catechism: designers must aspire to be self-effacing professionals who direct their whole intellect, talent, skill, and ego to diagnosing their client's need, then focus all their energies on creating the uniquely appropriate solution, while valiantly attempting to submerge any evidence of a personal style.

This particular line of illogic also holds that there is a single perfect answer to each problem and that, like snowflakes, no two are alike. Often the notion is carried further to claim that for every job there is one ideal typeface, one grade of paper, one photographer or illustrator, and, predictably, one designer— usually the one holding forth about all this. In this carefully considered formula, the slightest hint of the personality of the designer would, the theory goes, compromise the intended communication. The evidence suggests otherwise.

It is demonstrable that any reasonably alert layperson with some background in and exposure to graphic design—say, a corporate communications director—could, with some accuracy, pick out the work of most of our noteworthy practitioners from across the room, regardless of the variety of clients involved or the type of pieces (annual report, house organ, identity program, etc.). The matches he or she would make would not be perfect, but the odds favor a high success rate.

The fact is that Massimo Vignelli's work just doesn't look like that of Mike Vanderbyl, nor does that resemble Peter Bradford's, which wouldn't be mistaken for Woody Pirtle's, while Deborah Sussman's design is entirely unlike any of the above. Furthermore, even the product of a single design office varies greatly, not so much depending on who it's for, but on who did it. For more than two decades, Milton Glaser and Seymour Chwast produced an enormous body of marvelously thoughtful and varied work under the umbrella of Push Pin Studios, yet only the most myopic would mistake the projects of one for that of the other. Ivan Chermayeff approaches design differently from his longtime partner, Tom Geismar, and the results are identifiable. And Kit Hinrichs's work is clearly distinctive from that of Vance Jonson, Neil Shakery, Marty Pedersen, and even the other Hinrichs on the letterhead, Linda.

All the above designers consistently demonstrate their individuality in ways obvious even to the disinterested; indeed, they could hardly do otherwise. And that, I think, is all to the good. Rather than getting in the way of their clients' messages, their characteristics actually enhance them, much in the way that the distinct personalities of great actors can, if directed well, inform and augment the playwright's dialogue.

There are, nevertheless, a large group of designers, probably the majority, who have repressed their identities to the point where it would be difficult, if not impossible, to attribute their work from one piece to the next. I'm sure that many of these professionals would, in righteous defense, claim some version of the "doctrine" described above. I would also lay long odds that nearly all of them would eagerly trade in their anonymous purity for the reputations of our more identifiable designers. For their sakes, as well as for the benefit of our craft, I wish they would try.

I'm not, of course, advocating that we disregard our clients' wishes while we go about indulging our tastes and making personal statements on their time and money. Even portrait painters don't accept a commission and then paint a likeness entirely of their own choosing. I am, however, suggesting that we might abandon, or at least modify, our hype about what it is we do for a living.

Most people in the communicative arts have what literary critics are pleased to call an "authentic voice." Composers write scores for films on a variety of subjects with differing moods and themes, and manage to stay true to the spirit of each new project, as well as to themselves. Designers might well adopt that stance, if only because it is the only one that makes any sense, given our natures. And if the work has integrity, it won't in any way compromise its worth to the client.

To that point, it might be added that if the burden of choice and direction is to be placed anywhere, it is most often (and appropriately) put squarely with the client. For when the client intelligently selects the designer who most nearly parallels its requirements, it is defining that voice as surely as does an advertiser that picks, for example, Hal Riney over Joe Sedelmeier to present its message on television.

By deciding that what it needs is an annual report, that it should convey specific attitudes and attributes (strength, dignity, diversity, obfuscation, whatever) and that Generic Graphics Worldwide (GGW) is precisely the firm to produce the job, the client has already made the major decisions. If GGW has little personality of its own, but adapts with the versatility of a chameleon to each new project, it may be fairly assumed that the client is looking for one of two things, or a combination thereof: inordinate influence and control in which to express identity and judgment, or a designer to mimic that which is admired in other people's work.

Either way, these are not desirable ways to work. Better, by far, to be chosen because of who and what you are and do well. Given that the client has already exercised enormous influence over the result by defining the project and selecting the means by which it shall be accomplished, what remains is nevertheless crucial, and has everything to do with factors like skill, efficiency, long hours, and, most important, one's personal intellect, taste, sensitivity, and insight.

*Originally published in Volume 4, Number 1, 1986.*

# IN THIS CORNER: EDITORS VERSUS ART DIRECTORS

*Michael Anderson*

My career in journalism has seen a series of warring camps. The drawing of sides began in college: editorial or advertising? Later on: newspapers or television? Then: reporting or copyediting? Behind a desk or on the streets?

Those were the good old days. Now it seems that throughout the field of publishing there is a new line of death: print versus art directors.

The ascension of the art director—hell, the very title itself—continues to leave me bemused, bothered, and bewildered. The reason, put bluntly, is that I don't consider designing a page to be such a big deal. When I was coming along, you learned how to do layout; such knowledge was considered basic, like knowing how to write in inverted pyramid form. Granted, the instruction was pretty basic, along the lines of how to avoid tombstone headlines, and I will confess to snoozing during the sessions on the names of typefaces. (I was willing to concede that the value of an art director was the ability to distinguish Goudy from Caslon, until I caught one cheating by asking an elderly printer.) But like everything else in journalism, page layout was learned by doing (else what are college newspapers for?), and while you might not have the knack for it—the same way you might not be as good writing a soft feature as you were covering a speech—if you were a professional, you could do a competent job, when called upon. Otherwise, you stayed off the desk and let the news editors, the guys with the green eyeshades, wield their shiny metal rulers behind their picket fences of fiercely pointed pencils.

Of course, that ain't "art." News editors were concerned with news values: the weight appropriate to a given story, how much emphasis it should have, how to let the reader know instantly how important the paper considered this piece of information, and how to ease that reader into digesting it. A news editor never forgot that text is meant to be read.

Let me repeat that: Text is meant to be read. Text is not meant to be looked at. Text is not meant to be a "design element." Text is not meant to be gray matter interacting with white space and illustrations. Text is meant to be read.

I know, I know—art directors pay lip service to that. But how many of them mean it? And if they do mean it, how many operate under that principle? What is the most commonly heard defense from art directors when told that their designs make the page hard to read?

"But it looks good!"

Never mind that the typeface causes headaches; never mind that the columns expand and contract until the eyes cross; never mind that the story has to be sliced in half to fit the dummy. If the page is an object of aesthetic contemplation, well, why waste time reading it?

I understand. I have worked for extended stints as a news editor and know the daily challenge of juggling a set of stories, graphics, headlines, and logos into a coherent, pleasing design. Of course, you always want your pages to look good. All right, I admit it: I wanted my pages to be beautiful. I would start out with the haziest notion of how it could look, invariably waste a series of dummy sheets until: voilà! And to see those lines and squiggles, the sketch of my mental canvas, transformed onto newsprint—such a sense of satisfaction, of accomplishment, of (dare I say it?) artistic pleasure was not often to be had in this dreary world.

Pretty soon, that daily aesthetic euphoria became damn near the focus of the job. I would think about what I had drawn yesterday and how I could do something different today (heaven forbid you should repeat yourself!). I would think about horizontal and vertical, about white space and how to use more of it—but I really wasn't all that concerned about content. In fact, I kind of resented content. To tell you the truth, it just got in the way. The really grizzled news editors have a mantra: "It's just names and numbers"—slugs and story lengths. And where's some art for the page? And how to break up all this gray? What are these stories about? Who cares?

Who cares, indeed? I suspect the ascent of the art director is more than coincidentally connected to the maturation of the first generation raised on television. Certainly, among newspapers, the fear of video competition became acute about twenty years ago, and suddenly "redesign" became all the rage. The first impetus was to make gray, text-clogged pages more attractive and inviting to read. Today, redesign has become an end unto itself. It seems that the first impulse of an incoming editor is to redesign the publication: it is quick, relatively easy—though seldom cheap—and gives the illusion of freshness and change. (It is also far more easily accomplished than a true transformation of the publication: fresh editorial ideas, better writing, sharper editing.) It is a new skin for the same old vinegar. Design seems to have become an end in itself. Art directors have bewitched publishers and editors. Like "image consultants" in politics, they promise that presentation is paramount, style will always subdue substance, and bedazzled, unsophisticated readers will never know what hit them.

I'm not so sure. I think art directors are going to get pulled back into collaboration with—not to say submission to—editorial. The pull for the designer to try something new—it *is* damned dull doing the same thing over and over—becomes subversive: the art gets wilder, the type gets zanier, the layout gets harder to comprehend. But publications are fundamentally utilitarian. People buy them to read them—at least they want to read them; that's why the magazine stacks keep climbing in the closet. And if they're so hard to read, eventually they will stop being bought. Which would mean fewer jobs for art directors.

And that just wouldn't look good.

*Originally published in Volume 13, Number 2, 1995.*

# MODERN AND OTHER ISMS

# A POSTMORTEM ON DECONSTRUCTION?

*Ellen Lupton*

Theory and graphic design have always been a problematic union. Perhaps because graphic design is often approached more intuitively than intellectually, theory is rarely an explicit part of design practice. When theory does emerge as a topic among designers, it often serves to name a new style, a current stock of mannerisms. A conspicuous example of this surfacing of theory is the circulation of "deconstruction" within the graphic design community.

The term *deconstruction* was coined by the philosopher Jacques Derrida in his book *Of Grammatology,* published in France in 1967 and translated into English in 1976. Deconstruction became a banner for advanced thought in American literary studies, scandalizing departments of English and French across the country. Deconstruction is part of the broader field of criticism known as poststructuralism, whose theorists have included Derrida as well as Roland Barthes, Michel Foucault, Jean Baudrillard, and others. Each of these writers has looked at modes of representation—from alphabetic writing to photojournalism—as culturally powerful technologies that transform and construct "reality."

In the mid-1980s, graduate students at Cranbrook were engaged in readings of various poststructuralist works, finding in them analogues for their own ideas about communication. Meanwhile, artists, architects, and photographers in art schools and studios across the country were connecting similar texts to visual practice. "Deconstructivism" catapulted into the mainstream design press with MoMA's 1988 exhibition *Deconstructivist Architecture,* curated by Philip Johnson and Mark Wigley. MoMA used the term *deconstructivism* to link contemporary architecture to Russian constructivism, whose early years were marked by an imperfect vision of form and technology. The MoMA exhibition found a similarly skewed interpretation of modernism in the works of Frank Gehry, Daniel Libeskind, Peter Eisenman, and others.

The word *deconstruction* quickly became a cliché in design journalism, where it usually has described a style featuring fragmented shapes, extreme angles, and aggressively asymmetrical arrangements. This collection of formal devices was easily transferred from architecture to graphic design, where it named existing tendencies and catalyzed new ones. The labels *deconstructivism, deconstructionism,* and just plain *decon* have served to blanket the differences between a broad range of design practices and an equally broad range of theoretical ideas.

I take a narrower view of deconstruction. Rather than viewing it as a style, I see it as a process—an act of questioning. In Derrida's original theory, deconstruction asks a question: How does representation inhabit reality? How does the external appearance of a thing get inside its internal essence? How does the surface get under the skin? For example, the Western tradition has tended to value the internal mind as the sacred source of soul and intellect, while denouncing the body as an earthly, mechanical shell. Countering this view is the understanding that the conditions of bodily experience temper the way we think and act. A parallel question for graphic design is this: How does visual form get inside the content of writing? How has typography refused to be a passive, transparent vessel for written texts, developing as a system with its own structures and devices?

A crucial opposition in Derrida's theory of deconstruction is speech versus writing. The Western philosophical tradition has denigrated writing as an inferior, dead copy of the living, spoken word. When we speak, we draw on our inner consciousness, but when we write, our words are inert and abstract. The written word loses its connection to our inner selves. Language is set adrift. Grammarians, schoolteachers, and other "priests" of verbal correctness have long bemoaned the inaccuracies of the alphabet—its inability to consistently and concisely represent the sounds of speech. In written English, for example, the function of a letter pair such as *ph* is woefully at odds with our expectations of how these letters behave individually. Herbert Bayer's "fonetic alfabet" (1958–60) attempted to reform this situation.

The Latin alphabet is supplemented by a range of conventions with no relation to speech at all. Spacing, punctuation, the styles of letterforms, the conventions of page layout—these are nonphonetic devices on which the alphabet now depends. Writing is not merely a bad copy, a faulty transcription, of the spoken word. Writing has, in fact, changed the way we think and talk.

A work of design can be called deconstruction when it exposes and transforms the established rules of writing, interrupting the sacred "inside" of content with the profane "outside" of form. Modernist typography has long engaged in such structural games, from the calligrammes of Apollinaire, which use typography as an active picture rather than a passive frame, to the experiments with simultaneous overlapping texts produced within the "new typography" of the 1970s and 1980s.

Such self-conscious explorations of language and design within the context of modernism are matched by numerous developments within the "vernacular" field of commercial publishing, which since the early nineteenth century has expanded the limits of classical book typography to meet the needs of advertising and popular media. The early nineteenth-century display face called Italian deliberately inverted the anatomical parts of the "modern" letterforms that had been formalized in the late eighteenth century. The neoclassical fonts of Didot and Bodoni epitomized the tendency to view typography as a system of abstract relationships—thick and thin, serif and stem, vertical and horizontal. The designer of Italian turned the serifs inside out, demonstrating that the forms of letters are not bound by the authority of divine proportions, but are open to endless manipulation.

Within the context of philosophy and literary theory, deconstruction is just one question among many that emerged out of the body of critical ideas known as poststructuralism. Roland Barthes's theory of "mythology" looks at how images serve to validate key beliefs in modern culture—such as progress or individualism—making ideologically loaded concepts seem like natural and inevitable truths. Graphic design can reveal cultural myths by using familiar symbols and styles in new ways. A typeface such as Barry Deck's Template Gothic, based on an industrial stencil, calls into question the values of polished perfection commonly associated with technology. Deck calls his typeface "an imperfect typeface for an imperfect world," countering utopian beliefs in technology as social savior or corporate notions of technology as law and order.

It has recently become unfashionable to compare language and design. In the fields of architecture and products, the paradigm of language is losing its luster as a theoretical model—we no longer want to think of buildings, teapots, or fax machines as "communicating" cultural messages, in the manner of postmodern classicism or product semantics. Yet, the link between language and typography is quite different from the link between language and three-dimensional objects because typography is so close to language. In fact, typography is the frontier between language and objects, language and images. Typography turns language into a visible, tangible artifact, and, in the process, transforms it irrevocably.

For the design fields, deconstruction has been reduced to the name of a historical period rather than an ongoing way of approaching design. Derrida made a similar point himself in a 1994 interview in the *New York Times Magazine;* when asked if he felt that deconstruction was losing credibility in the academic world, he answered that deconstruction will never be over because it describes a way of thinking about language that has always existed. For graphic design, deconstruction isn't dead either, because it's not a style or a movement, but a way of asking questions through our work. Critical form making will always be part of design practice, whatever theoretical tools one might use to identify it.

*Originally published in Volume 12, Number 2, 1994.*

# FABULOUS US: SPEAKING THE LANGUAGE OF EXCLUSION
*Natalia Ilyin*

Something is happening to graphic designers: we are losing the ability to make choices. We used to speak to each other in controlled tones about the merits of a Brodovitch or the timelessness of a Lustig, as we cleaned our small round glasses or downed the chicken with lemongrass. Now we mumble that every administrative assistant with Quark is going to take all the business and leave us sitting quietly alone and sad, as the wind picks up the dust and scatters it meaninglessly across our archival copies of the American Can Company's annual report.

Up to this time, the language of design was based on exclusionary principles that we, as designers, all recognized. We went to school and learned and taught our clients what tools they needed to understand this language. We all agreed to use these principles, were welcomed to the long house, had a corner on the market of knowledge, and paid the Con Ed bill. It was fabulous us and not-so-fabulous them, and it was our job to keep them realizing that we knew more than they did.

Now that these principles, for which we worked long and hard, are being built into the software on everyone's desktop, designers find themselves displaced and are scrambling for another code that has value, one they can protect. Clean work is easy. Edgy, inclusive work is unintelligible to those who do not speak the language. Our exclusionary language is now a language of obfuscation, which clients pay money to understand. And they said the computer was just a tool.

Graphic designers, by nature, are in a bind. We need to be individuals because we spent all that time with painters in art school and, damn it, we're just as sensitive as they are, but we need to create work that communicates a specific idea not of our own choosing. We work for somebody else. This communicative activity, if not handled well, can result in a brush with the mainstream.

We need to feel that what we create is individual, specific, and inspired. But we need to be individual, specific, and inspired in a way that does not get knocked down at marketing meetings. We chafe at the restrictions of client, budget, and lack of vision, but without these restrictions, we are not designers. We need to speak the language of design (that confluence of influences, one-upmanships, and radical egalitarianisms), but we cannot afford to look as though we care about speaking it too fluently. We must constantly reinvent ourselves, because edginess is next to godliness, but we must espouse an appreciation of those arcane universal design principles that we, as individuals, choose to break because we're so radical. Design is a language of exclusion, even though it is, at this moment, a language of exclusion that is trying its best to be inclusionary. And there is the rub.

All communication happens through codified systems, or languages. Design, by nature, is a language about choosing. The choice between that photograph and this one, between Garamond and Interstate, puts a designer in the position of leaving something in and something out. What's left in generally has to do with the designer's spider web of educational impressions—eighth-grade teachers, various technologies, what's in *Bikini*. Choices that seem self-generated often depend upon who has been the teacher, on what has been the guide. What's left out is information that the designer finds unworkable: things that don't fit the prescribed boundaries of the set solution, images that don't communicate. In other words, we design along the boundaries laid out by our learned design language. We slice up a problem, organize it into concepts, and make these concepts significant—all because we agree as a group to organize the design of communication this way. Our agreement is never stated, but its terms are absolute.

Many languages develop around objective acts. But our language describes an act that is subjective—that exists only as a decision between what is perceived to be good and what is considered better. The Sapir-Whorf hypothesis suggests that the distinctions encoded in one language are not found in any other language. Over time, as graphic design became a profession, the linguistic act of deciding what's left in and what's left out developed into a specific language unto itself—into a series of codes for various species of designers. Sentences like "It's Vignelli-ish," "She went to Cal Arts," and "He worked for Roger Black" are shorthand descriptions of various design hierarchies. Most of these hierarchies can be traced back to the Bauhaus, to the beginnings of modernism, to a time when design took on the public good as an area of its concern, albeit an often patronizing concern. After years of telling the great unwashed masses what to do, some designers feel as though they must now give popular culture a chance to talk back, and are making a big effort to synthesize backwards and to show the image makers of our society the influences that are acting upon them. The language of design now includes a code for those whose design depends upon the codification of a lack of codification.

In the best post-everything tradition, designers are dealing with issues of meaning and nonmeaning in ways that can only be described as pertaining to a dominant style: a style of inclusion. What happens if I put together random images from influential childhood cartoons with wacky Fontographer errors? It's a design hierarchy allegedly based on a leveling of value. And, yet, that's impossible in the real world. All design is equal, but some design is more equal than others.

Even when inclusion is the style of the moment, the designer is making choices about meaning: there is always some choosing inherent in a design solution, always meanings that escape the designer's consciousness. These meanings happen when the designer's message is received by the person "reading" the work.

After ripping through the arts and literature, postmodernist black magic has seeped into the design world, and with it has come a style based on a leveling of authority. Designers who adopt a position of alternativism, who have read their graduate texts, and who are determined to show the dirty underside of design and its dominance are actually contributing to the very machine of culture they deride.

If the alleged objectivity of modernist design principles is a thing of the past, how do you make choices? And if you are still making choices without a measurement of value, of what value is your work? If objectivity is deemed impossible in our era, subjectivity is making the decisions. Is the opinion of a twenty-two-year-old brand manager just out of UCLA business school really as valuable as the opinion of an art director schooled in the constructivists, Derrida, Lacan, and the whole nine yards? Inclusivity breeds contempt.

It's an inclusivity based on fear. We're afraid to take a stand because styles change so fast. We're afraid we'll be refuted. We're afraid that our solutions—that our "design philosophy"—will have its moment in the sun, but then languish on the trash heap indefinitely. So we present the elements, albeit ironically, and force the reader to take the burden of putting together the text. It's an old postmodernist trick: throw the responsibility for choice back on the audience. That way, what the audience chooses to see is its own problem.

This approach is starting to get old, just like its progenitors: 1968 can't go on forever. Let's face it. Design is really a mild form of fascism: the fascism of valuing one person's viewpoint over another's. To be unwilling to accept this role of form giver, reluctant to take a stand on the slippery pile of mush that is popular culture, is to be unable to take the responsibility for choice. This unwillingness signals a breakdown of the hierarchies that are the language of graphic design and an introduction of the elements of a language that describes, but does not choose.

Graphic designers have the opportunity to influence the way average people are informed. This influence affects people, and it involves real responsibility—responsibility that has proved terrifying enough to drive the best design minds of the generation into a tailspin of tangential stylistics. Grappling with the issues confronting our society head-on takes guts. Presenting them airily to a reader already overwhelmed by a cumulative backlog of choices is the easy way out. Playing with the forms of the graphic design language is intriguing, but languages are created to carry meaning, and to deny responsibility for that meaning is to be ironic, elitist, and chicken. We need to stop pretending that we are egoless and egalitarian, and start saying something with our language of exclusion.

*Originally published in Volume 12, Number 2, 1994.*

# CONFUSION AND CHAOS: THE SEDUCTION OF CONTEMPORARY GRAPHIC DESIGN

*Paul Rand*

I n the torturous history of painting and design, from Cimabue (1240–1302) to Cassandre (1901–1968), communication between artist and spectator—even if one disagreed with what was being communicated—was rarely a problem. Today, with emphasis on self and style, rather than on content or idea, in much of what is alleged to be graphic design, communication is, at best, puzzling. Order out of chaos, it seems, is not the order of the day.

The deluge of design that colors our lives, our print, and our video screens is synchronous with the spirit of our time. No less than drugs and pollution, and all the fads and isms that have plagued our communities, the big brush of graffiti, for example, has been blanketing our cities from Basel to Brooklyn. Much of graphic design today is a grim reminder of this overwhelming presence. The qualities that evoke this bevy of depressing images are a collage of confusion and chaos, wrapped in a cloak of arrogance: squiggles, pixels, doodles, dingbats, ziggurats; boudoir colors—turquoise, peach, pea green, and lavender; corny woodcuts on moody browns and russets; art deco rip-offs, high-gloss finishes, sleazy textures; tiny color photos surrounded by acres of white space; indecipherable, zany typography with miles of leading; text in all caps (despite indisputable proof that lowercase letters are more readable); omnipresent, decorative letterspaced caps (optional style and weight), and—lest we forget—Garamond condensed; visually annotated typography and revivalist caps and small caps; pseudo-Dada and futurist collages; and whatever "special effects" a computer makes possible. These inspirational decorations are, apparently, convenient stand-ins for real ideas. And all this is a reflection, less of the substance, than of the spirit of graffiti—less of the style than of the quality.

That these clichés are used repeatedly, irrespective of needs, is what defines trendiness. The "Memphis" fad was also based on clichés and on outrageous, kitschy notions. (Occasionally, however, some potentially useful ideas seeped through—only proving that it takes talent to make something out of nothing.) The huge investments involved in the manufacture and storage of Memphis products have probably helped speed its demise. Trendy printed ephemera, on the other hand, which involves less capital, may take a bit longer.

There is something about graffiti and graffiti-like design that smacks of World War I Dada. But that was a revolt against the lopsided conventions of the time. The participants were often great artists and reformers: Arp, Grosz, Heartfield, Duchamp, Ernst, and Schwitters. And the work was not, in any way, trendy; it was serious, often amusing, and always interesting. Today's Dada, if it can be called that, is a revolt against anything that is deemed old hat. Faddish and frivolous, it harbors its own built-in boredom.

"I feel that the ideas I tried to outline . . . will strike many of you as consisting too much of the atrabiliar grumblings of a disgruntled elder,"[1] is how Roger Fry, the distinguished British critic, expressed the fear that his message might be falling on deaf ears.

Most of this "new" style of design is confined to pro bono work, small boutiques, fledgling studios, trendy publishers, misguided educational institutions, anxious graphic arts associations, and a few innocent paper manufacturers who produce beautiful papers, but then spoil them with "the latest" graphics, and who, undoubtedly, see themselves as the avant-garde—and are comforted by the illusion that this must be progress. Unhappily, this is infecting some of the graphics of the corporate world: annual reports, identity programs, direct mail, etc. Trendiness is seductive, especially to the young and inexperienced, for the principal reason that it offers no restraints, is a lot of "fun," permits unlimited possibilities for "self-expression," and doesn't require conforming to the dictates of reason or aesthetics. "Self-expression is real only after the means to it have been acquired,"[2] comments the author of a brilliant commentary on the foibles of education, *Begin Here.*

Lack of humility and originality and the obsession with style are what seem to encourage these excesses. The absence of restraint, the equation of simplicity with shallowness, complexity with depth of understanding, and obscurity with innovation, distinguish the quality of work of these times. The focus on freedom is just another sign that suggests a longing to reject the past—"the infinite greatness of the past"[3] is how Walt Whitman put it. All this, of course, carries little weight with critics who, out of hand, reject the styles of their predecessors, and respond to reason with disdain.

Added to this is the obsession with theory, which, instead of being fuel for action, as it was at other times—during the Renaissance, for example—is merely the vehicle for fathomless language, variously described as "extravagantly obscure, modish, opaque verbal shenanigans—and the authors as masters of impenetrability."[4] Although these descriptions are aimed at architects, they seem equally appropriate for graphic design theorists of the *new* (a buzzword often seen in advertising sometimes preceded by the expression *amazing.*) Reaching for the new is tilting at windmills; the goal is not what is new (original), as Mies put it, but what is good.

Twenty-eight years ago, my friend Charles Eames (1908–1977) spoke at the Pasadena Art Museum, concerning a growing preoccupation with the problem of creativity. "This preoccupation in itself," said Eames, "suggests that we are in some special kind of trouble—and, indeed, we are." A look at graphic design today suggests that, perhaps, we are even in greater trouble now than we were twenty-eight years ago. As a matter of fact, design today is reminiscent of the trials of an earlier era in which Edward Gibbon, author of *The History of the Decline and Fall of the Roman Empire* (1776), astutely described the arts in theater, music, and painting as "freakishness pretending to originality, enthusiasm masquerading as vitality."

Eames would probably turn in his grave if he knew what was happening even in academia today. "It is no secret," asserts the author of *Tenured Radicals,* "that the academic study of the humanities in this country is in a state of crisis. . . . Every special interest—women's studies, black studies, gay studies, and the like—and every modish interpretive gambit—deconstructivism, post-structuralism, new historicism [postmodernism] . . . has found a welcome roost in the academy [and in many studios], while the traditional curriculum and modes of intellectual inquiry are excoriated as sexist, racist, or just plain reactionary."[5] "It is also necessary," adds another critic, "to remind oneself of the dangers that ensue when metaphors substitute for facts, when words lose their meaning, and when signifiers and signifieds part company, with the deconstructionists' blessing."[6]

Today, the popular sport is to put down whatever isn't perceived as change, the very latest—subjects like the classics, the curriculum, modernism, functionalism, and, for example, the Bauhaus, into whose history is woven the very fabric of modernism, is seen as a style rather than as an idea, a cultural manifestation. Socially aware, and like neoplasticism and constructivism, it harbored a strain of the ascetic. To say that the Bauhaus (1919) and its ideology are defunct is to cast aspersions on its antecedents: on Ruskin and Morris, on the Arts and Crafts movement, on the Secessionists, on Hoffmann and Moser, on Muthesius and the Werkbund (1907), on Behrens, on the predecessor of the Bauhaus—van de Velde—the director of the Weimar Academy, on Gropius, Klee, Kandinsky, Moholy, Albers, Mies, and on outsiders like Malevich, Mondrian, van Doesburg, and Lissitzky. Cubism and some of its progeny—suprematism, neoplasticism, constructivism, futurism—were its aesthetic foundation. The Bauhaus Archives in Berlin, the refurbished building in Dessau, and original products now available to all are stark evidence that the Bauhaus is breathing vigorously.

"There are two principles inherent in the very nature of things . . ."[7] writes Whitehead, "the spirit of change, and the spirit of conservation. There can be nothing real without both. Mere change without conservation is a passage from nothing to nothing. Mere conservation without change cannot conserve." Elsewhere, he says, "Mere change before the attainment of adequacy of achievement, either in quality or output, is destructive of greatness."

Interminable disputes about whether or not design at the Kunstgewerbeschule of Basel is focused too much on form at the expense of other goals miss the point that Mies espoused: "Form is not the goal but the result of our work." Fads are governed by the same immutable laws of form as are other visual phenomena. Wishful thinking will not make them go away, and one can no more escape from the exigencies of form than from one's shadow. To poke fun at form or formalism is to poke fun at Roger Fry, Clive Bell, John Dewey, and the philosophy called aesthetics. Ironically, it also pokes fun at trendy design, since the devices that characterize this style of "decoration" are, primarily, formal. Furthermore, it denies what the great historian, painter, and architect of the Renaissance, Vasari, had already stated about design (form): "It is the animating principle of all creative processes." [8]

The quality of teaching in the university and art school is rarely taken to task. To teach in a university, practical experience, it seems, is not one of the prerequisites (at least, not long-term experience). Experience in the workplace, and a thorough knowledge of the history of one's specialization is indispensable, both for imparting information and for one's well-being. But such experience, with some exceptions, is rare among students as well as among faculty. Absence of these disciplines can only help perpetuate mediocrity, and ensure the continual flow of questionable work in the marketplace.

But for the familiarity with a few obvious names and facts about the history of painting and design, history is a subject not taken too seriously. This does not imply that just because some work is a product of the past it is privileged, willy-nilly, to join the ranks of the immortals. The historical process is (or should be) a process of distillation and not accumulation. In a certain sense, it is related to natural selection—survival of the fittest. Furthermore, to shun history is to reinvent the wheel—the probability of repeating what has already been done.

Gutenberg, Picasso, cubism, futurism, Lissitzky, and Tschichold are among the historical facts and figures that a student or teacher may be aware of. But what about the history of art going back to pre-Renaissance, which is so well documented? What about the history of design, largely a product of journals and a few isolated books, which is not so well documented?

Even though artists of the 1890s, like Lautrec, Bonnard, and the Beggarstaff Brothers, may be familiar to some schools, designers of the twenties and thirties are little known. If the artist happens to wear two hats—a painter as well as a designer—more time is spent discussing the relative merits of "fine" as opposed to "applied" arts than on intrinsic values. Mention of some of the Europeans (not necessarily linked with the avant-garde), whose work appeared in periodicals like *Gebrauchsgraphik* and *Arts et Métiers Graphiques* (before World War II), will probably be greeted with silence. With few exceptions, a blank stare is the usual reaction when some of these names are ticked off, from students and teachers alike.

This, by no means, is a complete roster: Ehmeke, Parzinger, Klinger, Arpke, Schulpig, Bernhard, Dexel, Buchartz, Leistikow, Zietara, Deffke, Mahlau, Goedecker, Ahlers, Hadank, Fuss, Koerner, Gipkens, Boehm, Corty, Garetto, Brissaud, Benito, Renner, Depero, Schleger, Koch, Schwichtenberg, Trump, Colin, Martin, Satomi, Scheurich, Bouté de Monvel, Berény, Kozma—designers, illustrators, fashion artists, and others too numerous to list. And, among Americans, in the thirties and forties, there were Jensen, Trafton, Bobri, Sinel, Switzer, and others like McKnight Kauffer, who spent most of his life in England. Designers like Dwiggins or Gill occupy a different category.

The purpose of listing these names should not be seen as mere pedantry; rather, it provides an opportunity to learn by example, by studying the work of an extraordinary number of out-of-the-ordinary talents.

Both in education and in business, graphic design is often a case of the blind leading the blind. To make the classroom a perpetual forum for political and social issues, for instance, is wrong; and to see aesthetics as sociology is grossly misleading. A student whose mind is cluttered with matters that have nothing directly to do with design; whose goal is to learn doing and making; who is thrown into the fray between learning how to use a computer at the same time that he or she is learning design basics; and who is being overwhelmed with social problems and political issues is a bewildered student; this is not what he or she bargained for, nor, indeed, paid for.

"Schools are not intended to moralize a wicked world," [9] says Barzun, "but to impart knowledge and develop intelligence, with only two social ends in mind: prepare to take on one's share in the world's work and, perhaps in addition, lend a hand in improving society after schooling is done. Anything else is the nonsense we have been living with." Further on he continues, "All that such Good Samaritan courses amount to is pieties. They present moralizing mixed with anecdotes, examples of good and bad, discussions of that catchall word *values.*" And, finally, he admonishes, "Make the school a place for academic vocational instruction, not social reform. . . ."[10]

This does not suggest that social or political issues are mere trivia. On the contrary, they are of real significance and deserve the kind of forum that is free of interference. Even though common decency implies continuing concern for human needs, social issues are not aesthetic issues, nor can they be the basis for aesthetic judgments. Where, for example, would Caravaggio, Lautrec, or even Degas be if work were judged on issues other than aesthetics? And where, today, would so many schools, studios, and advertising agencies be if important decisions depended on aesthetic priorities?

Coping with the problems relating to the understanding of design in business depends a great deal on how well informed, genuinely interested, and experienced a businessman is. Managers responsible for design are chosen, not for their aesthetic judgments, nor for their impeccable taste, but for their administrative skills. Few, if any, understand the intricacies of design, or even the role, beyond the obvious, that design and designers play.

Most managers see a designer as a set of hands—a supplier—not as a strategic part of a business. Their backgrounds are primarily those of marketers, purchasing agents, or advertising specialists, not of connoisseurs of design. It is their uninformed, unfocused preferences or prejudices, their likes or dislikes, that too often determine the look of things. Yet, much of the time, they are not even discriminating enough to distinguish between good and bad, between trendy and original, nor can they always recognize talent or specialized skills. In the field of design, theirs is the dichotomy of being privileged, but not necessarily being qualified—after all, design is not their business.

Bureaucrats largely responsible for the administration of design spend endless hours at meetings allegedly about design, in which miscellaneous subjects are discussed, and in which marketing, production, and administration problems are treated as if they were design problems. Whether or not the participants really understand the nature of the problems, or the implication of design, is questionable. If quality, for example, is the subject for discussion, it is dealt with only as an abstraction, with participants assuming the other person understands what is being discussed, when, in fact, nobody can be sure. Since perception is so intimately a part of taste and design, it is the experienced designer who might possibly point the way to meaningful solutions, and smooth the path for an administrator's needs.

Even though there are comparatively few experienced and really innovative designers around, there are, regrettably, even fewer administrators who are receptive to innovative work.

*Notes*

1.  Roger Fry, *Art and Commerce* (London, 1925), 23.
2.  Jacques Barzun, "The Centrality of Reading," *Begin Here* (Chicago, 1991), 25.
3.  Walt Whitman, *Passage to India* (1868).
4.  Roger Kimball, "Deconstruction Comes to Architecture," *Tenured Radicals* (New York, 1990), 123.
5.  Roger Kimball, *Tenured Radicals* (New York, 1990), xl, xiii.
6.  David Lehman, "A Scandal of Academe," *Signs of the Times* (New York, 1991), 243.
7.  Alfred North Whitehead, "Requisites for Social Progress," *Science and the Modern World* (New York, 1925), 289.
8.  T. S. R. Boase, "The Critic," *Giorgio Vasari* (Washington, D.C., 1971), 124–.
9.  Jacques Barzun, "Ideas vs. Notions," *Begin Here* (Chicago, 1991), 50.
10. Ibid., 208.

*Originally published in Volume 10, Number 1, 1992.*

# GRAPHIC DESIGN (IS) NOW

*Jeffery Keedy*

The negation of cognition thus correlates to the negation of language.
For when those two pillars of Western humanism, individual cognition
and evolutionary continuity, lose their meaning, language loses meaning. Existence ceases for the individuum as we know it, and all becomes
chaos. You cease to be a unique entity unto yourself, but exist simply as
chaos. And not just chaos that is you: your chaos is also my chaos. To
wit, existence is communication, and communication, existence.
— *Haruki Murakami,* A Wild Sheep Chase

There have never been more books, exhibitions, and schools of graphic
design than there are today. And there have never been more graphic
designers and clients. Never before has the average person been so aware of
design: thousands of people who never knew what a typeface was must now
decide which ones to put on their personal computer and many are doing their
own designing. The greater degree of awareness in the world and the profession
has significantly elevated the level of sophistication in graphic design practice and
theory in the past ten years.

I am sure there are plenty of "designasaurs" who would argue this point
with their favorite examples from the past, but that's not design—that's design
history. Contemporary graphic design is consistent with contemporary culture
and is therefore context dependent. To consider design outside its culture is to
consider it as an independent craft or art form, not as a means of communication.

Unfortunately, that is exactly what most of the current discourse on
design does, either in the form of beauty-contest design shows or vanity press
books that never address work in terms of the culture within which it functions.
Design, in this view, is predicated upon an assumed and ultimately arbitrary
universal standard of excellence. Although certain formal characteristics and skills
may apply, there is no such thing as a universal context for design. When context
is ignored, graphic design is just an artifact of speculation.

The context of graphic design today is one of considerable complexity, not
just in terms of the obvious technical aspects, but in terms of the designer's
relationship with his or her culture. Today's designer must be a "cultural general-
ist"; keeping abreast of contemporary culture is a job in itself.

Long ago, graphic designers were either scribes or printers (depending on
how far back you want to go), and the designer's relationship to the work fol-

lowed the "customer is always right" model. Later, in the "we know what's good for you" days of modernism, the graphic designer's role changed to that of educating the client about "good" design. Both of these models are problematic: each portrays the designer as either completely passive or dutifully pedagogical in relation to client and culture. Regrettably, graphic design practice and theory are still encumbered by these outdated attitudes.

Instead of embracing new ideas and supporting their development, most graphic designers have retrenched into past styles of the vernacular eclecticism or the old standard modernism. Outside of academia, new ideas (and new work) are greeted with skepticism and hostility. If the profession continues in this manner, it will ensure that graphic design is never considered seriously as a discipline or practice.

What we have now is a regressive protectionist trade mentality. Most of the hostility toward new work is fueled by anxiety over change—either technological or ideological—by theoretical explorations in deconstruction and postmodernism, or by the move toward cultural inclusion, known as multiculturalism. Change is inevitable, and no one should know that better than graphic designers.

Fortunately, there is a new attitude emerging that is not dominated by the past, but looks forward toward the future. Today there is a greater diversity of approach in new work because designers have agreed to disagree and reject stylistic conformity. When designers are engaged in creating new work, they are engaged in the real world, not the artificial world of their own self-aggrandizing profession. Increasingly, the biggest influence on new design lies in identifying the cultural context of a particular project, not in perpetuating the vicissitudes of the graphic design community.

Many graphic designers today think of themselves as producing a consistent yet evolving body of work, work that expresses their place in contemporary culture. They are not interested in passively serving a client or adhering to some kind of official design dogma. In this light, the "client" is no longer merely the person commissioning the work, but is also the entire cultural context that the designer is participating in and responsible for.

To understand new work, one must take the time and attention necessary to access the work on its own terms, within the context in which it functions—not by some vague notion of universal excellence or preconceived notion of appropriateness. Simplistic ideas of good design or problem solving are of little use in an era of increasing technological and cultural complexity.

As we enter the new millennium of the information era, the importance of communication is paramount. If graphic designers can learn anything from their past, it should be that the best graphic design doesn't use the past to solve the complex problems of the present: it uses the present to reveal the possibilities of the future.

*Originally published in Volume 12, Number 2, 1994.*

# NEWS FROM THE REVOLUTION

*Matthew Carter*

I n recent writing about type design, excitement about the state of the art is
often combined with an elegiac wistfulness about the state of the profession. I
seem to hear the monastery bell tolling behind Karrie Jacobs's statement "The
design of typefaces, once practiced by a small, cloistered group of men such as
Herman[n] Zapf or Adrian Frutiger, as patient and skilled as the monks who
illuminated manuscripts, has emerged as a counterculture project."[1] In an article
in *Eye* on *Fuse*, written in 1994 but still the *locus classicus*, Michael Rock began
thus: "Like enraged citizens, long denied political rights, bursting into the palace,
graphic designers have broken down the walls of the hitherto closed enclave of
letterform design and seized control." Wiping a tear from his *Eye*, Michael adds:
"But as exciting as the results of the type revolution have been, it is hard not to
feel a speck of remorse for the decimation of another craft, and another organized
group of craftsmen, by a handful of young punks with personal computers."[2]

We old punks, decimated or not, have to admit the galling fact that
graphic designers—that barbarian horde—stormed our palace long ago. What,
after all, do these (not inconsiderable) typefaces have in common: Centaur (1914),
Futura (1927), Peignot (1937), Sabon (1966)? Their respective authors (Rogers,
Renner, Cassandre, Tschichold) designed types as by-products of wider design
practices. They were no more professional, full-time, specialized type designers
than are most of the contributors to *Fuse*. Even harder to acknowledge is that a
couple of today's most important typefaces were the work not of type designers,
nor yet of graphic designers, but of total interlopers. Cheltenham, which at one
time had a claim to be the best-known type of American origin, was designed by
an architect, Bertram Goodhue. In a recent exposé, "Starling Burgess, Type
Designer?" Mike Parker makes a convincing case that Times Roman—yes, *Times
Roman*, no less, among the two or three most popular types of all—was the
brainchild not of Stanley Morison, pillar of the British typographic establishment,
but of Starling Burgess, American designer of racing yachts and airplanes![3]

"With the advent of fontmaking software and alternative channels for
distribution, typeface design has merged with graffiti," to quote Karrie Jacobs
again. I agree with her point, and Michael Rock's, that type design is now a
greatly expanded and demystified field open to all comers, and is much the better
for it. But if the implied corollary is that full-time type designers have suffered
from the same things that have benefited occasional type designers, then I beg to
differ. The "organized group of craftsmen," as employed by the big manufacturers
of typesetting machines, has gone along with the machines, but their extinction

began back in the days of photocomposition and was hastened by Adobe and Bitstream, companies that from their beginnings in the early eighties treated their typographic staffs not as assembly lines of letter drawers but as designers with individual responsibility, and credit, for their work.

The news from the revolution is not really that graphic designers, young punks, and graffiti artists have seized control of type design—although they may have seized control of some writing about it. The personal computer has liberated, not decimated, type design as a trade. Fontmaking software and alternative channels for distribution have been as much of a boon to the culture as to the counterculture by allowing type designers to earn a living independently, alone or in small studios. And obituaries of the craft may be premature. Designing or adapting types for publications, particularly in different size-dependent "cuts"; designing types to be legible on computer screens, often involving the intricacies of TrueType hinting; designing types with huge character sets that include non-Latin alphabets: these are examples of outgrowths of the typefounding craft still practiced, on personal computers and in parallel with the creation of original designs, by professionals who were, at last count as we went to press, alive and kicking.

*Notes*

1. Karrie Jacobs, "Electronic Youth," *I.D.*, vol. 43, no. 3, May–June 1996, pp. 48–53.
2. Michael Rock, "Beyond Typography," *Eye*, no. 15, vol. 4, Winter 1994, pp. 26–35.
3. Mike Parker, "Starling Burgess, Type Designer?" *Printing History*, 31/32, 1996, pp. 52–81.

*Originally published in Volume 14, Number 3, 1996.*

# RUMORS OF THE DEATH OF TYPOGRAPHY HAVE BEEN GREATLY EXAGGERATED

*Peter Fraterdeus*

Javian Tabibian, humanist scholar and restaurateur, dismissed me as "one of those computer addicts" when I tried to laud him on his "Twilight of Human ism" talk at last year's Aspen design conference (he saw *designOnline* on my name tag). "But," I said, as he turned away, "I'm a card-carrying humanist— here, look, I've studied Petrarch's handwriting; I write with goose quills and was a letterpress printer way before it was hip to deep-emboss logos from your Mac LaserWriter output."

I tried to tell him that I agreed with his analysis of the Internet. At least it was one of the most colorful and provocative descriptions I had heard: "The bastard child of the necrophiliac father War and the shameless whore Entertainment." That stopped the murmur in the big tent for a second. I think most people just figured he was some kind of academic with a socialist agenda and never gave it another thought. I, on the other hand, found his definition the high point of the conference, particularly after listening to Mr. Four-Million-Dollar-Video-Studio and Mr. Think-and-Get-Rich and the general run of "Business Is Good Business" corporate design apologists.

There are still some of us who do believe that the purpose of design is to help make a better world. Perhaps we are those who take seriously the relationship between the culture and the cultural workers whose artifacts help to define the culture (See *www.dol.com/worldstudio*).

### THE JET SKI AS CULTURAL ATTACK WEAPON

In northwestern Washington state, there is a quiet corner of Puget Sound that has taken a giant step toward balancing the all-pervading "mechanophilia" that seems to overwhelm our society and, all too often, our better judgment. This small community, which depends on its peace and quiet as a special quality to attract vacationers, has banned Jet Skis in the entire portion of the Sound under its jurisdiction, saying that the constant buzz of these obnoxious watercraft and their loud-mouthed and inconsiderate riders traveling back and forth across the waterfront have destroyed the tranquillity of the area, which is a natural treasure and a commonwealth of the community. Of course, the Jet Ski industry won't take this lying down! It's already in court claiming a constitutional right to "interstate travel" and so forth, arguing that "you can't fight progress." It seems that the predominant culture is largely made up of terminally immature kids who are forever rebelling against their eternally authoritarian elders. Of course, things are no different in the culture of typography.

### DEGENERATE TYPE — SIGNIFYIN' NUTHIN'

"[Degenerate type is] a form of canned cynicism which will doom its perpetrators to a special room in hell where lovely little children of all races, creeds, and religions are eternally bathed in gentle rosy and amber glows, singing 'It's a Small World After All.' There's no legitimate typographic reason to create an alphabet which looks like it leaked out of a diaper."

— *P. F. lecture notes for ATypI, Barcelona, 1995*

Trash type is proud of being the worst student in the class. As if it were more "legitimate" to create ugly little malformed splotches in Fontographer than to attempt to draw the Platonic nature of the alphabet from its essential causal form into a well-reasoned and deliberated family of symbols. Please, I'm not getting personal here. Some of my favorite people are making trash type these days. It seems to be the only thing small foundries can even sell! But we don't have to accept that these are anything more than accidental expressions of a technosociological transition.

> "Letters are programs, not results of programs."
>
> —*Erik van Blokland*

"Letters are things, not pictures of things," says Eric Gill. Perhaps the "fontography" buffs (sorry, Macromedia, it's a generic term now!) and "fontographists" are really just making pictures of things. The difference between a fontographist and a type designer is simple enough. Ask a fontographist to draw a three-inch-high Roman *S* with a pencil, without tracing. Soon enough, you'll know if there's any real knowledge of the shapes of letters there (although even many type designers don't know the true subtleties of these forms). Mangling Caslon and calling it a typeface is not what type designers do. Maybe it's what font designers do, but then who cares, since apparently anyone with a PC and a pirated copy of Fontographer can be a "font designer." It's time for someone to say, "The friggin' emperor's got no friggin' clothes on!" Nonetheless, graphic designers can't seem to get enough of these fonts. It's apparently related to the fact that in our Jet Ski society, no one can get enough novelty to satisfy that itch, that craving for the next one. And since our visual circuits are so overloaded with snap, crackle, and buzz, people don't even notice letters anymore, unless they jog our deepest reptile-brain fears of death and decay.

A bicycle ad in the *Chicago Reader* is lettered in a decaying, crumbling font, generating a deep subconscious response in me that says, "These letters represent some kind of danger. I'd better pay attention." As if they've just been run over by an eighteen-wheeler, and I'm still in the middle of the highway. And, of course, with the hundreds of millions of dollars spent, since the earliest days of advertising, on detailed psychological research to determine exactly what makes people buy, we can be sure that these fonts have caught the attention of the marketing people, who see their vast potential.

> "The grunge face Burner has been accused of being illegible, but this feature is built in intentionally. Graffiti as an art form is a way of expressing your message to those who will care to read it. Many of the pieces seen on subways and the like are overlooked every day by people who do not care to take the time to read. Burner allows the reader to become part of the message by forcing him or her to understand the type in order to get the message."
>
> — *http://users.aol.com/penultimate/chroma.html*

The wave of trash type and grunge "typography" is just that—a wave. The sound of it crashing on the beach of long-term typographic structure is not the sound of the whole beach being washed away. There is nothing more pretentious, to my view, than the designers (or worse, the purveyors) of trash type claiming that their wares are responsible for "changing the nature of legibility." For, as in language, while the styles and vernacular shift with the seasons, the underlying grammar and structure change very slowly indeed.

The question, at this juncture, seems rather to be whether there's any lasting value to the "new typography." In fact, as graphic design is really a fashion industry, one can't dispute that the new tools have widely broadened the palette for typographic designers. But there seems to be an unfortunate paucity of brilliant, clear hues. Instead, we are faced with an overabundance of murky industrial corruptions and mutations rendered mechanically possible by Fontographer. I suppose it really comes down to simple Newtonian (Isaac, that is) physics, where it is noted that it's much harder to create order than to create chaos. Chaos is the inevitable expression of the loss of order. In our typographic universe, sociological and personal chaos find expression in letterforms often artlessly drawn and mechanically rendered. Of course, there are exceptions, and if you browse through the list of foundries at Chris MacGregor's online font foundries Web page (*http:// users.aol.com/typeindex/*), you will find among the chaff some remarkable and useful designs being produced by small font offices around the world.

The nature of typographic design will change more in the next eighteen months than it has since the birth of printing, as design for online environments becomes more widespread and its strengths and limitations are tested and developed. The Web browser is the new "codex"—somewhere between a scroll and a folio, it challenges designers to think in a new dimension. The technological discussion about online fonts is starting to take shape, and, unfortunately, it is again an afterthought, arriving after the camel has left the corral. However, the inclusion of some form of designer control over on-screen fonts is inevitable, and with it considerations of moving type, random type, hyperspaced type. Through it all, the underlying issues of proportion, structure, and legibility will remain.

Good typography is in no danger of disappearing on the Net. Clear visual signs are a highly developed and widely understood method of message transmission, and if a typeface doesn't serve this purpose, it will quickly evaporate. There will always be market forces seeking to bypass the rational mind with the use of jumbled and degenerate typography, but it seems the argument is not with type design, but, indeed, with consumerism. However, if the folks in Puget Sound win their battle, there may still be hope, and with it, the potential for a rebirth of quiet places in the world, and a return to clarity, elegance, and skillful drawing in typography and type design by the turn of the millennium.

*Originally published in Volume 14, Number 3, 1996.*

# SOME THOUGHTS ON MODERNISM:
# PAST, PRESENT, AND FUTURE

*Milton Glaser, Ivan Chermayeff, Rudolph de Harak*

## MILTON GLASER

Growing up in the thirties and forties, one could not be immune to modernism. It was the pervasive Zeitgeist, the spirit of the time. It was the beginning of post-Bauhaus thought, the International School of architecture, the idea that beauty is the inevitable consequence of appropriate form. We were products of a modernist age without ever thinking about it. We ingested the philosophy of modernism and accepted the idea of reducing everything to its most expressive form. There was really very little to counter it as a proposition.

Yet, I have never felt that there was any single truth. Modernism offered me a set of conventions to work with or against, because in the absence of beliefs (even temporary beliefs), it is just much harder to act. Anyway, I tend to view all philosophical notions as sometimes useful and sometimes not.

My own training was not very doctrinaire. I went to the High School of Music and Art in New York where I received one body of instruction, and then on to Cooper Union where I got another, then to the Art Students League for yet another. I had a variety of educational experiences before I ever realized that design existed as a profession.

When I was growing up, there was a real struggle between notions of what was called "abstraction" and "reality." The question of how to view the world and represent it most convincingly is art's oldest question. More than any other artist in history, Picasso demonstrated clearly that you could, in fact, represent the world from innumerable vantage points, all of which turn out to be equally compelling. Understanding that I could change my vantage point was one of the instructive lessons of my life. It meant that I did not have to be loyal to a single belief.

There is a certain arrogance in the idea that one can develop a universal methodology that works in every case for every person. It does not make any sense. I have never been able to simply subscribe to the idea that any one principle, such as simplicity or reductiveness, can be universally applied to every problem. Life and people are too complicated. I must admit to one belief about design: First, you have to accomplish your intended task. Then, if you are lucky and talented, you may also create something extraordinary that goes beyond the objective task.

The responsibility of reflecting our time is another idea inherent in modernist thought. The truth is that people with talent do good things that last, and people without talent, no matter how much they follow the rules, do work that is discarded by history. There is no way to avoid being in your time. I do not think that anybody should worry about being timeless, but rather be concerned about doing the job at hand.

I wonder if one had to define modern graphic design for the last twenty years as opposed to the twenty years before that whether one would find much difference. Much of contemporary graphic design is a reiteration of fifties design thinking in terms of its appearance and vocabulary of form. Along these lines, one of the things that binds a lot of designers to a certain way of working is the fact that they cannot draw. As a result, they are limited in terms of their ability to create form. One way to deal with this limitation is to rely on geometric forms or existing materials.

Drawing was discouraged during the modernist era, and this impulse still continues. Imagine that designers should not be able to represent form through drawing. What stupidity! This is an example of ideology gone crazy. It is the aesthetic equivalent of eating yogurt, tofu, and wheat germ for life. This constraint results in a specific working method—collage. Finding things, cutting them out, and assembling them in new combinations is the basic design methodology of our time. It is a way of working that had its parallels in the fifties.

The modernist idea was not to imitate anything that existed in reality. Talk about limitation. It seems to me that the power of visual work is transmitted through the metaphors and re-creation of existing imagery. The idea that you cannot use the visible world as a subject is like saying you can only eat brown rice. Undernourishment comes from eating only one thing; you can become undernourished from having only one aspect of the visual world as a diet.

It is true that you can take a very narrow piece of the world and produce extraordinary things. The collage method can produce remarkable imagery. A whole generation of people are basically working off that idea. Drawing skills are technically significant and help in the understanding that occurs when you attempt to represent the world in some way. You cannot reject the body's form or the swell of a breast or thigh. Life is erotic, and the only thing that is missing from most modernist work is eroticism. You really want to feel that a work has passion and sexuality. Why give it up? This has to do with the idea of purity. The idea that modernism refuses to use the symbols and archetypes of history is its greatest limitation.

It is therefore understandable why modernism became a useful tool for corporate representation. Corporations do not want to deal with issues of individuals, or eroticism, or the messy side of life. So modernism became a wonderful way of detoxifying dirty people and dirty ideas. A corporation can represent itself through the vehicle of modernism as being progressive and above the human squabble without ever having to deal with human sweat. If we look at history, it is not surprising that the utopian ideals of modernism would be captured by people who want to use it for their own purposes. With all of that, the extraordinary unity of vision that modernism provided us with is beginning to erode. Its all-encompassing principles are being questioned. Postmodernism has been officially announced, but has not quite found its philosophical base. At the moment, it is addressing questions of style and fashion. Conversely, modernism is powerful and pervasive. Although I've had my own problems with modernism, I believe our world view is still a modernist view.

Modernism is about progress, the endless frontier, and ceaseless development. Modernism is essentially utopian. Its origins are in the idea of good coming from boundless technology. Despite its contradictions and the erosion of its strength, the announcement of its death is premature.

## IVAN CHERMAYEFF

I was brought up in a world in which "modern" was taken for granted rather than discovered. Modern was at my doorstep as a way of contemplating and dealing with the visual and tactile world. My father, Serge Chermayeff, was involved in the modern movement almost by default. Although he was not trained as an architect or designer, he worked his way into these professions. I was taught that modern art, design, and architecture are presentations of expression that are clean and simple.

For the past several years, however, there has been a betrayal of modern in the form of endless rationalizations about decoration, coupled with complaints about the coldness of modern design. Postmodern is a desire to return to the appearance of things, rejecting the idea of modern as a background for whatever else is going on. Modern is not an end in itself, but rather a framework in which to accomplish something else.

For example, I work in a completely white room. It was bequeathed to me and was once Marcel Breuer's office. But if it hadn't been white, I would have painted it white right away. The room is merely a canvas in which other things happen. It is not an end in itself. If it were, I'd have to take all the art off the walls and anything else that gives it focus. I would have to remove myself as well.

Painting and sculpture have had a tremendous influence on the way I look at design. I grew up with the usual gang of classic modern painters—Klee, Miró, Picasso, Léger, and Mondrian. The explorations that they made generally lead one away from a sense of coldness, repetition, and sterility, which can exist in modern art. As a young boy, Miró was my favorite painter, but as a young man, I went through a long period of thinking how wrong I had been. A decade later I came back to feeling that Miró had tremendous, original qualities—comic, fresh, vibrant, immediate. I understand his visual language and feel once again that he is one of the great painters of the modern era to whom I owe a great deal. That made it easier to intuitively understand the artists who came later: de Kooning, Tomlin, Brooks, Kline. With all their rawness and immediacy, the abstract expressionists still had the same predecessors. Modern art and design grows in a logical way. And that is the modern's virtue; it changes and expands, becoming

endlessly redefined and forward moving. It is an attitude that invites reconsidera-
tion and shifting according to time, yet holds on to the best of what has been
accomplished.

All my thinking about the process of design in the development of
graphic tone and composition comes more from painters than from any other
source. The strength of painters like Léger or Stuart Davis comes from the
simple directness in their development of forms and flat colors; the whole, a
bridge between symbol and picture, and a change from illustration to symbol
making. I would not say that I made the same explorations, but, nevertheless,
contemporary graphic design deals with similar problems, like eliminating
unnecessary elements.

I do not have the belief that there is a proper way to do things. What
makes graphic design so interesting is that there are few real rules. However,
having said that, there are nevertheless purposes. I am not sympathetic to pur-
poselessness in design. What is called "new wave" is a revisionist return to bygone
periods, arbitrary and incredibly boring. Art deco and art nouveau are important
to be aware of as styles. The Bauhaus and pop art are important as ideas, which
are greatly reduced in value when distilled into style alone. To bring any style out
of the drawer unrelated to the subject matter at hand is depressing. If there is a
single rule, it is that there should be some logic in the application of the past to
current communication needs. And this logic has to be based on more than
predilections of taste.

If one is drawn to anything in a positive way, it is because one immediately grasps the reason for its being. Then, one can analyze how successful or how
original it is. If it works, it looks good after a while, like the original Volkswagen.
Nowadays, there is an enormous volume of graphic design work that is at a high
level of professionalism. There is more good work around than ever before. But
the amount that is really refreshing, in a purposeful way, is not greater at all.

What has happened to modern design is that its horizons have expanded.
Some people have abandoned it because it seems not to be there anymore. But, in
fact, there is more opportunity for varied attitudes to coexist than when modernists were more doctrinaire.

An excellent example of a new modern spirit can be found in the work of
Grapus, a group of Parisian graphic designers who lend their talents to politically
significant causes. They go to great lengths to make their work appear immediate.
Their posters always look as though they were done in ten seconds flat. One
knows perfectly well that they aren't, yet their process demands and produces a
level of freshness that the others rarely reach so consistently. They believe that
something which appears "hot off the press" demands attention. This is a modern
thought.

The Grapus philosophy differs significantly, for example, from the theories about typography design emanating from Basel. The Swiss have too many
stylistic tenets that have to do with spacing, weight, and color. The Basel ap-

proach appears to spread like wildfire because it is recognizable, consistent, and, therefore, teachable. It is too easy and repetitive, and the levels of boredom attached to it are high. The essential difference between the modern tradition and the Basel style is that the latter abandons function altogether. This does not mean that modern design is void of style or artistry. On the contrary, modern design can include anything, including new wave graphic styles.

The refuge of the untalented is to make more of things, never less. Modern graphic design of the thirties did not. That does not make it less modern, but rather evolutionary.

The bulk of graphic design today is done without designers. Most houses are designed without architects. In architecture, for example, despite the modern legacy, the building that goes on in the name of capricious fashion is more notorious than any other kind. It is successful because it demands a lot of conversation and gains high rents for its developers.

Similar practice occurs in graphic design. There are those who rest on their fashionable accomplishments, while a few others attempt to push boundaries.

### RUDOLPH DE HARAK

In the late forties, as a beginning commercial artist in Los Angeles, I attended two lectures that introduced me to modernism and had a profound effect on my life. The first was a lecture by Will Burtin entitled "Integration, the New Discipline in Design." Burtin not only spoke about design and communications, but also presented an exhibition of his work, which guided the viewer through a series of experiences that were described as the four principal realities of visual communications. They were the reality of man, as measure and measurer; the reality of light, color, and texture; the reality of space, motion, and time; and the reality of science. He was the first person I had heard use the term *visual communications.*

A short time later, I heard Gyorgy Kepes speak. At the time, I didn't fully understand everything he was saying, yet I knew that his words were very important to me. I recall my excitement, as I was able to draw parallels between what he was saying about the plastic arts and what Will Burtin had said concerning the realities of visual communications.

It was the beginning of my realization that it was possible to communicate visual information that transcended common conventions and could become art. I discovered the possibility of having a viable vocation and at the same time to be able to experience deep fulfillment. These lectures were so important that they inspired me to leave my job as a mechanical artist and commit myself totally to design.

As I became more involved with this profession, I realized that my deepest concerns with design were centered on what I felt were the mysteries of form—discovering new forms and using them to construct creative and meaning-ful solutions to design problems.

I attempted to evolve forms that covered the entire emotional spectrum and were also impeccable in their sense of order. This, to me, was the essence of modernism, and toward that end, I wanted to create constellations so rich that they could communicate content. I was searching for what I called "the hidden order"; trying to find some common principle or scheme inherent in all things that would answer questions that maybe I hadn't yet asked.

The Bauhaus was perhaps the most profound example of modernism in its break with the rigid ideologies of "grand manner" art education. Dedicated to research and instruction, its objective was a social reconditioning through a synthetic curriculum. Simultaneously, all the arts were examined in the light of contemporary conditions.

Modernism is also exemplified in the International Style of design that developed following World War II. Its mostly Swiss contributors included such notable designers as Max Bill, Josef Müller-Brockmann, Armin Hofmann, Max Huber, Richard Lohse, Hans Neuberg, Siegfried Odermatt, Emil Ruder, and Carlo Vivarelli. These modernists breathed new life into design, cutting away all unnecessary graphic appendages and leaving only the essentials. Their work, which manifested itself in this timeless style, was thoughtful and systematic. The work was beautiful, thoroughly crafted, and communicated complex information quickly and simply. Like the Bauhaus, it was an essential development and a strong reflection of its time.

In the forties and fifties, I believed that modern design was a means to precipitate reactions and new actions. At that time, there was a sense of ur-gency—a design revolution that was alive and aimed at developing openness to what many considered radical forms of communication. The goal was to create a platform for design from which could be communicated bold, new graphic ideas. I think that platform today is firmly rooted, thus expanding the possibility of producing intensely creative, dynamic, and even bizarre ideas. There is now much more awareness and acceptance of good design.

As times changed, so did my design philosophies. Now I am more inter-ested in the process of problem solving. This is not to say I don't want my design to be beautiful. But, in the past, I was preoccupied with finding something profound and revealing within a form. Today, I am much more concerned with the clear, direct communication of an idea.

Twenty-five years ago I said in a lecture, "The attitudes that forms com-municate dictate the ultimate validity of a design. Form is necessary and vital to the expression of ideas. Without it, content is barren. So, in an effort to effect a solution to any visual problem, the designer relies on his abilities to create new forms or use existing forms in unique concepts, and manipulate them."

Just a few years ago, at another lecture, I made quite a different statement.

"Design is a problem-solving process, but, for many of us, it is much more than that. It is also a very personal process of searching for and developing new concepts that serve to clarify and extend ideas. Herein lies the creativity in design.

"The climate that the designer works within is very complex, and, as in all creative fields, at times painful and frustrating. The designer's work must satisfy the tastes and opinions of the client, but most important, it must successfully reach and communicate to the audiences for which the work is intended. Even though the design work should also be self-rewarding, it is frequent that personal preferences have little meaning in the solving of design problems."

The differences in these two statements, made more than twenty years apart, are apparent. Yet, because my fundamental belief in modernism has not changed, I believe that they mostly represent a shift in emphasis and priorities.

Before I became fully aware of the International Style, and the Swiss pioneers in particular, my design inclinations moved in a somewhat similar direction. Before we had Helvetica in the United States, I primarily used sans-serif typefaces such as Futura, News Gothic, and Franklin Gothic. When Helvetica was first introduced, I specified it almost exclusively because it had a purity and uniformity that signaled no-nonsense information without embellishment. It is the way I feel about the old Remington typewriter face—beautiful, direct, and systematized. Typography is a profound issue, and when I started in this field, I felt that developing an understanding of all typefaces would be an extraordinary, time-consuming challenge.

It was preferable for me to work with just a few typefaces on a consistent basis, thereby developing a more intimate understanding of the letterforms. The challenge and ideal solution to a book design, for example, would be to set the entire book—titles, subtitles, text, and folios—in one style and size, establishing priorities of information through position and spatial relationships.

I am not implying that this approach was better than others, but it gave me a more disciplined position in which to understand type and to achieve viable solutions. Moreover, in designing a record cover on the music of Mozart, I was never interested in using a typeface that would be representative of the eighteenth century. I can no more identify Mozart with Caslon than with Futura. If I were to follow this design philosophy to its conclusion, it would be logical to put flames on the word *fire* or ice caps on the word *cool*. I believed the problem-solving process requires intelligent selection of a typeface that functions most appropriately for an overall design concept.

Changes in style, or new preferences in typefaces or color, have little to do with the basic responsibilities of problem solving in visual communications. The designer making a poster today has the same responsibilities to communicate clearly as El Lissitzky, Rodchenko, or Cassandre had decades ago.

I don't believe in change for the sake of change. Change comes about through a natural process of development or because something needs improving. Modernism suggests movement that is ahead of its time. If we do something that has been done before, we are not being creative; we are being redundant. Creativity, which is what modernism is all about, is a constant searching process that promises a greater chance for failure than it does for success.

*Originally published in Volume 5, Number 2, 1987.*

# GYORGY KEPES REVISITS THE VISUAL LANDSCAPE
*interview by Rudolph de Harak*

I n the mid-1940s, I was fortunate to attend a lecture given by Gyorgy Kepes. Shortly thereafter, I read his book, *The Language of Vision.* These experiences had a deep and lasting effect on me, both personally and professionally.

Through the years, I have always remained on the alert for his writings, lectures, exhibitions of paintings, and photography. During a discussion this past spring, Steven Heller told me of his wish to have an article about Gyorgy Kepes published in the *AIGA Journal.* With great enthusiasm, I volunteered to visit him in Cambridge and do this interview.

For those who are unaware of Gyorgy Kepes, let me simply say that he is a visionary and visual experimenter, whose achievements in various media are extraordinary and of great importance to this century. These include painting, graphic design, photography, writing, and teaching.

His roots are Hungarian. He had an academic art education in Budapest and an early professional life that included working with some of the outstanding avant-garde artists in Europe. Chief among these was László Moholy-Nagy, with whom he worked closely in Berlin at about the time the Nazis came into power. He again worked with Moholy-Nagy as head of the Light and Color Workshop at the New Bauhaus in Chicago (later renamed the Institute of Design). He left to become the founder and director of the Center for Advanced Visual Studies at the Massachusetts Institute of Technology (MIT), where he remained until his retirement in 1971. During his entire pedagogic career, spanning almost fifty years, and the years since his retirement, Gyorgy Kepes has never ceased his visual experimentations with light, color kinetics, his photography, and his paintings.

**Rudolph de Harak:** Could you give a brief summary of your background? That is, your beginnings as an artist and the motivations that brought you on the long, rich journey to where you are now.

**Gyorgy Kepes:** I was, for some reason, starting as a painter. I have to begin with how I responded to my own early childhood reality, as a budding painter. I use it as an analogy to what happened in England in the early part of the nineteenth century, when some of the natural environment was polluted, degraded, and confused by too fast and too reckless industrialization. The smoke and dirt that was gradually taking over London was, in a mini scale, the same situation of my own childhood. I dare say I almost had a love affair with the environment of my early childhood because we lived in the countryside. When we moved to Budapest, away from this environment, I missed it. As I sometimes review my own evolution, I come to the conclusion, again and again, that my motivations and my achievements, if any, were a result of this seeking for the richness of the lost paradise of my childhood.

Quite frequently, when I'm lecturing, I use the term *homeostasis*—automatic self-regulation. We all know when we are overheated, we perspire. When we are too cold, we start to shiver. There is an inner regulation in everybody's life, physically and also emotionally. If we are overcommitted to social existence, we seek quiet solitude. If we are alone too long, we seek company. So, as a young person, each time I lost something, I tried to replenish it or regain it. I found that whatever I did in terms of thinking or painting, it was partly this inner mechanism—to find a complete, more balanced sense of life.

And so, looking back, as a young boy in 1908 or 1910, when I first started to look at art, when we first went to the big city . . . I had to find for myself this feeling that I could run when I wanted to run, that I could see the open sky when I wanted to feel a sense of freedom. Whatever I did as a painter or a budding thinking person, I tried to replenish the missing part of my life . . . something which created for me a sense of fullness.

My early life in Budapest was not optimum because it was also a difficult historical moment. The First World War had arrived, and we had difficulty just finding enough food. I sensed a certain curtailment of my birthright to be happy and to be fully satisfied. This experience and this interpretation stayed with me.

**RdH:** How old were you when the war came?

**GK:** It was 1914, so I was not quite eight. I have strong memories, but it has no great validity for anybody else.

**RdH:** At that early age, were you already painting?

**GK:** I have painted since I can remember. I don't know what made me paint. It was partly a kind of vanity, that I was a little different from the other little boys, because I could paint a little better or have a more mature skill to render images. For some psychological reason, I had an ability to draw. My parents, uncles, and aunts looked at me as a budding genius. And I believed them. This was later a rather serious handicap because it was too early to have an inner maturity. I didn't have a message inside.

**RdH:** What form did your drawings and paintings take?

**GK:** I was drawing gypsy children, landscapes, and animals . . . and, when the First World War came, then, naturally, soldiers. There were no master-pieces, but I was invited by some of the people in my school to bring in drawings for an exhibition. I still have a little catalog.

**RdH:** Did you go to art school in your early teens?

**GK:** No. In my early teens, I went to *gymnasium,* which is the equivalent of high school. There I had the opportunity to study Latin literature. I never regretted it. I was not a good scholar, but I felt at home there because the teachers were kind and helped in scaffolding my confidence. There were also some stimu-lating minds among the teachers who helped me to orient myself to an under-standing in social territories. I had, for an odd, unexplained reason, a strong sense of social justice.

**RdH:** Do you feel that developing a sense of social justice and human values at a very young age can be traced to your parents? Were they quite liberal?

**GK:** My mother was deeply involved in poetry and interested in literature and art, and she had a great impact on me. My father also liked poetry, and he was interested in reciting poetry.
Everything has a role in one's grown-up life. I think this variety of being encouraged and discouraged as a young boy to make paintings, and brightened by one's own activity, still remains. I was not, and am not, a very self-certain person. When I am painting today, I still struggle, and this is both good and bad as far as I can tell.

**RdH:** When you finished gymnasium, did you then go to art school?

**GK:** I went to the Art Academy. That was, for me, a very important step in life. When I started to get a sense of myself, I knew I wanted to be a painter. Also, my parents encouraged me; so when I went to the art school, it was a major step.
It was really a very good school. The professors were the prominent artists of Hungary. There was a good system. There were several weeks of entrance examinations, which meant that we all went into different rooms and drew from a model, made compositions, or whatever else we chose to do. The professors evaluated this work and chose students for their own class. There were maybe five

hundred applicants, and the total number accepted was eighty or ninety. So we felt potent and confident that we made the grade. Also, some of us, luckily, were chosen not by one professor but by two or three, so we could choose our own professors.

**RdH:** Then, your education in the art school was essentially classic?

**GK:** It was great in terms of my needs. It was not avant-garde. It was nothing that demanded great guts to fight it out.

**RdH:** The reason I ask that question is, in view of the direction that you took, and your later connections with artists like Moholy, what was it that somehow turned you around, that made you start thinking and acting as an artist who broke with grand manner styles?

**GK:** It was not entirely a personal decision. We were in the Academy, accepted for a year to work and prove ourselves. After one year, five or six of us students were given a studio to share. I remember them as really wonderful people. One student later became an important film designer.

Another was a really great painter, later killed in the war in France. We had an interesting, complex life. I feel that the nature of the gymnasium school and that of the Art Academy had a great deal to do with my searching for idioms and meanings that were not given by our professors.

Later, we collectively started to explore new ground. We got hold of some books on the cubist artists, and we started to imitate cubist and constructivist art. The Academy was under the Ministry of Fine Art and Education, which was a very typical bureaucratic hierarchy. When the Minister came to visit the school and saw what we were doing, he forced our teacher to resign, and we were practically kicked out from the school because we were not behaving as dignified university students should. We were happy because we were more than ready to leave the climate of this school.

So, by some accidents, I had two levels of education that helped me to grow up as a painter. The official education was a formal, academic education where I learned to draw well. But I also had this revolutionary upheaval among my colleagues in which we explored the avant-garde in art.

**RdH:** When you finished with the Academy, you would have been about twenty, and that would have brought you just about to the time of the Bauhaus. What was your understanding of the Bauhaus at that time?

**GK:** I had very little knowledge of the Bauhaus in the school except for a couple of its books. But I got involved during this same time in a so-called avant-garde revolutionary movement. There was a strong-minded, gifted Hungarian

writer/artist who was a key man in the Hungarian avant-garde. He was at first a
writer and a poet. He really made a major impact on this generation. He was a
socialist and a propagandist of a new kind of life. He got involved during the
short intermezzo of the communist regime in Hungary. Then he had to leave
Hungary, and he went to Vienna. After a few years, he returned to Budapest and
was greeted as a hero by my friends and myself. He organized a group of socialist-
oriented writers, poets, and artists. That was my real education.

**RdH:** When you finished with the Academy, you already had developed
certain avant-garde philosophies and attitudes. You also had the classical skills of
an artist. What did you do with them then?

**GK:** The inner revelation came: I didn't want to be just a painter. I was
emotionally involved in the Hungarian peasant's life. I saw their sufferings, and I
felt both sorrow and anger, and decided that painting was not for me anymore. It
was too static and too limited in terms of social message communication. I
decided to become a filmmaker. I wrote to Moholy-Nagy, whom I had never met,
but assumed had a strong social commitment. He invited me to work with him
in Berlin. So I left Hungary and went to Berlin.

**RdH:** About what year was that?

**GK:** The beginning of 1930, when I was twenty-three years old. This
was, for me, a very important experience, but not always rewarding. He was a
very able and excitable, creative person. He was also a very skilled self-promoter.
Inevitably, we had some conflict of interest in many things. I designed a great
deal with him, and we had conflict credits for our work.

**RdH:** Was he much older than you?

**GK:** He was eleven years older. He was very alert, alive, social, and able.
He loved to be with people. He was a very bright manipulator, in the best sense. I
had a different nature, but I still learned a great deal from him, not necessarily to
do with self-evolution.
    I didn't know anything about photography at this time, and he didn't
either, but Lucia, Moholy's first wife, was a photographer and was teaching him
photography. She's still alive and resides in Switzerland. She must be around
ninety. Their marriage didn't last too long because Moholy met a young lady who
was a sister-in-law of Gropius, and they became friendly lovers.
    So, this was an exciting chance to explore new territories. I was never
committed to photography or committed to anything—just trying to find my
own heart and meaning. And I was working for a while, learning the technical
skills in photography. I also participated in exhibition design. I didn't like this

type of work because my own inclinations were more to lyric poetry, the small-scale emotional expression, and not the structured environment. I later changed my mind.

**RdH:** This was a very turbulent time. It was the early 1930s, and the Nazis had just come to power. Who was in Berlin at that time besides yourself and Moholy? Was Gropius also in Berlin?

**GK:** Yes, Gropius was in Berlin, as was Breuer. I met quite a few people. I had a great love for Soviet films, and I met Dovzhenko and Dziga Vertov there. Have you ever seen *The Earth*? It's a film by Dovzhenko. It's one of the greatest films I have ever seen. I was deeply impressed by the film, and so deeply impressed by Dovzhenko and his lady, that I tried to orient myself to filmmaking. It was in 1930, but I became very sick and returned to Hungary.

The period in Berlin was an exciting time, not just for me, but for practically anybody who was there. It was the last tick before the death of Germany, or at least the Weimar culture. It was, for me, important on many levels, but it was also useful as a historical encore. Hitler was very visible, and I had no kind feeling toward him. If one finds the diametrical opposite of friendship, that was in my heart.

I had great respect for the work of John Heartfield. He was designing covers for the magazine *Neue Russland* and doing much better than I could do. But I felt that if he could do it, I could also. So I went to the editor and I told him I would like to make the covers for the magazine. He told me that he'd made a temporary commitment to Heartfield, but that Heartfield was much too busy, and he was sure that he would be happy for me to do them. And that's what happened. I took over, and I did maybe a year's magazine covers. It was not my greatest creative challenge, but I still enjoyed doing them for two reasons. First, because politically I was on the same wavelength. I was interested in doing something where I felt it may help a little to change the mood of history. Secondly, it was a good feeling to be in a situation where I could, practically every week, meet somebody else from Soviet Russia. And it was there that I met Dovzhenko and Vertov.

**RdH:** Did you ever meet Rodchenko?

**GK:** No, I never met Rodchenko. But I had a great admiration for him. I was very surprised because at the end of his life he lost his creative vigor. He was much stronger as a young man.

**RdH:** When did Moholy-Nagy come to the United States?

**GK:** Actually, we came to the States practically at the same time. I came in 1937, and he came in 1937, too. We went independently to London. After I returned from my excursion to Hungary, because of my sickness, Moholy decided he had to get me out of Berlin as soon as he could. He wrote to me, inviting me to work with him again. And I accepted his invitation and went back to Berlin. But it was not a Berlin where I could enjoy a single second. And when Moholy went to London, in I think 1937, he asked me to come to work with him again. I went to London, I think, in 1937—no, 1935, I think, because I stayed in London for a while. Sometimes, chronology is very confusing.

RdH: But you both, then, found yourselves in London around 1935 or 1936.

GK: And he was doing some work for various companies, and finally he was asked to be something like the art director of the Simpson-Piccadilly, which was a store like Saks Fifth Avenue. As he was a guiding spirit, he put me in as the chief designer of everything, from window displays to graphic design. I enjoyed the London life and was also inclined to have a great liking for English people. I made friends in London—mostly scientists and writers. My London life was one of the important intermezzos in my existence.

RdH: You met your wife there?

GK: Yes. I was working with Simpson-Piccadilly at the time. Then, Moholy got an offer to come to the United States. First, Gropius was asked to take over the architecture department at Harvard. And Gropius decided that he would take it, but, at the same time, he was approached to start the new Bauhaus in Chicago. Gropius then suggested Moholy, and Moholy took over the school as an organizer. I was asked by Moholy, still in London, to come over and to be the head of the Light Department. We did not know what to teach. We did not know America. Neither of us had ever been here, and it was an interesting excursion in the wilderness.

RdH: Did you speak English at the time?

GK: No, very little actually. I went to the Berlitz School in Berlin, and when the teacher heard my accent, he told me we Hungarians are hopeless. When I went to London, my total vocabulary was maybe twenty words. But I survived, and there were a fair number of German immigrants in London at this time, so I had no serious difficulties.

RdH: When you came to America, did you have any problem working here because you were an immigrant?

**GK:** No, because Moholy had a rather tricky mind. He arranged it for himself, and for me too, to sneak into the teaching profession. I came legally to the U.S. on some kind of immigrant visa. I had to still wait for a few years to get my citizenship, but there were no difficulties with me teaching. It was an interesting, undesigned event because I did not know what I was bargaining for. I hardly knew anything about America. As a young man, I read Walt Whitman and Emerson in Hungarian. I hardly knew anything of American history—just a few writers. But teaching is a compulsive enterprise. When you are forcing yourself to teach, then you force yourself to learn. So I learned a great deal about history and about myself.

**RdH:** What was the nature of the problems that you gave to students? You were in charge of the photographic department?

**GK:** I was in charge of the Light Department. That was a new term that we introduced. Moholy was interested in light. I had a rough time at the beginning because if one tries to fit into a preconceived notion, and this is not the right notion, then you get into difficulties. I arrived without really knowing too much about America.

The school was an exciting challenge, but not always positive. I mean, Moholy was a very brilliant mind, but also a hard-hitting salesman for his interests. He was not getting along too well with the students. After maybe half a year, the students started to plot against him. It was an unpleasant kind of confrontation.

I don't know who has survived from this time, but there were a number of bright young Americans who knew something of the Bauhaus, and they assumed that we would have a new Bauhaus.

But after a year the school collapsed because the trustees withdrew all the funds. I started a mini-school, maybe fifteen or twenty students.

**RdH:** Was this the time that you were working on *The Language of Vision*? You evidently started that book somewhere around 1939.

**GK:** I think 1938, if I am not mistaken. *The Language of Vision* had a simple history to it. In Chicago, I was asked to give a course for the Art Directors Club. You may remember the name of [Egbert] Jacobsen—

**RdH:** Yes, of course.

**GK:** He was taking my course and was also helpful in selling *The Language of Vision* idea to people. So I started this book, with some help, because my English was more than primitive, but less than good. I had some help with the English part of it. But it was an exciting time. I was very young, I worked hard, and had roughly sixty teaching hours a week. I gave courses every evening for the Art Directors Club and every Saturday. . . . It was a full load. And, at the same time, I did some work. You may have seen some of it. Container Corporation work. I considered myself a designer. If anything, I wanted to be a visual poet. But I had to face necessity, and I did whatever I could do.

**RdH:** Because your book had been very highly acclaimed, you were then invited by MIT to come to Cambridge. Is that correct?

**GK:** Yes. Roughly correct, not necessarily in chronology. Because I got into what they call a confrontation with Moholy at the end of my Chicago work. I resigned, and . . . (At some time, it would be good just to publish the correspondence.) I felt that Moholy was too much in a rush to do things just to survive. I was too young to work in this improvised dream there, and I wanted to keep my principles. I confronted Moholy, and we decided, that for us and the school, it would be better if I left. It was not a simple situation, but I thought it wiser in any case. And so I left the School of Design, or the New Bauhaus, and made my living with these various teaching possibilities.

After I published *The Language of Vision,* Bill Wooster, the dean of MIT, called me and invited me to visit MIT, and I came to see him. It was during the war, and most of the young people were in the army or navy. It was not a school time. It was in 1943, I think. I was not too impressed, and I was hesitant because Brooklyn College, where I was teaching, was full of bubbling energy. It would be difficult to go to this sleepy place. I called my old friend Marcel Breuer, who lived in Cambridge, and asked him what would be his suggestion. Should I accept it? He told me that between Brooklyn College and MIT he would not hesitate for a second and suggested that I take it. And I never really regretted it for a second . . . the School of Arts. It was an exciting new vista for me.

At MIT, I had some difficulty in finding my own kind of inner balance. I did not know what to do. Luckily, I still had some friends from Europe. I had an old friend, Bruno Rossi, who was one of the top physicists, and he came to MIT the same month that I did. Through him, I met some of the top physicists. I came to MIT with a rather worried feeling that there are intellectual giants, and I am just a primitive, at least in terms of knowledge. But in meeting with some of these giants, I discovered that they are, in a certain way, primitives because their aesthetic awareness was really close to zero. Gradually, I developed an almost complete commitment to MIT, and I still love it.

**RdH:** Now, you stayed on there until 1974 or 1975?

**GK:** MIT had a regulation that you cannot stay longer than age seventy—no, sixty-five. But I got an extension, and I was teaching there until 1971, I think.

**RdH:** Since then you have given yourself almost entirely to painting again?

**GK:** Painting, and sometimes I write short communications, but not with full conviction.

**RdH:** It's over forty years since *The Language of Vision* was published. It was packed with your enthusiasm, your commitment, and energy. I felt it was a most important book, written with a strong hope for the future. It was concerned with the many aspects of the process of seeing, and through your concise explanations of the psychological and physiological elements of this process, a new visual coherency was defined. Additionally, I believe its intent was that a new and broader-based understanding of the plastic arts would strongly contribute to a richer understanding and practice of human values. In other words, a better integrated and emotionally healthier society would result. Were these your goals? And, if so, after these forty years, to what degree do you feel your goals in that book have been successful?

**GK:** The answer is, to the first part, those were the goals. But life was editing my goals, and many things that I was completely confident about in 1939, when I started to write this book, were fading a little. I still believe that nothing is independent. We are living with an interdependence of every culture and social phenomena. And for me, art is not an isolated entity, but it has a very strong interconnectedness with everything else. As a young man, I felt more confident that this can be realized, in real terms and in the real full sense of those terms. I am now fading a little in my confidence, but still haven't given up my original convictions. First, visual art seems to me, the image making, a key issue in one's intellectual and also ethical orientation. And I think that it would be a great benefit for all of us if we could re-pose our interest in these issues I believed in so many years ago. So I did not give up my beliefs, but I had to edit in a certain minor key.

**RdH:** How do you feel about the International Style of graphic design? By this I mean simplicity and clarity of image, with emphasis being placed on the underlying grid system and extensive use of sans-serif type, usually an asymmetric arrangement. This, of course, generated by the Swiss.

**GK:** I have a mixed response and a mixed-up response. I like it, but I feel it lacks physiognomy. Expressive power. I don't imply that one should go back and try to make illustrations of graphic design. But I feel a little . . . oh, not negative . . . but doubtful that there is a final word that that's what we should do, and that's the only thing we could ever do. I have to think it over before I carry on.

It's always difficult because I like the work. Actually, I like your work immensely, as you know. But maybe some new input should come in from the art side. Not from typographical or graphic design, but some emotional impact from social or psychological reasons. But I feel that it's a certain standard that took over the graphic field entirely. As I am primarily a painter, not a designer, I feel often almost let down that there is not a stretching out. It's all of a coordinated design, but not a courageous exploration.

**RdH:** My next question has a bearing on the previous one. Because of the enormity of considerations in graphic problem solving, the need to express information and ideas quickly, which would also imply the requirement of great coherence in communication: What do you feel is the role of aesthetics in this context?

**GK:** You may recall that I was almost preaching at the end of *The Language of Vision*. I implied that there is a major social task in communication, and the clarity of communication is an important asset in this communication system.

I am now in a dilemma, because I like the Swiss attitude toward design, but I still feel a little letdown when I compare what happens in a kind of typographical design with what happens in graphic art in very general terms. I would like to see more courage in stretching the present graphic standards. But I could not dare to make recommendations on how to do this expanding.

**RdH:** Did you feel perhaps that, when you think of some of the graphic expressions of, let's say, Alexander Rodchenko or El Lissitzky or Piet Zwart . . . Do you feel that perhaps the stretching out, as you call it, was manifested more in their type of work than in the Swiss design?

**GK:** No. It's more a question of the stage of history when these early pioneers in clarity in typography did their job. It was less competitive. They coexisted with Lissitzky, who was, in my reckoning, maybe the most potent figure in such territory. This has not been my involvement for a long time, and I have to think it over before I make a nonsensical statement.

**RdH:** Let me get back to this question again. In other words, we both agree that we understand that the whole communication problem today is very complex because a greater amount of knowledge and information has to be imparted to a greater number of people. And because there is so much more information floating about, one has to digest that data much more quickly. So what we're really looking for, in a sense, are methodologies that can solve or shortcut communications problems. If that is the case, and if communications is really the prime issue, my real question is: What role does aesthetics really play in that? I mean, we understand that we want simple type and clarity. But how do aesthetics balance in that? Do you have any feelings about that?

**GK:** I have some deep feelings. First, I would like to edit it for my own sake, that we in every profession assume that our profession is a lifesaver. Let us say that you have a commitment to an avant-garde typography, and I had the same, and we assume that it will really give a new compass to life. I have no such feeling anymore. I think the interconnectedness, with the different attitudes to life . . . a graphic attitude, or moral attitude, or aesthetic attitude together should find a common denominator. And I think that the Swiss idioms did bring some quality that I myself admire and sometimes envy. I wish to be a Swiss typographer. But when I see too many of them, I feel that the spectrum of graphic communication is potentially richer than these idioms.

**RdH:** The next is a three-part question. The first: partly because of what you've already said about your response to the International Style, from a very personal point of view, how do you respond now to postmodern design?

**GK:** I have a much greater genuine response to the International design, the Swiss design, than to the postmodern design in architecture. In fact, I was irritated and still am irritated with this kind of collecting different past idioms and trying to make a hodgepodge out of it. I feel much more sympathy and a warmer response to what you are doing, or what people are doing, who know the whole spectrum of design and choose, in an appropriate moment, the right idioms.

**RdH:** Then, perhaps this next section of my question is already answered. First, the question was how you responded to postmodern design. Then, objectively, do you feel that it's helped to clarify or strengthen visual communication?

**GK:** Before I can answer: do you mean postmodern in architecture?

**RdH:** I was really speaking typographically, but I think that there is a connection between postmodern architecture and postmodern graphic design.

**GK:** There must be. As I mentioned before, the postmodern design and architecture is not warming to my heart. I was involved in a number of confrontations on what they call postmodern architecture. It came like a forest fire. It just came through and took over the whole design field. And, as my old friends, like Gropius, Breuer, and others of them . . . they were not postmodern architects. They were doubtful about it, and I belong to the same group of doubtful citizens.

**RdH:** Do you have a feeling of where design will go from here?

**GK:** I don't have a very strong sense of the direction. But I know, whatever I know about history, that there are certain types of oscillations or changes from one extreme to the other, and in between we are just filling in time. There was a revolutionary mood when Piet Zwart, El Lissitzky, Rodchenko, and these people were working. They did not assume that there was a wholesale new attitude. But they tried to do their little bit to go ahead. I don't really know what the future can be, but I know what I would like to see in the future. I wish to see a still greater clarity and also a greater sense of vitality. Because what has happened in most of the newer work, if I am correct . . . the sensuous richness was a little subdued, into a preconceived geometric. Does it make sense for you? In Lissitzky's work, I feel there was a great deal of imagination and guts, and sometimes an incredible high crescendo of vitality.

*Originally published in Volume 6, Number 3, 1988.*

# LIFE, STYLE, AND ADVOCACY
*Dan Friedman*

At first, I was reluctant to talk about lifestyle. I thought it would be superficial. But then I realized it would be at the very heart of my larger agenda. I was given just ten minutes to talk about the way I live. But it was necessary for me to begin with some observations about design and culture, in general, and our profession, in particular, because these things very much affect the way I have chosen to live. I also showed images that indicate how our homes express our lifestyles; how they reflect our disposition, creativity, knowledge, taste, wealth, and view of ourselves in relationship to the rest of the world.

We exist in a culture that generates all kinds of recipes for how we should look. Like changing channels on TV, we are shown that everyone can aspire to various lifestyles, from the look of Ralph Lauren to the look of Guns n' Roses. Our consumer society classifies all of us by style.

So it seems only natural that designers would also fall into this business of creating style, even while maintaining to each other that we possess keener sensibilities and that we are above such things previously described as fashion. To the contrary, we seem to admire most the work that packages a message in a new look even if we can't always tell what that message is. We see this development everywhere from Los Angeles to New York and from Michigan to Texas. Even one of our foremost architects, Philip Johnson, has gotten into this game. Six years ago, his office made its first proposal for a project in Times Square in the postmodern style when it was at the height of its popularity. Recently, the same firm made a new proposal for the same project, which indicates that a deconstructivist style is now better. It is no surprise to me that the biggest contribution designers seem to be making these days is in promoting styles.

What we don't seem to realize is that, culturally, much of society has moved way ahead of the designer. There was a time when things were the other way around! Designers and artists were visionaries leading society. I think we should aspire to do that again. The early modernist movement still provides a noble message about the role of design in affecting culture and lifestyle. The spirit of early pioneers such as Ruskin, Gropius, Wright, Schwitters, or Le Corbusier was that design—like art—would be a service and inspiration to humanity. And designers would reflect this spirit in every aspect of their work, their lives, and their ethics.

I was lucky early in my career to get to know other pioneers such as Armin Hofmann, Paul Rand, and George Nelson. I admired them mainly because of their passion, their dedication, and for the manner in which their work was an inseparable part of their lifestyles. I, too, developed this idea that my lifestyle and design style would be effortlessly integrated. Each would be unified within the other. I saw graphic design as something integral to larger environmental and social issues, so it seemed only logical to me that our homes and personal style would likewise express the same criteria. This was the foundation of modernism, which I have always embraced.

But I don't think that the first pioneers of modernism would have anticipated how our profession, and even the lifestyles of its practitioners, would have become so thoroughly dominated by purely economic and corporate values. For example, I learned in the mid-1970s, during an association with a New York design firm, how my idea of integrity somehow mutated from service to the public good into service to the corporation. In my opinion, this is a process in which designers eventually become willing to look and act as bland and predictable as the work they create. I always point out that modernism forfeited any claim to a moral authority when designers sold it away as corporate style. If you want to discuss dangerous ideas, I would say, despite indications of change, that this practice has now dominated our profession for more than twenty years and is celebrated every year at the AIGA *Communication Graphics* show.

If consumer society has brought us to one end of a spectrum, excess of style with limited substance, then corporate society has brought us to the other extreme, blandness of spirit at the expense of personal value.

In the late 1970s, my personal, domestic landscape became my primary source of experimentation and a laboratory for studying issues of design. I expected this expression of my lifestyle would lead me into some new design profession; I certainly no longer wanted my profession to define my lifestyle as I did earlier in my career. For me, my home is like a diary. It is always changing, it makes references to the world around me, and it provides a very private way of trying design ideas. Since there are always more ideas than space, I accept complexity as a necessity. I create an extreme caricature of the beautiful modern American home in order to bring into question our notion of what is a beautiful modern American home. There is something very satisfying about applying my design skill to things where you actually live every day, rather than those bits of corporate paper that end up in the garbage. And the more I make it look like something no one else in their right mind would want to achieve, the more visits I seem to get from journalists, art collectors, and even architects from around the world who take it very seriously. My home has become the ideal place to reexamine the relationships between design, art, nature, culture, technology, and modern urban living. It helps me focus my pursuit of an art that has meaning and function and a design that has poetry and value.

This activity all comes together into a kind of grand assemblage; it seems a result of some primordial explosion of energy, radiating with intense color and complexity. I have created elegant mutations of a hypermodernist world that deconstructed in my imagination into a wild ritualistic playground. You can walk in my door and find the coherent, integrated world of modernism brought to its wildest extreme. I choose to celebrate progressive optimism, fantasy, and playful exuberance. I reject solutions that revert to excessive historicism and nostalgia. This is not an easy route when most of our culture has moved in the opposite direction. Therefore, I see myself as a radical modernist, one who still believes in an idealism bound to a moral imperative, even if it might take some sort of apocalyptic process for it to happen. The objects I live with do more than function; they express ideas and tell stories. My goal has been to signal a realignment with the spirit of primal societies—the spirit through which one is surrounded, not by art or design, but by objects that are artfully conceived, culturally significant, useful in daily rituals, related to human scale, and energized by magic.

So, is this the work of some crazy schizophrenic lost in his personal metaphorical space, or is there really insight from one man's lifestyle that other designers can use? Like all of you, we have moments when we ask ourselves: How do I fit into the grand scheme of things? What do I want to do professionally? What kind of lifestyle do I desire? And, of course, how much money do I need to make? But there are other questions that I think I only fully resolved in the midst of my odd domestic experimentation, and I gather they will be questions you too may be asking:

How can I make my profession an expression of my lifestyle rather than the other way around?

Why are there so few graphic designers whose lifestyle I truly want to emulate?

Why do good designers have a relatively minor impact on our overall environment or on our popular culture?

What happened to our sense of humor?

Why must a bottom-line mentality tend to squeeze out artistic and humanistic concerns?

Are very personal forms of expression inappropriate to impose on jobs for clients, or are these expressions better left at home?

Why have designers allowed themselves to become servants to increasing overheads, careerism, and predominantly corporate goals?

As someone who has successfully spent most of the last decade in both the worlds of art and design, I now believe our most pressing issue in the next decade is not about art versus design but is about reinvesting both with a moral authority and a higher vision. It has always been my goal to inspire my peers to perform with a sense of quality, exuberance, freshness, danger, responsibility, and optimism. I now dream of designers becoming advocates. I'm not talking about the few attempts some of us make that we refer to as pro bono work, but truly a change of mind set that reorients us away from purely aesthetic or narrow corporate values toward educational, technological, cultural, informational, environmental, social, and even domestic values. I think this would really be the way to enhance our lifestyles and to work us out of the corner in which the profession finds itself. If it's our priority, I expect in the 1990s that this endeavor could be leveraged into an industry and could even be profitable.

*Originally published in Volume 7, Number 4, 1990.*

# TASTE IS JUST A MATTER OF TASTE
*Dugald Stermer*

L et us now, briefly, praise bad design, or, more properly, *nondesign*; meaning those printed communications that appear to be untouched by the educated designer's hand, yet do their jobs quite nicely, thank you, all the same.

For example, newspapers used to be remarkable bastions of nondesign, with layout by editors who guided our eyes by placing what they thought important at the top and filling the rest of the page willy-nilly with what fit. Let's not quibble about the *London Sunday Times* and Stanley Morison; the papers I grew up with were entirely unfettered by their influence. Of course, there are nicely designed-by-designer papers—the *New York Times* and *Los Angeles Times* being two—but mostly we are being greeted by printed happy talk like *USA Today* and its ever-increasing clones, not bringing us hard information so much as reassurance.

Blissfully, much, if not most, of the material upon which we rely for hard information remains designer free: classified advertisements, telephone books, *Racing Form,* shopping guides and grocery throwaways, the dictionary, *Old Farmer's Almanac,* etc. And there are other pieces of informative ephemera that probably should be left alone, like menus.

Stereo and electronics ads in the newspapers seem to do the job pretty well; one would be hard pressed to figure how Jim Cross, Massimo Vignelli, or Deborah Sussman could improve on their effectiveness. Admittedly, on television they are, like used-car commercials, nothing but nasty; but in print, with all the models depicted and listed along with their features and prices, they make comparative shopping fairly simple.

There is no question that any decent journeyman designer could slicken up the Brooks Brothers, L. L. Bean, J. Press and J. G. Hook magazine advertisements and catalogs, but something is very likely to get lost in the transition—like tradition, which is the better part of what they have to sell. The same cannot be said for those tired Neiman-Marcus pages, which only serve to sustain a slightly seedy—and entirely inaccurate—image of the store and its merchandise.

It is splendid that some noteworthy designers have, thanks largely to Saul Bass's pioneering efforts, been able to pick up a few bucks designing ads, posters, and titles for the movies. Many of these have been extraordinary. But nostalgia aside, those old posters—lurid, tinted, and retouched monuments to cinematic heroic realism—were and are perfect evocations of the spirit and content of the films they flogged. One cannot imagine Bass or, say, Mike Salisbury doing justice to the epics of Cecil B. DeMille, much less Busby Berkeley.

Then there is *kitsch,* or that which becomes chic through the aging of what was considered bad taste initially: airport gift-shop merchandise will do for an example, or seashell sculpture, or statuary containing clocks and thermometers—that sort of thing. But kitsch, unlike nondesign, is a self-conscious style, one that is embraced as good by virtue of its extreme badness. It is an amusing pastime to try to predict the kitsch of the future. Is the old Peter Max sufficiently bad, or too bad, to ever be collected in that spirit? How about the new Peter Max? LeRoy Neiman? Your work? Mine? Then, too, I have a pair of Walter Keane cuff links that I am insufficiently hip to appreciate and would be willing to talk trade with anyone who owns anything to do with Tom Mix.

But kitsch aside, there are other forms of print which are, by their natures, too immediate and urgent, too much a product of volunteer effort or cottage industry, to be treated to sophisticated design techniques and technology. In this category fall political broadsides and posters (of dissent usually, as distinct from campaign literature), announcements of community gatherings and issues, T-shirts and bumper stickers commemorating cultural events and tourist attractions (Carlsbad Caverns, Winnemucca's House of Reptiles), and all manner of other memorabilia.

Some of this material, in fact some of everything under discussion herein, can be surpassingly lovely by anyone's standards, though that is generally unintended and serendipitous. Only misfortune rewards professional designers who would attempt to mimic innocence and naïveté. The outcome will always be as graceless and disingenuous as commercials using adult actors' voices to sound like children.

But who said everything had to be "designed" anyway? Sure, design has to do with communication, but not necessarily vice versa.

*Originally published in Volume 4, Number 4, 1986.*

# PICASSO REX

*Brad Holland*

When I was living in Chicago in the mid-sixties, an artist I knew, a bebopster known to his few friends as Waynesville, wrote a letter to Picasso challenging him to Indian wrestle for the title of World's Greatest Artist. As far as I know, Picasso, who seemed forever in the company of matadors and photographers from *Life* magazine, never replied, and the last I heard of Waynesville he was pasting up catalogs of tractor parts on Michigan Avenue and dreaming of escape to some Caribbean Eden where he would shack up with illiterate women and paint savage masterpieces.

For him, Picasso was the true existential hombre. If you were an artist in those times, eyeing a serious perch on the totem pole, it seemed that in one way or another you had to size up Picasso like no other single figure. Still, for me, his influence had no meaning at all until I was seventeen. I had been indifferent to the clichés of academic modernism. In my small-town midwestern childhood, Picasso was a remote figure of no consequence, except as an occasional figure of fun to farmers or workers at the local cutlery plants, for whom his paintings of women with their preposterous anatomy and their flounder eyes represented the foolishness of modern art. He didn't fare much better in the grade schools and the high schools, even where modern art was taught. In our school he was embraced with a big academic bear hug as the benign father figure of self-expression, a kind of colorful soul brother to John Dewey.

But, from a chance conversation on the Chicago El one morning, I learned that in the world I had chosen to leave Ohio for, Picasso was the very Newton, even the Napoleon, of modern art. He embodied the values that had enthroned him. The bohemians and art students I knew on the North Side of Chicago all bombarded me with the various imperatives Picasso had tossed around like casual thunderbolts: that modern art is about form, not literary or psychological values; that figurative art is merely bad literature; and, fundamentally, that after cubism there can be no more representational painting since you can "make wine from grapes, but never the reverse." I picked up the anecdotes, metaphors, Picassoisms, and various tidbits collected by Sabartes, Cocteau, Gertrude Stein, and the rest of their merry band, all published in the vast Picasso literature that flourished during those last decades of his life.

Cocteau, the busy disciple, frequently referred to Picasso not as a mere artist, but as a "creator." Of course, I suspect Cocteau felt himself the only-slightly-less luminous half of a twin star of which Picasso was, by concession, the brighter. Picasso defined their relationship in his own terms. Upon hearing of Cocteau's death, he dismissed him as "the tail of my comet." A hell of a way to send off a pal, I thought, when I read it in the *Times*. If you were Picasso's friend, you wouldn't want to die before he did. But it was an elegant cruelty. It had a well-sharpened edge, as if Picasso had prepared it and kept it handy for any of the various pretenders who crowded around his throne.

From the generation of Cézanne and Gauguin, Picasso certainly inherited the revolution in art that, for many, he came to symbolize. But those of us who were born at midcentury found that those revolutionaries most identified with the modern era in art were all people the age of our grandfathers. They were lions already, safe in our textbooks. Picasso was even gilded with wealth and fame virtually unprecedented for an artist. Still, he had maintained much of the attractive air of danger and romantic sleaziness that had characterized his early days. This was something none of his contemporaries had done in quite the same way, not even Pound in the asylum. Eliot, Stravinsky, Matisse, and Braque all may have been great artists, but Picasso had stepped out of the art books, his life a masterpiece of popular mythology.

When I first became aware of him, around the fifth grade, he was flagging but still battling, down on the canvas one minute, up the next, ducking, clinching, and using rope-a-dope tactics against the likes of Jackson Pollock and Arshile "If Picasso drips, I drip" Gorky. By the mid-sixties, there were other challengers. Ad Reinhart, for one, announced, as if he were a thunderbird climbing atop the totem pole, that his black minimal paintings had made him the ultimate artist. The art magazines and galleries set up a chorus behind him, but it was a hollow claim and he might as well have challenged Picasso to Indian wrestle for it. The old man, in his shorts and bare chest, had outfoxed them all, years before, by redefining the rules of the game. To be a serious artist, you had to be a revolutionary. The catch was that if you did, you became part of Picasso's revolution, dust in the tail of his comet.

As soon as I understood the grip Picasso exercised on his successors, I marveled that Freud, whose intellectual turf was just next door to Picasso's, evidently showed no interest in getting the Minotaur onto his couch. The mythology of Picasso seems so ripe a subject for Freudian unraveling that had Picasso slain his father, married his mother, and been blinded on the road to Paris, he could not have provided a more archetypal case history.

An artist's life is often more accessible than his work. Fame in art, even posthumous fame, is probably incomprehensible to many people except as a success story. The work itself may seem mystifying, beside the point, or even a bit silly, but there's something satisfying in having a dramatic hook on which to hang it. In the case of Gauguin, it's his escape to nature; van Gogh, his struggle with sanity. In the case of Picasso, the theme is that of the child prodigy who never grows up, never has to, because he subdues and gobbles everything in sight.

Picasso the Wonder Child makes his first appearance in his father's studio. It's a tidy little story and gives the impression that all his later triumphs in the world were prefigured there. The details are relatively well known.

He was born Pablo Ruiz. The name Picasso was his mother's. His father, Don José, was an academic painter and teacher; in Picasso's description, an authoritative but ultimately weak figure. Picasso grew up in and around his father's studio, in Málaga and Galicia, drawing constantly and studying art at Galicia's university. Here, according to the story, Don José recognized his son's genius, saw that he had been mastered, and announced that his own work was finished. He gave Pablo his paints and brushes and never painted again. You can almost see the limp brushes spring back to life in the stubby little hands.

Picasso seems to have loved this story. He is said to have told it often, although his best friend from childhood, Manuel Pallares, swore it never happened, that Picasso had made it up "out of whole cloth." But, of course, there was no need for Picasso to make it up. He could simply have borrowed it from legend or mythology.

It is, after all, a story probably as old as puberty, the story of the miracle child incarnate as a brilliant protégé. In the Renaissance it was a common story, told about Raphael and his father, about Leonardo, Verrocchio, and others. It was probably told when Jesus astounded his elders at Bar Mitzvah, or earlier, when Oedipus astounded his father otherwise. Before mass education many children were apprenticed at quite early ages, so it's perfectly believable, even predictable, that some of them would become early masters. What makes this myth compelling isn't the idea of the prodigy, it's that of the little genius who hauls the father figure down from his chair and climbs into it himself. It is a myth bound to be attractive to the young. But in those waning days of fin-de-siècle Europe, when Picasso and Freud were under parental eyes, when even that midnight rambler, the sexagenarian Prince of Wales, was reduced to the status of bad child by the memory of the saintly Albert, the myth may have found a special resonance, particularly for an ambitious son like Picasso with an ambitious, puttering father ahead of him on the ladder.

But Freud at least claimed to feel guilty over the sense of release his father's death brought him. Picasso dispatches the problem parent with seeming efficiency. In a series of tactical little moves that make you suspect Don José didn't hand over his brushes easily, if ever at all, Picasso dismisses his father as a retired pigeon painter, takes his mother's name, and leaves for Paris for his big showdown with immortality.

This is virtually, in parable form, the story of the eventual steamrolling of the beaux-arts by the avant-garde. Picasso seems to have told the story from his early days in Paris, when he was fashioning a folk image of himself that would serve him out among the philistines, where fauvist or cubist breakthroughs could not be counted on to cut much ice.

In the everyday world, where the nuances of art history are just so much intellectual filigree, Picasso is so accessible that he virtually symbolizes the overthrow of old humanist European values, even elbowing aside his predecessors. For example, the paintings of Cézanne and Matisse really embody the values that cubism merely made obvious. Historians say cubism released art from the iron sleeve of realism and rediscovered the power of primitive fetishes and monkey masks. But on a layman's level, it is much more appealing as a story of how genius landed a tomato between the eyes of craft. Hardened into cliché, conventional wisdom now defines genius not as the effort of development, but as the naive directness of every child, something you are born with, and which would flourish naturally if not tied to the railroad tracks by the villain, craft.

Picasso said that when he was a child he drew like Raphael, that he spent his whole life learning to draw like a child again. So generations of artists since have denigrated craft as if it were merely a refuge for Sunday painters and commercial artists. It was as if Baby Ruiz had begun redefining art in the cradle, rather than gaining confidence as a young boy drawing in his father's studio. Craft has, in fact, become the "Picasso's father" of contemporary art. Well meaning, but dull by common consent.

As a practical matter, however, craft has been so long in the wastebasket that should you try to find an artist to teach you even the simple technical skills, you are likely to stumble into a twilight world of traditionalists who, if you were to beam them five hundred years into the future, would still want to paint like Rembrandt, brown soup and all.

When I was twenty, working in Kansas City, and struggling to teach myself how to turn oil paint and canvas into something I wasn't ashamed of, I heard from a friend about an artist in Mission Hills, Kansas, who supposedly knew the secrets of the old masters. It wasn't Renaissance secrets I wanted to know, but I had never studied art and I was laboring over images that I still lacked the technique to articulate. So I grasped at the straw.

I hiked and hitchhiked the ten miles or so to his home and found a stiff, gracious man who painted slices of nature so delicate that they virtually advertised sensitivity: a honeycomb, a chain looped over a branch, a bird's nest

rendered in silverpoint. Sometime during the afternoon, he prodded me for my
opinions about modern art and used my answers as cues to give me his. He
shrugged off Picasso the way an out-of-pocket nobleman sitting at an oyster bar
in New York might dismiss the usurper sitting back home on the throne. Picasso
wouldn't last. Art lovers would ultimately shake off his seducer's spell and would
return to solid craftsmanship, nineteenth-century realism, and, one presumed, to
honeycombs and birds' nests.

He seemed to feel that he and his fellow artists were the keepers of certain
rare and endangered secrets. The local Plaza Art Fair was coming up, he told me,
and he invited me to meet some of his artist friends there. They swapped "tricks
of the trade," he said. I suddenly felt as if I had opened the door to the lodge of a
mystical brotherhood, hoping for some transcendental experience, and, instead,
found the members handing out lapel pins and practicing special handshakes. I
left after a few hours, grateful at least to have learned that I could do worse than
to teach myself. In short, by the time I wanted to learn how to gesso panels and
size canvas, craft had been left to artists who were determined to fight on to the
finish, like those Japanese soldiers flushed out of the coconut trees on some remote
desert island. Plucky little fellows, still shooting and awaiting new orders from
Winslow Homer.

This reality belied one of the curious myths of the avant-garde at midcentury: that their progressive art had to advance bravely against the awesome
wall of academic realism. It's true that traditional artists were still painting
truckloads of turgid landscapes and farmers with red noses in the style of George
Luks, but they were fast becoming the in-house Amish. The glamour had passed
to the avant-garde.

The war had left America the leading nation of the world, and, among our
other obligations, we had shouldered the burden of developing an art movement
to symbolize our invisible power. If abstract expressionism sprang up overnight as
corporate America's status symbol, it was by the 1950s a style as rigidly insinuated into the art world as the perpetually drugged-looking Christ Pantokrator
had been in the mosaics of Byzantium. Young people my age, with no more
background in art than some high school classes where they copied jet planes and
cocker spaniels from magazine photographs, wandered into art school believing in
the mercy of education, and within weeks were spouting certainties about vibrat-
ing colors like Josef Albers himself, and belittling craft as if they had personally
led the enslaved artists of the nineteenth century out of Pharaoh's Egypt.

The study of craft had required that an artist internalize his or her experience. There were no shortcuts. Like shooting a gun, you simply had to learn the
indefinable skill. But the strength of modern art was its theory of cultural revolution. And theory is didactic. It's well suited to mass education. You can even give
true-false tests on it.

So theory gradually became the currency of contemporary art. Art history
was flattened out until it appeared to be not just a jumble of styles and insights

from various periods, but a linear record of slow and painful innovation by great men who broke the rules of their day, driven—one can only guess—by some vague collective urge that led, by jumps and false starts, to the consummate cubist liberation to which we were heirs. It reminded me of social Darwinism, where sponges and bony fishes all led to the modern Western capitalist.

All this meant that artists, for whom craft had been discipline, were now cut adrift to search consciously, rootlessly, for style. As if style could be found somewhere else than in the tension between discipline and invention. This flattening out of art history ironically left painters with no context in which to work but the history of art itself, everybody trying to grab himself or herself a place on the totem pole.

From cubism on, the various movements of the avant-garde have been a monument to the logic of revolution, each movement claiming to be more radical than the last, with Picasso, the survivor, emerging almost inevitably from the skirmishing as the no-nonsense jungle dictator, the Fidel of modern art who still wore his fatigues to the office. The revolution, over at the beginning, had given way to style.

There is a story, reportedly reliable, that a photo of Picasso's palm was once taken to a gypsy to test her skills. She wasn't told whose hand it was, but concluded, apparently with ease, that it belonged to a gangster with genius. This, in the fewest possible strokes, is the folk image of Waynesville's existential hombre. The breaker of rules who leaves everybody else playing by his.

I saw a fine art postcard the other day of a young man in a black leather jacket sitting in a drab room. He had an Elvis hairdo, a cigarette dangling from his lips. He cradled a rifle in his arms. He wasn't a mass killer. Not even a slasher of tires in some midwestern parking lot. Just a fashionable New York society photographer posing for his own camera. Self-portrait of the artist as rough trade, with the brand of Picasso still smoking on him.

I suspect that the trail of the avant-garde has led, finally, not to abstract expressionism, nor any of the other isms of art—not to pop or graffiti—but to mass culture itself, to the modern rock-and-roll urban circus, where everything from the pose of the outlaw to consumer purchasing to "lifestyle" is rationalized with sociological seriousness as a form of self-expression. Thirty years ago, it might have been the dream of every bohemian artist to be seen getting out of a stretch limousine wearing blue jeans and sneakers. Today, it may well be the dream of half the people in the country.

The magic moment of modern art had come in that age of Cézanne and Klimt, when something as innocent as raw color on a canvas could still make people's eyes pop out on springs, when people had to sneak into Freud's office to tell him about their dreams. By the late twentieth century, when movie stars line up beside Johnny Carson's desk like crows on a fence to tell a nationwide TV audience about their private lives, when terrorists with a real sense of mission gun down tourists at airports to make media statements, you are as likely to shock the middle classes by saying please or thank you as by anything you can do with your art supplies.

For two years—from the day I first had modernism explained to me to the night of my visit to the honeycomb artist of Mission Hills—it bothered me that I didn't really feel I owed anything to Picasso. Everybody else seemed to think he or she did. I remember hiking down the dark roads of the Kansas-Missouri border, feeling like Dorothy heading home from the land of the tin woodsman. I was certain something had happened, but not quite sure what insight to draw.

There was never any epiphany for me. Just a series of realizations over the next few years that I was at home outside art schools and galleries, outside the orthodoxy of cultural revolution, and equally at home outside the circle of anyone still waiting for the Ash Can school. I realized that what I wanted to learn I would have to teach myself—that in the end, that may be the practical definition of modern art.

There are several advantages to stumbling ahead on your own. You can rummage as carelessly through art history as you want and draw from any period. I drew from the wounded lioness on an Assyrian wall, from the earnest crosshatching of Little Orphan Annie, from the soulful funeral portraits of the artists of the Faiyûm school, or the postcard I found somewhere in Missouri of a fur-bearing trout. From Giotto, Diego Rivera, and Saul Steinberg and from dark, stoic Kathe Kollwitz, who, with a style older than Picasso's father, was modern for no more complicated reason than that she lived in our time.

In these dying years of the twentieth century, we ought to find it adolescent of modern art to have tried building a theory of transcendence on intellectual scandal. Not many people in any age are genuine rebels, and injecting those who aren't with a theory of cultural revolution will not suddenly make them want to land the present on its head. Ask Mao. When journeymen artists have to behave like revolutionaries simply because it's a job requirement, you can hardly be surprised to find them reducing revolution first to style, then to fashion, and ultimately to advertising. Art, new art, new improved art.

If postmodern art resembles anything now, it's not perpetual revolution in art, but revolution-as-ritual—the artistic equivalent of the Eucharist or carnival—in which the slaying of the decadent beaux-arts is reenacted by careerists, many of whom have government grants to do so.

Rousseau, who thought himself a painter in the academic tradition, supposedly told Picasso once that they were the two great artists of their time. "I in the modern style," he said, "and you in the Egyptian." No babe in the woods, that Rousseau. Like Evil Knievel, Picasso came roaring across the Grand Canyon of art history and landed with great fanfare on the other side—like everybody else I applaud. But when the chips are down and I'm sitting stupidly in front of a blank canvas, I can take no comfort from the fact that a hundred years ago Picasso took the brushes away from his father.

*Originally published in Volume 4, Number 3, 1986.*

# DESIGN 101

# BACK TO SHOW AND TELL

*Paula Scher*

A year ago I relived an experience I had in my ninth-grade Algebra II class. The occasion was a seminar on graphic design education at the Maryland Institute of Art where some practicing designers and design educators shared a common stage. The premise was sound: to generate debate between these factions. However, what resulted was disappointing. Instead of meaningful discussion and clear explanation, the design educators gave pompous presentations on the structure and curriculum of their schools, supported by pedantic visuals and charts. They spoke in jargon I've never used professionally and didn't understand. These lectures were so abstruse that I hadn't a clue as to what was going on in their schools. I wondered if the students did either.

The Algebra II syndrome (a compulsion to hum sixties rock and roll and make spitballs) is my reaction whenever theoretics (theoretics as an end in itself) are applied to design. At Maryland, my feelings were compounded. The first was one of shame. That's what happens when I'm bombarded with incomprehensible language. Boredom follows shame: I tune out and squirm in my seat. Then I realize I'm really angry. Boredom is anger. I'm angry in this case because the speaker is supposed to be talking about graphic design, not quantum physics.

*Semiotics* was one of the favorite words bandied about the Maryland session. In fact, some of the educators took great pride in the fact that their schools were breaking new ground in this area. If so, why couldn't any of them make the idea understandable? At the risk of losing anyone who has read this far, the following is a dictionary definition of semiotics: "A general philosophical theory of signs and symbols that deals especially with their function in artificially constructed natural language and comprises syntactics, semantics, and pragmatics."

How does it really apply to graphic design? I thought it would be fun to call seven of my favorite "award"-winning designers and ask them to define semiotics. Four said they didn't know (one of them didn't want to know); two said that it may have something to do with symbols; and one said she knew but didn't want to answer. If one asks the same designers how a symbol "works," they'll give articulate answers and use good examples to illustrate their points.

It's not just the exclusionary language that bothers me, but the process of making more complex the difficult act of explaining graphic design principles to would-be designers. Obviously, my reaction is based on a personal teaching style that might be termed *extended apprenticeship.* Call it what you will—a style, method, or philosophy—it is a hands-on process that has produced tangible results.

In 1982, I was asked to teach graphic design to seniors at the School of
Visual Arts, New York. The media department has a loosely prescribed curriculum, with an emphasis on doing—there are few, if any, theoretical courses. The
school hires working designers who represent a broad range of experiences and
approaches. Hence, the instructors are completely responsible for course content
and are encouraged to teach what they know best. The students have a certain
choice in what they take. After the foundation year, they audit classes to see
whether they feel comfortable with the approach being taught.

When I first saw the work by the students entering my class, I thought
that they were unprepared to enter the job market unless radical improvement
occurred over the year. No amount of theoretical instruction would help. Therefore, I created a series of complex assignments that were extensively critiqued.
The challenge was to pinpoint what was wrong and show how it could be made
better. My method was to use simple language and strong visual examples to
illustrate my point. In effect, I became the client. But I also became a graphic
fascist, disallowing typefaces, reordering elements, dictating style and content.
The students were forced to design and redesign, yet, in the process of following
these directives, they made their own discoveries, which had surprising results.

The approach I instinctively used was the old apprentice method. Do
what I do, and watch it come out your way. This method requires total commitment. The teacher must "give it all away" (style, conceits, tricks) or the premise
won't work. It's sometimes threatening. It can be intimidating to watch as a
student easily accomplishes something it took me fifteen years to master. But, in
the end, and in a relatively short amount of time, some potentially good professionals emerged.

At the Maryland Institute seminar, one educator presented a chart showing the spiraling growth of students as they absorbed the design theories of
successive courses, culminating in graduation—meaning the students were
qualified to enter the profession. What hogwash! There was no mention of talent.
All the theory in the world cannot replace talent. Talented students can overcome
any form of education unless they've been bored out of the profession.

I abhor the charade at the Maryland session. These academicians, I believe, have created designspeak to give credence to the profession because they're
embarrassed that it was once called commercial art. Is it necessary to indoctrinate
students with jargon just to compensate for a sense of professional inferiority?

My point comes down to this: designers learn by doing. They can learn
faster when someone gives them a way to do it. When they learn how, they can
understand it. And when they understand it, they can teach somebody else.

*Originally published in Volume 4, Number 1, 1986.*

# IS DESIGN IMPORTANT?

*Gunnar Swanson*

Designers and design educators spend much time and energy talking about developing public awareness of design and how to gain recognition for design. We rarely ask whether design is important.

Imagine, for a moment, design education without the promise of a job as a designer. The idea seems every bit as stupid as dental school without the promise of fixing teeth. Neither dentistry nor graphic design is important unless you have a toothache or need your product promoted. However, we consider other areas of study to be worthwhile whether or not they lead to careers in, say, psychology or history.

Could studying design be of general, not just professional, interest? Do we really have anything to offer outside of the sometimes questionable promise of a job? If we answer no, it is because we underrate the potential of our field. Design is at an intellectual crossroads where anthropology meets communication studies, art meets marketing, and cognitive psychology meets business. It is in the position to become an integrative educational field, a liberal art for the next century.

From the time of Aristotle through the nineteenth century, the liberal arts were a set of studies that defined a generally educated person. They comprised the range of knowledge of humankind. An educated person could know, at least in outline, what was known in all fields of study, but this is no longer possible. In the meantime, *liberal studies* has often come to mean an approach to education that can be likened to ordering from the menu of a Chinese restaurant—one from column A, one from column B, and so on.

It is time to reexamine our notion of general education. One approach is a liberal arts program that centers on subjects that involve integration of the traditional areas of knowledge. Design could be one of them, a place where manufacturing meets philosophy.

Wouldn't such a change in emphasis in design teaching cheat students of professional training at a time when entry into the field is harder than ever? Working designers struggle to stay on top of a changing vocation. Vocational training in times of rapid change will almost certainly be out of date before the training is completed. Learning how to keep learning should be every student's primary educational goal.

It has become a cliché of career counseling to point out that most of today's jobs won't exist in fifteen years, and most jobs that will exist in fifteen years don't exist now. We can expect the statement to remain true, although the time period will shorten. Although there may be graphic designers in fifteen years, most of them will likely be doing something very different from the present vocation of graphic design.

The design students of today will be the inventors of the design field of tomorrow. A general education is more conducive to the flexibility needed for such invention than is vocational training, with its narrower concerns. A general education focusing on the issues of design—form and meaning, vision and under-standing—would serve our next generation of designers better than what we now offer them.

I would like to think that we assume that design students would benefit from studying anthropology. Then the leap I am asking for would be considering whether anthropology students could benefit from the study of graphic design. But I'm afraid we have further to go than that. Although rhetoric about general education is widespread in the design field, I have observed a distinctly anti-intellectual streak in many design teachers. In the mid 1970s, an industrial design teacher of mine told me I was "too articulate" and that great design happens when designers have no other way of expressing themselves than with form. Paul Rand, perhaps the best known living graphic designer and design educator, wrote, "[A] student whose mind is cluttered with matters that have nothing directly to do with design . . . is a bewildered student"(*Design, Form and Chaos*, Yale University Press, 1993, page 217). Many design teachers and design students see "academic" classes as time stolen from their true purpose—the design studio.

Rand is hardly alone in his denial of "matters that have nothing directly to do with design." This attitude places design education firmly in the realm of vocational training and assumes a stable list of things that do have something directly to do with design. Clearly, such an assumption should not be made. Many designers are naturally suspicious of the idea that the study of design might inform other areas of study; after all, very few academic studies have direct value for design. We are doers, not theorists. The empirical evidence is that design and ivory-tower thinking have little in common, but it is the fact that graphic design is not part of the mainstream of academia that has marginalized design's interests. For instance, it is not surprising that most studies of type and comprehension seem irrelevant to designers' concerns, since designers generally do not participate in such studies.

The interests of the design business have traditionally driven design education. It is time to reconsider whether this approach is really in the interest of design education, design students, and, for that matter, the design business. The pace of development of the design business has, in the past, allowed for the kind of consideration and analysis that a maturing field needs. However, the current changes in design leave little time for practitioners to reflect, and that is unlikely to change. The room needed to grow could be provided by design studies that are independent of vocational concerns. Without such a balancing force, the graphic design business is in trouble. With it, we could discover that design is, indeed, important.

*Originally published in Volume 13, Number 1, 1995.*

# RETARDED ARTS: THE FAILURE OF FINE ARTS EDUCATION

*Frances Butler*

**A**ll material images—whether made of paint, print, film, or electronic media—exist finally as a representation of values held by the society in which they are produced. The people who make images are usually trained to do so in two different schools—popular arts (crafts, decorative arts, architecture, graphic design, industrial design) and fine arts (painting, sculpture, and whatever has been absorbed into the fine art fold at the moment). At least since the middle of the nineteenth century, the fine arts have towered over the popular arts in terms of cultural prestige. The difference between the two schools lies not in technique—photographic technology produces both fine art and advertising, ceramic technology produces pottery and sculpture—but in intention, either proclaimed or perceived.

The intention of fine artists has been the representation of power or morality, and their products gain value by being confused with the subjects they represent. I call this the DeBeers phenomenon. DeBeers, an international diamond cartel, markets a product that is extremely common, highly compressed carbon, by employing a two-edged technique: (1) the extreme, and arbitrary, limitation of both production and distribution of the product, and (2) continuous reiteration, through advertising, of the product's fabricated function as an index of great love (the message being: Diamonds = Rarity = Value = True and Lasting Love, or "Diamonds Are Forever"). The fine art product slides down a similar sluice of language, from picturing value to being valued, regardless of whether the materials or skill employed would make it so. Meanwhile, the intention of popular arts products has always been to serve and drive daily social usage.

The fine arts are incorporated into higher educational institutions to enhance their prestige, but fine arts education lags ten to twenty years behind that of the popular arts, both in technology and in theory. Why? To describe the fundamental epistemology of fine arts training is to describe the reason it is now irrelevant, unable to devise any new representations of cultural value except through the cannibalization of the popular arts. This failure is especially grievous because our highest values, once religious and political power, have been joined, if not replaced, by the value accorded innovative thought, fueled by the new scale of data available on the information superhighway.

The epistemology of educational programs called the humanities, including the fine arts, is rooted in ancient prejudices that downgrade democratic or body-based intelligence and favor reflexive abstraction, linearity, limited access through specialized language, and an institutional hierarchy granting credentials only to those who have been trained by the institution itself. Marshall McLuhan was devising his version of this ancient prejudice in the mid-twentieth century, although the seeds of understanding the importance of nonlinear physics, thought, and language had already been planted at the turn of the century by Einstein, Wittgenstein, and de Saussure.

In the following three-quarters of a century, educational programs based in physical and physiological materiality (the sciences) have accepted high-speed movement, relativity, and lack of (cognitive) templates as the nature of the material world, including the human mind. Cognitive research has demonstrated that thought is a relative process made of responses newly generated moment by moment, using every part of the body, in which even memory is reconstituted, virtually from scratch, each time it is activated. The dissolution of time and space, discontinuity, and nonlinearity have been shown to be the nature of the mind, not the traces of barbarism. The fine arts and the humanities, however, have refused to abandon their ancient, privileged fields.

In fine arts departments, courses called "critical theory" still use the texts of Marshall McLuhan, John Berger, Judith Williamson, and the work of their acolytes. A course developed in the fine arts department at my former university in 1994 is centered on the texts of the dreamy mandarin Roland Barthes—floating high above human experience in a mist of logocentric abstractions—and uses de Saussure's semiotic diagrams (which for the last decade have been useless, rooted as they are in an earlier model of the human brain, with no reference to parallel cognitive processing). This course is typical in warning its students that the popular arts are not only epistemologically suspect, but socially corrupt as well.

Meanwhile, the producers of popular imagery—from *Sesame Street* to the Yellow Pages—have continued the ceaseless generation of nonabstracted, use-based, visual products. Material that is not simply jumbled together is usually structured by metaphor. Filmmakers and advertisers have spliced naked bodies or big-eyed children with products ranging from nose-hair clippers to spaceships, all in contexts spanning bathrooms to the houses of Congress, leaving their audiences to fill in the gaps.

Those who teach the production of popular imagery discuss the basic material components—scale, light, hue, texture, composition—still relying on such naive texts as *A Primer of Visual Literacy* by Dondis Dondis. (The book's title demonstrates a misunderstanding of the differences between visual perception and literacy, which fortunately goes no further than page one.) When popular arts faculty do discuss the transmission of societal value through imagery, they often emphasize the material and the experiential bases of image making and reception. The few courses on the social importance of popular arts that do exist were initiated in design schools in the 1970s, when perhaps design faculty did not need the cloak of prestige thrown over their subject matter. Unlike theoreticians in fine arts programs that depend on extensive, authoritarian bibliographies to validate their dominion, popular arts teachers were usually practitioners rather than, or in addition to, writers or critics. Their validation came from real experience in their field.

In 1978, I developed a course at the University of California at Berkeley, College of Environmental Design, combining studies in the nature of the materials, technologies, economic and institutional systems, and audiences that support the fine arts and popular arts. At that time, the literature on the materiality of the popular arts consisted of a few books: early anthologies from the Winterthur Museum, eighteenth- through twentieth-century manuals on mechanical or chemical processes, and studies in a few anthropological journals. Visual anthropology (now renamed critical theory) was dominated by institutionally biased texts lamenting the demise of linear thinking: the work of McLuhan; John Berger's *Ways of Seeing*; *Mythologies* and *The Empire of Signs* by Roland Barthes; and Michel Foucault's *The Order of Things*. It was possible, however, to use texts by the natural philosophers, such as Basil Bernstein, Mary Douglas, or Daniel Sperber, which emphasized perception and experience over institutionally transmitted learning in cognition, memory, and thought. I admit that the students found the range of readings and images confusing. I see that confusion as proof, not of the deficiency of the students, but of the failure of traditional instruction in the humanities. Their education had trained them to embrace linear thinking in place of the fluid, additive, nonsyntactic, and, above all, extremely sophisticated thought processes that are the natural birthright of all humans.

We need to scrap all bias toward linear structure in thought and begin the development of a "capture" system that will lead to enhanced opportunities for high-speed juxtapositions of information. The problem with such accelerated metaphoric thought is the lack of processes through which those ideas could be mentally reconstructed. But with the invention of increasingly rapid and invasive recording devices, *captures*—or bits of recognition and/or recombination that parallel the actual structure of the brain—could eventually become the unit of ideation and communication. The next chore will be generating indexing notions that are neither wide open nor exactly closed, that aid thought and conceptual research. Such indexing notions could be coded by basic visual components:

shape, scale change, value, texture, or sound. As they do not have to unlearn the strictures of abstraction—outdated ancient epistemologies that strain metaphoric captures through a sieve of linear thought—the practitioners of the popular arts are perfectly placed to begin that exploration.

*Originally published in Volume 13, Number 1, 1995.*

# ZIGZAG THINKING

*Roy R. Behrens*

A mong the most eccentric forms in design history is Gerrit Rietveld's zigzag chair. "It's not a chair," he said, "but a designer's joke"—it is "a tiny partition in space that leaves the space untouched." It is the hummingbird (a creature once characterized by James Russell Lowell as a "zig-zagging blur") of chairs.

In the late nineteenth century, American artist Abbott H. Thayer zigzagged with his children through Europe by starting at an arbitrary point, then following a random rule like "three turns to the left and two turns to the right." During World War I, research by Thayer contributed to "dazzle camouflage" in which ships were painted with erratic zigzags and steered in unexpected paths, in order to divert the aim of German U-boats.

Among zigzag thinkers, the most celebrated is American illustrator Rube Goldberg. In one of his absurd cartoons, a man pulls his tooth in the following way. He ties himself to a chair, then wiggles his shoe, which has a feather attached, which tickles a duck, which shakes an alcoholic drink tied to its back, and then falls forward, spilling the cocktail on a squirrel in a revolving circular cage. The cocktail makes the squirrel drunk, which spins the cage, which turns the crank on a phonograph and plays a song called "You Poor Little Shrimp." The music enrages a dwarf, who gets hot under the collar, and flames from the dwarf's collar ignite a fuse, which causes a cannon to fire. The cannonball is attached to a string tied to the man's tooth, and, at last, the tooth is extracted.

Goldberg reminds one of the experiments of Karl Duncker, a gifted German psychologist whose sole legacy is a lengthy paper entitled "On Problem-Solving." He emigrated to America from Berlin in 1938 and taught at Swarthmore College until his suicide two years later. In one of his experiments, each subject was asked to build a pendulum, using three objects that were provided: a cord, a nail, and a pendulum weight. The problem can be solved, of course, by using the weight as a hammer to pound the nail into the wall, and suspending the weight from the nail with the cord. However, Duncker found that if he presented the weight already tied to the cord and called it a "pendulum weight," only 50 percent of the subjects could think of using it as a hammer, or as anything other than simply a weight. Duncker concluded that in solving problems or creating new ideas, sometimes it pays to be naive, to be an outsider—that sometimes it helps to be ignorant of the customary way of doing things.

"In order to think new thoughts or say new things," wrote Gregory Bateson, "we have to break up all our ready-made ideas and shuffle the pieces." Zigzag thinking breaks routine and reassembles the dissociated pieces. It creates strange categorical bedfellows and often produces outrageous results. A combination of wit and nonsense, it is segue thinking or thinking by deftly caroming from one category or frame of reference to another, from one expectation to another.

In recent years, zigzag thinking has been touted as primitive thinking because of its resemblance to *bricolage* in *The Savage Mind* (1966) by French anthropologist Claude Lévi-Strauss. That term was derived from an earlier word for unanticipated diversions, such as a ball rebounding. *Bricoleurs* are cobblers or jacks-of-all-trades, who, like Goldberg's inventor and Duncker's subjects, work with whatever they happen to have and use whatever procedures they know. As in Goldberg's cartoons, the result is an often astonishing mix of previously unrelated ingredients.

The affinity between bricolage and Dada is self-evident, and the use of chance in modern art is well established. In modern graphic design, eccentric invention is often expressed in visual puns, shifts of emphasis, and planned incongruity, as shown by the frequent reliance on "play" in the works of Saul Steinberg, Herb Lubalin, Paul Rand, and Milton Glaser. But it is equally evident in Herbert Spencer's *The Liberated Page*, Steven Heller and Gail Anderson's *Graphic Wit*, and Bob Gill's *Graphic Design Made Difficult*.

Gill's unusual solutions are usually reached by approaching a problem with as few preconceptions as possible and attempting to see it with innocent eyes. "The prerequisite of originality," said Arthur Koestler, "is the art of forgetting, at the proper moment, what we know," and Gill's most reliable strategy in the practice of graphic design is to "forget all the rules you ever learned about graphic design," which is also the title of one of his books.

At the moment, zigzag thinking not only survives, but is blossoming in the postmodern design marketplace, albeit disguised by such curious names as *appropriation, ad hocism, historicism, decontextualization, eclecticism,* and *retro design*. Prominent among postmodern eccentric thinkers are British designer Neville Brody, profiled in John Wozencroft's book *The Graphic Language of Neville Brody*; and California-based designers Rudy VanderLans and Zuzana Licko (dubbed by one critic as "the new primitive"), founders of *Emigre* magazine and authors of the recent book *Emigre: Graphic Design into the Digital Realm*.

Known for unusual uses of type, Brody avoided typography as a student; he hated it because it "was a boring field to work in, overladen with traditions that would repel change." When Licko was in school, she disdained calligraphy, which, in retrospect, "contributed to her unique approach to type design, since conventional type design is rooted in calligraphy." And while VanderLans was originally trained in the Swiss modernist tradition, he strayed while he was working at the *San Francisco Chronicle*—the same newspaper, by the way, that published Goldberg's first cartoon—where the editors, trained not as designers but as journalists, were "breaking every rule in the book of typography" and where "all the things that they had taught me in art school about legibility and good type and bad type were swept aside."

Brody, VanderLans, and Licko are the design equivalent of "outsider artists," and much of what they have accomplished has come from zigzag thinking—pursuing conflicting directions at once, using the methods of nondesigners to create esoteric forms that only designers can appreciate, and (in the case of those who embrace the computer) diverting design to the digital realm.

*Originally published in Volume 12, Number 4, 1995.*

# SKETCHING: CONVERSATIONS WITH THE BRAIN
*Christiaan Vermaas*

Too many designers or art directors look to the work of their colleagues in search of visual solutions to the problems they have to solve. Others simply look to their own equipment and tools, or one design philosophy or another, to come up with their answers. This way of working creates results that don't solve problems or propose innovative methods, but only refer to other design solutions.

This becomes even more troubling in design education, where departments turn into houses of worship promoting existing design trends or current methods of production. If schools of design are necessary, and I am not convinced they are, we have to be very careful with the education of the next generation. Those young people need to find their own ways of solving the problems of the future. Perhaps the most prudent—and maybe the most idealistic—strategy would be to learn from the past, but not imitate it; use the tools, but not become overpowered by them; know the theories, but not live them. This would be a wish of mine, and I have pursued these goals over the last several years as a teacher in graphic design at schools in various countries.

In my teaching, I have tried to offer my students a process that could help them find and develop their own problem-solving techniques. To ignite their creativity, I encourage them to use pencil and paper; to sketch while thinking when solving their assignments. A familiar reply from my students when I suggest sketching is that they have already taken a drawing course. But drawing is different from sketching. Drawing is more self-contained, and a very important and essential visual foundation for a career in design. Sketching, however, I view as a visual search for a solution to a given problem. Sketching is thinking. It is about what you know, what you have seen before, what you admire and dislike, and what you can find from within yourself, your mind. Small strokes made with whatever on whatever, which are taken in by your eyes, to be answered again with new sketches. You end up with a visual document of a conversation between the big ideas inside you and the small ideas that are left on the surface of the paper. It is a way of talking to yourself by slowly drawing your brains.

While you are sketching, the visual realm reigns, theories are neglected, and all other tools and accessories are kept away until the appropriate time of execution. It is always a pleasure for me, as the instructor, to read the small sketches of the students, to understand how their minds work, to start to know their skills, lackings, and desires, and to better help them after this visual insight. When they sketch, their final products maintain their personality and can still be successful in solving the design problem.

To be more specific, here in Mexico, young students like the ones I work with are overwhelmed by influences from the Western world. I don't like to see that happen because Mexicans are made out of both a Latin (Spanish) and indigenous (Indian) culture. So Western design is an outside view, imposed on them but not from their cultural base. I have tried to address this conflict by discarding those tools that carry with them the constraints of a specific way of working and monopolize the freedom associated with paper and pencil. And this trick worked. The final results reflected both the conquest of Cortés and the revenge of Montezuma. Simple sketching led to a much fresher kind of visual result, a result that shook off the incestuous burden of Western design, the heavy influence of tools, or the weight of an overbearing philosophy. The students found they had plenty of stories inside themselves that they discovered by starting to sketch.

*Originally published in Volume 13, Number 1, 1995.*

# SPEAKING IN TONGUES

*Véronique Vienne*

Imagine speaking in Cooper Black, a typeface popular in America in the mid-sixties, when English became my second language. I could handle written English, but had never been taught to pronounce it. When I moved to the States in 1965, I literally had to "read my own mind" whenever I wanted to speak. To sound as colloquial as possible, I would mentally set the words in what I thought were very American typefaces—Cooper Black at first, and later Caledonia—and would simply read them aloud, as if they were projected on a panoramic screen inside my skull.

A born skeptic, I needed to see things in writing. I had, as they used to say, a "visual memory." In Paris, I had studied graphic design, and European designers were my heroes. I aspired to follow their example. László Moholy-Nagy, Mehemed Fehmy Agha, Alexey Brodovitch, Will Burtin, and Herbert Bayer had made a name for themselves in the States in spite of their native accents. So, I figured, I too could find a place in American culture without becoming truly assimilated. I decided I would be safe in New York as a magazine art director and soon became engrossed in editorial design. For two blissful decades I forgot I was French, until 1985—when I bought an answering machine.

One day I dialed my home number by mistake and heard my own re-corded message. A woman with a thick French accent muttered something about being unable to come to the phone. Perhaps I had the wrong number. But I left a message anyway. When I got home that evening and switched on my machine, the same woman's voice came back. As I stood there in the kitchen with my finger on the playback button, I felt the closest thing to an out-of-body experience. Who was this woman speaking on my behalf?

No one recognizes his or her own voice on tape. Ears are designed to pick up the vibrations produced by the displacement of molecules in the air. When we speak, we think we hear, but actually we feel. The bones in the head, the chest, and sometimes the whole body resonate like musical instruments. Our own voice is not a sound—it is a physical sensation. We are deaf to ourselves.

That night I felt a sense of loss. The woman on the phone was right: I should give her a call. But first I had to take speech lessons.

To change the sound of your voice, you first have to change the shape of your mouth. You must recondition the muscles involved with speech. I needed a workout. My teacher asked me to rub my tongue, stroke my palate, and poke my fingers down my throat. "I am not studying to be a dentist," I reminded him.

"Look," he said, "you can't act like a Puritan if you want to learn to speak like one."

So, armed with three fingers, a mirror, and a flashlight, I ventured past my lips. It was a dark, moist, and crowded place—there was hardly any room to exercise. But I was determined, and bravely tried to do calisthenics with my tongue, breath, and hard palate—while my teeth, on the defensive, were ready to bite my hand.

"Repeat: *Is this an apple?*"

"Es theese an apol," I said.

"Say: *Happy*."

"Oppee," I said.

"Listen,"

"Leesson!" I cried.

It took one year for me to learn to say *listen*—and another year to learn to listen to the sound of English words without frantically spelling them in my mind. "Don't let your thoughts get in the way," my coach would say. But he was wrong. My mind was more nimble than my fingers. Forget about tongue exercises. I felt often that I was reaching inside my brain to perform microsurgery. I had to reprogram my way of thinking. Imagine what it takes to turn a graphic device into a resonating entity.

The brain handles language in a very peculiar way, Sandra Blackeslee reports in a recent *New York Times* article. "Each person appears to have a unique pattern of organization for language ability—as unique as facial features or fingerprints. . . . While it is true that some people have essential language areas on the left side of their brains . . . some people have them on the right side and others on both sides." Shifting concepts around in the brain to reorganize your speech pattern can be a colossal undertaking.

Little by little, written words developed a life of their own. They gained in color, texture, and resonance. They became opinionated and started to walk off the page. I lost control. No longer could I bring myself to enlarge, stretch, wrap, tilt, reverse, and manipulate text the way I used to. Pull-quotes became powerful and vivid enough to occupy an entire spread. Photographs lost their visual integrity—they were now only visual excuses for captions. I emphasized words in titles, not according to their meaning, but according to their pitch and tone. And one day, punctuation became the raison d'être—the breath, the beat, the rhythm of a page.

I may never get another job as an art director—no editor wants to work with a designer who cannot be objective about commas—but I hardly miss it. I discovered a splendid world out there—a world where each written word is worth a thousand pictures.

*Originally published in Volume 9, Number 3, 1991.*

# ON LEARNING TO DRAW WITH JOHN GNAGY

*Michael Bierut*

In the early 1960s, my alma mater, St. Theresa's in Garfield Heights, Ohio, had no art program. The reason was that the diocese's spartan budgets precluded activities deemed "nonessential." Actually, the severe and terrifying Ursuline nuns that ran the place probably felt uncomfortable teaching subjects with ambiguous right and wrong answers. A few more hours of catechism every week would do our immortal souls more good. Besides, the horrifying chaos of paint, paper, and paste was more typical of the moral slackness and outright nihilism St. Theresa's associated with public school kids, who got to wear whatever they wanted to school and had alcoholic parents.

My only clue that I had nascent art ability was from my first-grade teacher, a much sought-after "lay instructor" named Mrs. Kinola. She was impressed with some drawings I had done of classroom objects as part of a spelling exercise and sent them home to my parents with a note on the order of "Michael looks like a real artist!"

But what did it mean? As far as I knew, there were no artists in Garfield Heights. Most of the adults I knew were either housewives or men who did things with big machines. What did artists do?

Like most of my friends, I liked to get up early on Saturday morning, say, 5:30 or so. The shows on before the cartoons had a faintly doomed and tragic aspect. Even then, I could sense that those time slots were some sort of filthy and neglected holding cells for unwanted programs.

Then I discovered John Gnagy.

Although I had never seen an artist, I knew immediately that John Gnagy was one. Not only was he standing in front of an easel, he was wearing a coarse flannel shirt and a goatee. This last detail seemed especially telling as I had never seen a living person with facial hair in my life; beards were for people like Abraham Lincoln or Jesus. John Gnagy was, like them, definitely not of Garfield Heights.

On each episode of *Learn to Draw with John Gnagy*, he would demonstrate, step by step, how to make a drawing. The viewer was meant to follow along at home. Electrified by my discovery of this potential mentor, I joined in enthusiastically. I still remember his authority, lack of condescension, and patience as he showed how a blank piece of paper could be methodically transformed into a still life, landscape, or portrait. I vowed to organize my schedule around this program.

After watching in rapture for several weeks, I began to make some realizations. First, the most striking quality of Gnagy's work was its realism, a characteristic all the more miraculous because the drawings were created (more or less) right before your eyes. Circles would become ripe apples, squares, homey little farmhouses. But it sometimes happened too quickly to follow, and the most dramatic transformations seemed to occur during the commercials. Second, art appeared to require special tools. Gnagy referred regularly to special chalks and pencils, not to mention something called a "kneaded" eraser and a completely incomprehensible item called a paper stomp. I gamely played along at home with my No. 2 Mongol and shirt cardboards, but it was obvious I was in over my head. The solution was a boxed kit advertised on each episode that contained all the necessary tools as well as an instruction book. After much campaigning by me and, no doubt, much research by my parents, I got the Learn to Draw kit for Christmas.

I carried my copy of this book around religiously for two years, studying every detail with a fervor that would have impressed even the nuns at St. Theresa's. With the book, I was no longer bound to the television show, the schedule of which had gotten more and more irregular. Some weeks, it wasn't on at all. No matter, I had the book. I attempted each drawing at least once (including the impossible *Harlequin Dane,* "the aristocrat of dogs"). My favorites, like *Whistle Stop* or *RFD America,* I repeated over and over again until I knew them by heart, like a piano student and the "Moonlight Sonata."

I recently discovered a copy of *Learn to Draw with John Gnagy* in a New York art-supply store. Although it appeared to be a new edition, it was completely—I guarantee, *completely*—unchanged from the edition I dog-eared so zealously back in Garfield Heights. As I turned the pages, I grew more and more dizzy with déjà vu; the effect each image had on me far exceeded anything the smell of madeleines could have done to Proust.

The seven drawings were particularly potent. Seeing *Covered Bridge,* for instance ("A scene that features depth by the use of 'aerial perspective'"), I realized that one image constitutes my total personal experience with that particular subject. In other words, although I would have sworn otherwise, I've never seen a real covered bridge. Other designers have similar memories. "Did you have John Gnagy when you were little?" I would ask. A positive response invariably took the form of a dreamy, unfocused look, and a murmured, "Oh God, that drawing of the Great Dane."

The one thing that impresses me most profoundly about John Gnagy now, though, isn't an image or a drawing. It's a particular attitude about art, specifically the idea that it could be demystified. I expected Gnagy's book, twenty years later, to be quaint and comical. Instead, it seems sincere and heartfelt. His goal was "to help you awaken that hidden talent so you may find happiness and genuine fun in the world around you through the hobby of drawing and painting."

Perhaps, in the end, John Gnagy somehow drove me out of fine art and into graphic design. I eventually became a good artist by high-school standards, which basically meant I could draw realistically. Gnagy knew all along that this is what we all secretly want to do anyway, and so he taught drawing in terms of design; a circle that had to become a pumpkin was just a problem to be solved. And there was a secret to the process, nothing mysterious, and it was promised on page 3: "ON THE NEXT PAGE IS THE SECRET OF REALISTIC DRAWING."

And sure enough, turn the page, and there it was: "SHADING IS THE SECRET OF REALISTIC DRAWING."

By the time I got to college, realistic drawing was considered a pretty cheap commodity. What was valued in the fine arts department seemed to be self-expression, or individuality, or passion, or something rather mysterious. Graphic design, on the other hand, seemed to be taught more in the tradition of John Gnagy: methodical, straightforward, and, to quote Gnagy, "genuine fun." So I became a graphic designer. And to fine artists, especially the most eccentric and broodingly tormented, I ask, what's the mystery? It's all on page four.

*Originally published in Volume 7, Number 3, 1989.*

# THE EXPERIENCE OF SEEING

*Leo Lionni*

As visual artists, what characterizes and differentiates us from others is how we extract from the seeing process—how we manipulate it, how we produce signs that communicate, how we produce analogs for the things we have perceived, and how we develop visual metaphors. How we process the information that our mental images give us, so that we may produce paintings, sculptures, photographs, films, and, naturally, the printed page, is indeed the common bond of visual artists.

When we mention the word *seeing* we somehow identify with a camera. We think of silent, cold images that are projected onto our mind. We don't think of feeling. And, yet, seeing is always accompanied by feeling. Feeling is the invisible side of seeing. It is what makes our mental images different from those that form in a camera.

Much of my work as an artist has been based on the assumption that mental images, rather than bursting into our consciousness as complete gestalts, evolve gradually by a process of step-by-step definition.

I believe that the first step in this process is profoundly conditioned by an initial feeling. Before an even rudimentary image, what is experienced is like an internal gesture that demands to be made concrete in space. The first phase in the emergence of our imagery is therefore something like a presymbol, an *Urgestak,* which, like an embryo, contains all the necessary information for its subsequent development. Obviously, because of the lightning speed of mental time, the recognition of this rudimentary stage in the evolution of images is an almost impossible undertaking.

When we demand from an artist his or her intuitive understanding of the essence of things and events, we really refer to his or her ability to recapture that first moment in the birth of mental imagery, when the essential gestural quality of forms is revealed. At that moment, a house is no more than a feeling of being contained and the sense of the space that contains us. Only later will specific informational details be added: a door, windows, a roof.

It is my contention that all art reaches inward toward the feelings that anticipate and accompany the birth of our mental imagery. To recognize these feelings and to give them form, to find ways of expressing them either in isolation or embodied in the traditional forms of the particular processes of our art, is something that all of us are somehow, and in different measures, engaged in. It is ultimately what we qualify as self-expression. It was Walter Pater, I believe, who wrote, "All art aspires to the condition of music." I would rather say that all art aspires to the condition of poetry.

In the first of last year's seminars that I conducted at Cooper Union, I asked the students, "Do you envisage yourselves as poets or as businesspeople?" Most did not understand the question. The question, intentionally provocative, had never occurred to them. They had never considered that the option was meaningful and that sooner or later they would have to make a choice.

They were unaware of the fact that the particular school in which they were working had, in effect, made the choice for them, that the portfolios that would finally represent their attitudes would make the choice obvious.

When I asked more specifically whether they would prefer editorial work or a job in a design studio to one in an advertising agency, they began to understand the implications of the question. They believed that in the latter, self-expression was totally ruled out. On the other hand, the word *design* appeared to mean a disengagement from the trivial demands of communication. And editorial excluded the no less trivial demands of the marketplace.

Conditioned by the somewhat rarefied, ivory-tower atmosphere typical of most art schools, they did not realize that their assumptions were only partially correct. They believed that the answer to the question, which of course was meant to be no more than directional, should be clearly the poet. They would have been ashamed to choose the other option. Who wants to be called a businessperson?

I use the word *directional* to qualify my apparently absurd question. In its context, poetry and business are obviously meant as metaphors that serve no other function than that of a signpost. We know very well that there is frequent trespassing and compromising between the poetry and the business of design, between the need for self-expression and communication, for monologue and dialogue, for ambiguity and clarity.

A Container Corporation ad may qualify as art, or exploit elements of Art with a capital *A,* but we cannot forget that it also serves a precise economical purpose. But so does a Schnabel painting. A book cover may be pictorially poetic and personally expressive, but it must be legible and successfully compete for attention. Only purely experimental graphics can permit themselves the luxury to point exclusively at themselves.

I frequently climb onto the wall that separates poetry and business, for I still have a home on each side. To stand on top of the wall and look both ways is always a rewarding and salutary experience. The two landscapes have more in common than we think.

When you paint, it happens that once in a while you decide to place ten or twenty paintings around the walls of a studio to see what they have in common, how well they express you, where they are situated in the world of art, how they compare with previous work. You want to see if you can discern, within the totality of their form and contents, a continuum of style. The questions that arise are, of course, not always so clearly articulated, and there are apt to be many others, more difficult to express. But the ones I mention somehow seem to be the first ones to come to mind.

When you make children's books, as I have been doing these last twenty or so years, this process of critically exploring your own work is much slower. For someone like myself, who produces one book a year, it is only after five or six years that I can hope to gather some ideas of where I stand and where I am going.

When you write novels, the intervals are even longer. Since one book may take as many as five years or more to produce, this self-assessment may happen only once in the latter part of your lifetime.

If you are involved in professional graphic design, the process is more complicated for other reasons. The varieties of subject matter and of the formal restrictions and necessities are apt to be far more complex. The work is not self-imposed, but derives its very existence from outside sources; the formal solutions are conditioned by the whims of clients and by the demands of the marketplace. Often self-expression lies hidden so deep inside the ink of the printed page that it is virtually irretrievable.

When one is engaged in various fields of artistic endeavor, as in my case, the problem takes on surprising new and even more diverse aspects. One is apt to discover not only unifying formal characteristics and patterns of stylistic development within the perimeters of each particular field, but the cross-fertilization among them. The critical process then not only reveals new aspects of one's hidden identity, but often the hitherto unrecognized formal affinities among the various forms of artistic expression.

It was after my fifth or sixth children's book, almost forty years after the beginning of my involvement with the visual arts, that one day I decided to line up my books—first the covers, then some inside spreads—to see whether I could find unifying elements and, if I did, whether within these unifying elements I would discover my preferences, attitudes, work habits, and feelings.

What was extraordinary about the results of this exercise in self-criticism is that I discovered not only what my books had in common, but how they related to my paintings, sculptures, photography, design, even to my taste in music. And, more surprisingly perhaps, to my choices and manipulation of content. What was exhilarating was not so much that the connections were there, but that they were so clearly visible, so easy to recognize.

The next step of course was to ask myself what these common formal attitudes were, where they originated, and what they meant. Pretty soon I found myself involved in a process of self-analysis that went well beyond the confines of art. It was inevitable that ultimately I should find myself sitting in my room on the van de Velde Straat in Amsterdam, almost seventy years ago, staring at three frogs hopping around in an aquarium, which I had transformed into an island, a slice of nature, the world.

What I discovered is that all the varied attitudes, which together could be grouped into a general concept of style, had their origins in those distant formative years. By style, I not only refer here to the formal mannerisms in the arts, the personal manipulations of the products of the seeing process, the preferences of gesture, color, space, and composition, but the total of our ways of acting, of being, not only in relationship to art, but to life itself. For, to be significant, the two must coexist harmoniously. After all, they flow from the same person, and share the same original impulses and influences.

This brings me back to my previous considerations about seeing and feeling. To retrieve from the world of our early experiences the memories of things seen does not seem all that difficult to do. To find in our memories the feelings that were part of those visual recoveries is more difficult. Under normal circumstances, to remember feelings, to relive them in our imagination, is almost impossible. Yet, to relive the original experiences in seeing, without reconquering those feelings and without being able to find and isolate the visual gestures that conditioned them, is of little or no use to the artist.

*Originally published in Volume 4, Number 3, 1986.*

# ON DESIGN EDUCATION: THE CASE FOR PROFESSIONALISM

*Sharon Helmer Poggenpohl*

Design education is rife with problems—and possibilities. We are still struggling to articulate what graphic design is—what its limits are. The confusion that exists between art and design doesn't help clarify matters. That we were once "commercial" or "applied" artists simply muddies the issue. First of all, I would carefully discriminate between design and art. These are very different activities with different purposes and criteria for performance and evaluation. What they do share is aesthetics and the visual world. Historically, design has been the stepchild of art. I think the time is ripe to align graphic design with other design professions, such as architecture, interior design, and industrial design, and to take a stand as a design professional, rather than a quasi-art practitioner.

From a humanistic standpoint, I can only teach so that each student becomes all he or she is capable of becoming. I am interested in and committed to education, rather than technical training. Many students I speak with believe they will start with low-level, menial jobs. This is depressing. Going to college for four years and then hoping for a paste-up job may be realistic for a mediocre student, but this should be seen as a fallback position rather than a goal. Their sights need to be raised; they need to envision themselves as professionals. They need more confidence.

Graphic design is a synthetic process that uses objective information from behavioral science and perceptual psychology; technical information about reproduction processes; knowledge of various communication codes such as typography, photography, and diagrams; visual aesthetic sensibilities; problem solving; project development; and human interaction skills. How you define graphic design impacts directly on how you educate your students. What items on the above list are teachable in a four-year time frame? In what emphasis and proportion? In what synthesis?

Tom Hine, architectural critic for the *Philadelphia Inquirer*, in reviewing the *Design Since '45* show, likened designers to "exotic menials." That phrase rings in my mind. I hate it. In our culture we have little real power. We are exotic because we use and understand visual language that the culture at large does not understand. We are menial because we are regarded as technicians, at best, or as hands, at worst. The culture is driven by words and, yet, we know that design significantly affects people's lives. We collaborate on or create visual images that sell products, services, and ideas. We direct, orient, inform, and persuade. But we have few corporate vice presidents among our ranks. Graphic designers in university settings are slow to gain promotions and frequently make less money than their peers in more respected academic departments. Even within advertising agencies, the proportion of word people to image people is nowhere near equal at the top. It is time to take off our blinders.

We either accept the role our culture has defined for us, or we work to change it. And one of the most dramatic places to effect change is in education.

There are always a few unique, self-made graphic designers who have bootstrapped it to the top (the top of what? we might ask) and think that because they've done it, anyone can do it. This is wishful thinking. At any given time, there are thousands of graphic design students at private and state universities studying design. They are at the mercy of what they know about graphic design—its objectives as a profession, its performance characteristics, the variety of ways in which it intersects with the larger culture. And they know precious little, because graphic design is a largely invisible profession. (It is sometimes difficult to recognize this invisibility as we are in the middle of graphic design and we tend to communicate more with each other via trade magazines, design exhibits, and journals than we do with the culture at large.) The students have few expectations concerning their education until it is too late to do much about it. Kathy McCoy spoke eloquently of her own experience in this regard at an STA Education Conference last year.

If we take a larger view of graphic design, one that goes beyond our own personal sense of success or failure, then we care about graphic design as a profession and about how thousands of students are educated to enter the profession. This is not to say that any one of us or any committee of us would be so bold or so ignorant as to think we had the one true recipe for graphic design education. Any definition of graphic design is fairly broad and somewhat fuzzy. Within this universe of activity, a university can stake out a territory that it believes it can address based on faculty, institutional policies of the parent school, location, student body, and the like. Defining the universe helps each school to see where it fits and could help students locate their best fit within education. Programs that are prominent have carved out a special technological thrust or philosophical position or intellectual connection. They seek to differentiate themselves within the education marketplace.

Graphic design programs need help. I recently participated in a self-study for the Department of Housing and Applied Design (Graphic/Interior) at the University of Maryland. It exhibited a pattern of problems common to many schools—too many students (438 were in graphic design), insufficient space or equipment, etc. Feedback in the form of critical comment and positive suggestion can be used to consolidate goals and can be used as a lever on the parent institution. I know of no professional graphic design organization, other than the AIGA or STA, which could help to make visible and public what design is—define the universe of activity and provide counsel to existing programs.

I am not unaware of the friction between design educators and design practitioners, but, in fact, each has a special role to play in education—in the universe of experience that a graphic designer needs. Sorting out the territory and discussing the overlap is a much-needed dialogue.

Design programs are the interface between the aspirant and the profession. They need critical support in order to define themselves and gain the financial support and respect of the larger academic community. They need access to thoughtful individuals who understand both university structures and the needs of the profession.

There is much to be done with regard to design education, but it is possible to identify objectives, tasks, and expected results. These can be prioritized and subjected to scrutiny concerning their financial and human requirements and their timeliness.

In closing, let me share my largest and boldest thought. Graphic design has largely developed as a cottage industry, but the culture is now evolving into an information economy. Designers can either seize the moment to have impact on the culture by becoming more visible, more professional, more creative, and more accountable, or we can ignore the opportunity and be swept aside by computer technicians, information and marketing experts, and others. Our individual efforts need focus and orchestration, and that is what the AIGA can provide.

When you have ideas that run counter to prevailing thoughts, you always wonder if you see a pattern that is just emerging, if you need new glasses, if you labor under some peculiar delusion, or if you genuinely have a relevant grasp of a problem and a glimmering of its solution.

*Originally published in Volume 2, Number 4, 1984.*

# FUTURE SHOCKS

# THE PLACE OF ORIGINALITY IN THE INFORMATION AGE
*Paul Saffo*

Does technology extinguish creativity and originality, or does it expand them? The history of technology and creativity over the last few centuries suggests that the answer is less bleak than today's information-age fears might indicate. Our response to a given new technology typically repeats a pattern of initial resistance, followed by uneasy accommodation and eventual acquiescence. Ultimately, we achieve a seemingly irreversible integration of the new technology into our creative lives, as once-offensive tools become seamless extensions of artistic reach and creativity. Be it bulldozer, chain saw, or laser printer, each new technological threat has been tamed into a useful tool for creative expression.

Three centuries of mechanical innovations have insinuated themselves into virtually every corner of physical creative expression. We have made a reluctant peace with the artifacts of the industrial revolution. The machine has extended the power of the hand in precision and speed, making the scarce common and the dear cheap—often at great aesthetic cost, but also creating newer wonders never before possible. Could a scrivener's unaided hand have delivered to us the photomosaic of earth shot from space by the Apollo astronauts that so reshaped our consciousness and influenced the environmental movement in the 1960s?

Above all, the machine has created an astonishing abundance. We live in an age of *profligate reproduction,* a world of enabling, multiplying machines, their output exceeding the wildest dreams of nineteenth-century industrialists. The machine breakers of Lyons feared deprivation of wealth and security from loss of work, and of expression from being reduced to mere machine tenders. But mechanization has been so complete that we no longer tend the spinning frames—they tend themselves. As it has always been with technological revolutions, the present danger is that we will be done in by the success of our inventions, creating more subtle and insidious forms of servitude than the machine breakers ever imagined.

The engines of this profligate reproduction have also drastically altered our notions of creativity and originality. Technology has made precision in multiplication the province of the machine, forcing the essence of human creativity to retreat slowly from the hand to the head. The merits of this retreat are fertile grounds for debate. But the debate is also something of a red herring, for the most important issue of all may lie in an unexamined assumption that seems to be shared by technophile and technophobe alike: no matter how precise our machines become, the familiars of the industrial revolution will never invade the last sanctum of creativity, the human mind. This smug, industrial-age assumption is blinding us to more fundamental shifts in much the same way that fear over becoming machine tenders blinded our predecessors to the impact of technology on consumerism.

This time, the transforming agents are the microprocessor and the communications laser. These and the artifacts of the information revolution are not simply extending the means of profligate reproduction; something utterly new is afoot. The machine age of profligate reproduction is yielding to an information age of infinite recall. This shift will do more than redefine design. It will cut to the very heart of what we mean by creativity and originality, and it will do so by invading the once-exclusive province of the mind.

Human culture has been shaped by a dance of two opposing forces: memory and forgetfulness. Memory gives us context, while forgetfulness provides an opening for invention and originality. Successful creativity occurs when the two are balanced and originality is set within the larger context of tradition.

Memory was once the exclusive domain of the intellect. Homer and his contemporaries carried epic poems and culture in their heads. The result was captivating, but transmission was laborious and imperfect. On the bright side, the process conferred an imprecise patina to culture that itself encouraged and enabled further creativity. On the down side, though, the sum total of human knowledge that could be preserved was limited to what could be recalled from frail memory and stored in one human lifetime. Every information innovation since then has nibbled away at the margins of memory. In the *Phaedrus,* Plato expressed the fear that writing would make human memory lazy. In fact, the "memory arts" became the central tool of scholarship until well after the invention of the printing press, a response to the human need to deal with burgeoning paper-based information.

Gutenberg's invention of movable type in the mid-1400s triggered a newer revolution that extended and complexified human knowledge and thought even further. But it, too, merely augmented memory, making the mind more important than ever. The advent of printing as a medium triggered a shift from the use of the mind as storage to the mind as processor of print-based information. These advances all enhanced creativity. Aided by the press and the book, the creative mental horizons of our ancestors grew by leaps and bounds.

Each of these information innovations also triggered fundamental shifts in cultural world views. Writing set us on a path of history. The formal memory arts led to a systematic though static medieval world view, while the press added a radical new Renaissance dynamism, setting us also firmly on the path of acknowledging individual originality and creativity. The press was the first industrial replication machine, with its pieces of type amounting to standardized parts centuries before the idea occurred to the captains of the industrial revolution. As a replication machine, it was also a star-making machine, for the notion of authorship barely existed before the multiplication of texts invented the audience. The

book and its replication led to a cult of the individual and of individual originality unprecedented in human history.

Now we are on the verge of an information revolution that is so great as to
amount to a difference in kind. A triad of information technologies—communications, processing, and memory—is reshaping both the real and the symbolic
world. We are entering a hyperdynamic world of connections, relationships, and
abstracting tools that help us make sense of the information flooding about us.
Already, the dominant form of information storage in our society has ceased to be
either the fragile and forgetful patterns of memory or yellowing paper and aging
books. Today, more information is stored in digital form than in all the libraries
of the world combined.

But this is much more than a memory revolution. We are in the earliest
stages of creating in a world of infinite recall, where all can be stored and nothing
can be forgotten, no matter how profound or banal. This digital shift to infinite
recall will upset the apple cart of originality forever. For starters, the line between
original and derivative works will blur as link-building information systems
relentlessly identify the origins of ideas that perhaps the originator and creating
designer had forgotten or never known. We may one day critique art the way the
IRS conducts tax audits. What seems like luck, inspiration, and risky happenstance at the moment of creation could take on the aspect of plagiarism and fraud
when viewed in perfect unblinking twenty-twenty digital hindsight.

Imagine clients routinely demanding an affidavit of originality from
designers. Indeed, plagiarism itself could become a profoundly relative sin,
differing only by degree from more venial derivations, and the causality of plagiarism might be determined more by happenstance and not by the original
designer's intent.

Will the act of creativity be reduced to assembling old ideas like so much
digital clip art, as the once-sustaining web of tradition becomes a suffocating
blanket of electronic recall? In *Choruses from "The Rock,"* T. S. Eliot articulated a
very modern fear: "Where is the wisdom we have lost in knowledge? / Where is
the knowledge that we have lost in information?" To this we might add, "Will
vast memory and infinite recall leave room for invention and creativity at all?" Of
course, this coming world of infinite memory and recall is not without its advantages. Think of the fruits of creative labor lost when the library of Alexandria was
torched in the seventh century by Muslim invaders, or when Spanish padres
burned the Mayan codices in the 1600s. Even modest recall and reproduction can
preserve ideas from the ravages of foolish contemporaries who would censor what
their descendants may see.

Now, in an age of digital storage, duplication is so facile and storage so
cheap that the notion of a single original will all but disappear. For, as the music
industry has discovered to its alarm, digital technology makes each and every
copy equal in quality to the initial master. Just as digital reproduction and
replication extend rather than extinguish the original, I wonder if the coming

new world of infinite recall will be more likely to extend and redefine originality than to eliminate it. *Origin* is defined as that from which anything derives its existence, source, or cause. The mechanical age, with its profligate replication and reproduction, turned origin into a point, leaving us with an obsessive illusion of individual creativity. And history became a pattern of multiple points of originality with patterns of copying and duplication fanning out from them.

This, however, is a myth. I think plagiarism has become so devilish an issue today because true, strict originality is vanishingly rare. We swim in a sea of culture, of memories old and new, and all our acts flow out in response to what we experience. In the coming age of infinite recall, I think we will rediscover a preindustrial fact: origin is not a point but a continuum, and the process of originality is much more linked than we imagine. For a world of infinite recall is a world of infinite unity, of deeply interconnected relationships. In this new world, originality is going to be recognized as an additive and transformative process, with multiple paths and forks along the way, as new and old divide and recombine in infinitely intriguing complexity. And this new understanding will lead us to realize that creativity and originality are much stranger and scarcer than we ever assumed, and much more precious than ever.

Eventually, we will look back on the closing half of this century and realize that we suffered from something of a cult of originality. And as the cult subsides, perhaps the litmus test of individual creativity will cease to be originality above all. Instead, the test will be passion—passion, surprise, and insight. The growing emphasis in the design industry on collaboration is evidence that the shift is already under way. We worry about working together today as a team. Perhaps we will also come to value vertical collaborations with thinkers long dead and with visionaries yet unborn.

Of course, nothing is new. You can reach back to the caves of Lascaux or the century-long process of building a medieval cathedral to see this kind of multigenerational collaboration taking place. With luck, perhaps the deep interconnections revealed by the coming age of infinite recall will also turn back and recombine into a new power of vision that will help us bring sense and control to the existing industrial forces of infinite replication. That, I think, would be the most welcome and creative act of all.

*Originally published in Volume 12, Number 1, 1994.*

# OWNERSHIP, AUTHORSHIP, AND CREDIT IN THE DIGITAL AGE

*Jessica Helfand*

Can design be its own reward? Or does our behavior bespeak a yearning for public recognition in order to feel professionally—if not altogether personally—validated? Each year, a host of juried competitions reinforces these inclinations with the promise of ceremony—ceremony that increasingly seems to take its cue, oddly enough, from the entertainment industry. In the design professions, award recipients are fêted by banquets and lavishly printed books, their names and titles recorded, and repeated, for posterity. Is it this reinforcement of the celebrity ideal that makes us so possessive on the subject of credit?

The issue of celebrity—or the public acknowledgment of credit—is a delicate one, reflecting a kind of unflinching territorialism more suited to birds, wolves, and political candidates. Such desire is driven by a need to establish parameters, to stake one's ground, and to be duly recognized for it. In the civilized world, territory has typically been marked by emblematic symbols that denote ownership: flags surrounding a castle, a gold band encircling a finger. These are gestures that establish moral, physical, or political boundaries. Over time, such gestures become part of our cultural lexicon and we learn to honor and respect them.

But in the gold-rush mentality of the virtual world, things are not so easy to define. Here, the "posterity" referred to above is merely symbolic: in truth, you are only as good as the thing you designed fifteen minutes ago. Recent advancements brought about by information technologies now enable increased access, independence, and customization. What that really means is it's all moving and changing, incredibly fast, and whatever you design won't be around for very long. Or it will, but it will mutate over time into something perhaps quite alien from its original incarnation. Therein lies the beauty, if not the insanity, of designing in an interactive medium: like a relay race, the baton is perpetually on the move, from you to your audience to another designer to another audience. In this new democracy, territory itself is transient, intangible, chameleonlike. So how are we expected to take—or give—credit for something we can't possibly expect to quantify?

As projects themselves grow more complicated, so does the issue of credit. Who designed what? And where? And for how long? What do we call all these designers, each of whom contributed a critical component in an overall process that might span weeks, months, or even years? In the design and development of Web sites, for instance, the careful engineering of templates is an architectural challenge requiring sophisticated computational skill. The person who resolves the intricate ways in which varying types of content will become visually manifest may be a programmer, a systems engineer, or a client with a particular talent for coding. Occasionally, it may be a designer.

As in most industries, credit remains, in the end, largely contract driven. The stalemate between new media practitioners and many (though not all) of the lawyers with whom they must negotiate lies in an antiquated contractual vocabulary. Corporations have adapted boilerplate legal language to describe services, to calculate fee structures, and to restrict reproduction rights. Confidentiality and ownership clauses reflect the finite world of print and the age-old word of the law. What they seldom do is address collaborative efforts and acknowledge the complexity of their resulting forms.

The issue here is not so much about who did what, but about how we talk about who did what. If seeking recognition is the only way to validate what we do, then sharing that recognition will always be perceived as minimizing the value of our achievements. And that is shaky ground, indeed.

*Originally published in Volume 14, Number 3, 1996.*

# THE ENVIRONMENT OF SIGNS: A MEDITATION

*Sven Birkerts*

The instigating image for this little collection of observations: I remember reading somewhere that the great humanist scholar Erasmus was seen crouching down in a busy thoroughfare trying to make out what was printed on a sheet of paper caught in the mud.

All of our reading or decoding of signs can be seen to take place in a semiotic environment, and the nature of that environment determines a good deal—though not everything—about how those signs are registered. Contents aside, the inscribed symbol itself has a certain specific gravity, a ground of implicit significance against which, or with the aid of which, its encoded meaning is received. When Erasmus famously bent over to read a printed scrap in the street, print was new in the world, and the simple fact that something was printed already signified. It was a short leap from that sense of signification to the higher level where a more concrete meaning was felt to reside. By vivid contrast, we live in an environment of signs that is utterly saturated. Where so many signs—words—vie for attention, the mainspring of attention itself is spent. Even contents of unarguable importance are diminished, robbed of their due focal claim, by the superabundance of signs.

But this is intuitively obvious to anyone who looks. Less obvious, perhaps, is the fact that what I am calling the semiotic environment has not only become saturated, but has begun to alter its fundamental nature. It has—and this is somewhat elusive—moved from fixity toward fluidity, from stability toward flux. This is a direct consequence of technological transformation—the advent of electronic communications media. Formerly, that semiotic environment, however dense or thick it was, was composed entirely of stationary elements—on billboards, in books, in newspapers, etc. (I am considering signs to be strictly visual entities here.) And from that we deduced certain useful truths about the nature of information and our relation to it. Fixed in place, cumulative, information was an accomplished thing—it was there, to be found, arranged, annotated, and stored.

Obviously, stationary signs are still everywhere around us. But they are being superseded by different, younger signs—signs that behave in a fluid manner, mysteriously. Keystrokes bring them into view from some unknown holding place; other keystrokes vaporize them back. Information, the very idea of information, changes. Information seems to possess agency, motility. Words are no longer passive elements to be arranged and sorted; they no longer just lie there. They are now vital elements in a process that we sense exceeds us. They move out from, and back into, a reservoir that is both invisible and infinite (like the child's conception of God). Everything has been recontextualized. Signs have been given a new relational life; the technology makes them sites of possibility. Each word, almost, can be seen as itself and as a potential link, an integral part of any number of pattern systems, any of which can be rendered active by a user's whim.

The whole electronic transformation is still in its very early stages, but already it influences how we read and absorb signs. The stationary look of a printed page, for example, signifies differently now that the printed page is no longer the only—or even the main—way of transmitting information. The page itself is now value laden; it telegraphs: immutability, control, a presumption of finality, of having the last word; also rigidity, datedness, the quixotic attempt to arrest what is likely a movable, mutating thing. The page hasn't changed its look, but changes in the larger environment have determined that it should strike us differently. We project these valuations, of course, on the most subtly subliminal levels.

Are we looking at new life for the word, the sign? In a sense, yes. Rendering the word fluid through new systems of presentation is a way of revitalizing things—of shaking a mixture that may have become a bit stagnant. The momentum of our time clearly runs counter to the fixity of tradition, counter to what many have called the "oppressive" sense of hierarchy enshrined by the canon (the very emblem of sclerotic fixity). Deconstruction was, in academe, the applied nitroglycerin, blowing away the very premises on which any such hierarchy could be based. Electronic communication, in its lateral and branching nature, cannot but further the change. And to some extent—who will deny it?—the change is healthy and liberating. But we have to reckon with the Pandora effect: once the demons of fluidity have been let out of the box, there is no getting them back in.

Yes, the sign is made more supple, is now reconceived as a wondrously mutable thing—but as the semiotic environment is transformed, all signs seem to lose gravity and authority. Where all is shifting, no expression can sound definitive; there is no last word, ever, just the next word. And this has negative as well as positive repercussions. It may—because how we think and speak and write is how we are—significantly lighten our sense of presence in the world. Expression is tethered to our inward perception of the world; change the former and you will affect the latter as well.

There is another way to conceive this same process, and that is as an injection of bits into a world hitherto composed of atoms. I refer to the distinction between things that actually exist—that have matter, atoms—and information that is simply a function of code, of lines of ones and zeros, that has no material base. A string of printed words on a page has atomic existence; a string of words on a monitor has only "bit" life. It is a shadow without an actual sponsoring body. As more and more of our communication is carried out by way of the bit, the semiotic environment must suffer some alteration. We cannot yet guess what this will be. The formerly material order is overrun with ectoplasm. Doesn't a sign signify differently when we know, however subliminally, that it doesn't really exist?

Some would say that it is then more purely signification, that the material impediment has been shorn away; that it is closer to pure thought. But do we say that money is more purely value now that it is freed from having to represent bullion reserves, now that it can just be? And hasn't thought always aspired to the palpability of print in order to validate itself? We need to look more closely at how the materiality of a sign influences, or conditions, its signification. Inflation—the situation that arises when the marker of value bears less and less relation to value—can affect the psychic economy as traumatically as it can afflict the fiscal economy.

Sketchy as this bit of speculation may be, it would be sketchier still if I did not allow for the possibility of the saving paradox. Which is, simply, that whenever relativism threatens to run rampant, the idea of absolutes starts to look more attractive again. Absolutism, of course, carries a negative valence—and so it should as a manifestation of extremism. But relativism, which we credit more positively, should have that valence, too, for it is simply the opposite pole. In any case, I'm contemplating tendencies here. When everything is mass-produced, then the handmade acquires value. When letters were all typewritten, the handwritten communication took on special meaning. And when more and more communication is conducted in bits, the atom-based modes of expression will gather new, different significance.

Electronic communication will wreak havoc on the culture of the book.

As the printed artifact loses prestige and relevance, as book reading as a mass phenomenon declines, certain books will—in certain sectors—acquire a compensatory aura. When the world reconstitutes itself online—if it ever does—then book culture will resemble, again, the undemocratic early centuries of print, when the bound object was only for the elites. If there is a silver gleam in this cloudy picture—and the picture itself is my own dark imagining—it is that what is prized by the elites is very often sought after by everyone else. I sometimes fancy that the book will one day be reincarnated as something that looks and behaves in every way just like . . . a book.

*Originally published in Volume 15, Number 2, 1997.*

# SMOKE AND MIRRORS ON THE WORLD WIDE WEB
*Daniel Drennan*

The World Wide Web has arrived with great fanfare and promise, and many in the design and publishing industries are blinded by the hype that the Web is literally to be the *last word* in publishing. The learning curve required for publishing on the Web is strikingly similar to the early days of Macintosh design, when the tools drove the designer—little or no control of typography, a hardly robust graphics format, as well as arcane and obtuse programming codes. Fortunately, these issues will be resolved as the technology behind the Web advances.

More serious problems, however, stem from the analogies made by those currently vaunting the new medium: the Web is like publishing, it is like a worldwide library, it is the online equivalent of newspapers and magazines. The Web is none of these things. It *is* a vast dumping ground of unformatted ASCII text, with low-resolution images, digitized video, and sound haphazardly piled on top. Text that in its unedited, unorganized, and undesigned state is hard to read on-screen, harder to digest as information, and perhaps hardest of all to navigate.

The intellectual and monetary value placed on computer-based information is derived from its completeness and organization. Government databases, airline reservation systems, and online information services (for example) all stockpile data that retain value based on their breadth, design, and cohesive structure. Unlike a library, the Web makes no claim to organization or thoroughness. Contrary to libraries, which boast more robust networks for sharing information, the Web provides software "crawlers" and other "agents" that randomly stockpile information that is incomplete and inadequate to begin with. Whereas books in libraries include references, indexes, and other alternative channels that can be searched, most of the Web remains haphazard and chaotic—undesirable qualities when talking about the value of information.

The design of useful information systems relies heavily on the dynamic nature of that information. A lesson can be learned from CD-ROMs, which too often provide shovelfuls of data without the interface needed to extract useful meaning from them. By the time a CD-ROM is delivered, the facts and figures they contain are often stale or outdated. Depending on the data contained therein, this may or may not be a problem. However, this inherent drawback is taken into consideration when CD-ROMs are designed.

Now we are presented with the Web, which runs over the worldwide backbone of the Internet and promises to deliver all kinds of information to our virtual doorsteps dynamically, but which in actuality only provides the same hardwired, static information that a nonnetwork-based data medium such as CD-ROM gives us. This static nature is the very antithesis of the "hyper" qualities ascribed to the Web. Most of the Web is not at all like a true spiderweb—yielding, pliant, and self-maintaining—but is more like a Tinkertoy construction—rigid and prone to breaking. The Web is not delivering edited and precisely honed information dynamically culled from users' requests. Instead, it is pulling a Dumpster full of useless and duplicated data up to her virtual door, and asking her to be thankful for the privilege of rifling through the chaotic mess. Designers looking to the Web as a possible medium need to think in terms of information design—the current crop of Web pages, reworked from their static, two-dimensional print predecessors, will be a worthless pile of broken spokes as the Web advances and evolves.

Of course, the Web is in its infant stages. Barring oft-predicted problems such as too little bandwidth, it will end up banal and commonplace like the overlooked services that grew up alongside it, such as Minitel. If not co-opted by powerful government and commercial interests, it will end up an affordable publishing medium servicing anyone who has something to say. If not dominated by elite members of a computer-savvy online population, it will evolve into an expressive medium open to most, if not all, of those who desire access. Finally, if it is not overblown by hypemongers, it will settle down into a niche and operate within a paradigm suited precisely to what it can and cannot do.

*Originally published in Volume 13, Number 2, 1995.*

# WHERE THE DEAR GOD LIVES

*Robin Kinross*

So, everyone—real estate agents' secretaries, refugee-center information officers, technical writers in electronics multinationals, editors in sleepy publishing firms, subsidy-seeking dairy farmers, primary-school kids, and architects—now designs texts for multiplication, and sometimes even typefaces, too. Everyone is his or her own PageMaker, his or her own Fontographer. Is there any place left for the professional typographer? Shouldn't we bow out gracefully, glad that the people are in charge of their own print and multimedia destiny?

In this brief discussion, I want to shift the terms of the argument as it has developed over the past few years by raising some questions about just what it is that typographic designers have been doing. This may, I hope, provoke some embarrassment. But honest self-examination will help us to find ways forward, and I think that in the present great democratization of text and image production, there are new roles for the professional typographer to play.

A glance at the history of Western typography reminds us that the profession of typographer has suffered an ill-defined, precarious, and brief life. The story starts properly only in the mid-1920s in Europe and the United States, when a few thoughtful and articulate practitioners began to try to bridge the gap that had opened between the old printing-trade workers and the new machines. Into this widening crevice, taste and style were dropping—and disappearing. The matter is usually put in aesthetic and visual terms, but at least half of this historical complex has to be understood otherwise: as an issue of human ambition, commercial and technical constraint, social struggle, and labor relations.

This process can be seen clearly in typeface design: a special domain within the larger field of typography. In sixteenth-century Europe, design and production of punches (the male forms that shaped the female matrices from which masculine type was then made) was undivided work. It lay entirely in the hands of punchcutters (all men, as far as we know). In this realm of the miniature image, drawing for production wasn't necessary or possible. Gradually, the making of type was brought into a larger system of manufacture by the type foundries. Then, at the end of the nineteenth century with Linn Boyd Benton's invention of the pantographic punchcutting machine, typeface design was split off from production and routinized. The way was open for the "artist"—who could merely draw letters—to design typefaces. Production lay in the hands of technical managers and drawing-office functionaries. So, although the artist-designer might supply a nicely finished set of letters inked on board, the translation of his desires—the final forms of the letters, and, crucially, the space around the letterform as it sat on its "body"—was then in the hands of the women (as they often were, certainly at Monotype in England) in the drawing office.

In the early to middle years of the twentieth century, this system resulted in some marvelous things. One thinks of typefaces such as the Akzidenz Grotesks from Berthold in Berlin, or Franklin Gothic and News Gothic from the American Type Founders company (ATF) in Jersey City, Imprint and Plantin from the English Monotype Company, the Janson and Garamond typefaces made at the Stempel Foundry in Frankfurt. One can find authors for some of these great works: most notably, ATF's house-designer Morris Fuller Benton—son of Linn Boyd Benton. But they really are company typefaces.

Meanwhile, these companies were beginning to enter into more or less fraught dealings with artistic advisers and freelance designers. These designers drew the best they could and fired off pleading memos from the sidelines of production. But execution of their designs was out of their hands, and often they seem not to have quite understood, or were, anyway, out of sympathy with, the processes and ethos of the company drawing office. Notable among these frustrated men were Stanley Morison at Monotype in England and Jan van Krimpen at Enschedé in Holland. The Americans tended to be of a more open-minded and robust disposition. The shining example here is W. A. Dwiggins, who was happy to engage in dialogue with the technical staff of the Mergenthaler Linotype company. Frederic Goudy, who started out as a simple artist, became "art adviser" to the Lanston Monotype company and later resorted to making matrices and casting type himself.

Outside this rarefied zone of typeface design, one could make the same sort of commentary for the typographic designer proper: the person who tried to design and coordinate whole pages of text and image. However precise the layouts (and often they were far from exact), final control lay in the hands of the compositor at the machine keyboard and in the hands of the men (few women entered these fumy, inky, light-industrial workshops) who made up the pages, ran the presses, guillotined the sheets, sewed and stuck them (yes, that work was reserved for nimble-fingered, ill-paid women). As with the typeface designers, I think one would also tell a rather sarcastic story of artist-designers trying to get their dreams turned into reality, hoping for the best in processes they didn't quite understand, with lots going wrong on the way, and saved—if the designer was lucky—by compositors and printers who, after long years of apprenticeship and induction into a literate and proud trade, really did know their business.

In the 1960s, this young and unstable system began to unravel. Here again there was a complex of factors at work: the end of metal typesetting and letterpress printing, the introduction of computers into the processes of text composition, the end of the post-1945 economic boom, the end of job securities—of wide economic margins and social quiescence. The details of typesetting, which the compositor had known sometimes just tacitly—the space around punctuation marks, where to break words, good form in a paragraph of unjustified text, how to make up columns of text, and so on and so on—now began rather dramatically to be exposed: by suddenly not being tended to. Typographers had always had these details decided for them by compositors. If a typographer had ever thought about this state of affairs, he or she had usually been glad that it was so. Only the more hardened and obsessed of them had tried to instruct compositors in this microdomain. But now text composition and printing began to be done by people without the old skills, and trade boundaries and protections began to collapse. Or this work was done by frustrated and fed-up old compositors on new machines and with new materials whose constraints had been determined by engineers ignorant of semantic detail: that rich web of meaning that it had been possible to create on a Monotype or Linotype machine. I am thinking of things such as small capitals, nonlining numerals, ligatures, alternate dashes, and the diacriticals and nonstandard characters that are necessary for setting all the world's languages, except English.

The 1970s were for text composition, as in some other areas of human endeavor, a time of shame and despair. Certainly this was so in Britain. Books might be set in a single master typeface, ripped off by engineers from a mid-twentieth-century imitation of an eighteenth-century model, and justified without word breaks. One of these books I've kept for the record. It is called *Principles in Design,* and was published in 1979 in London by the Design Council.

Since the mid-1980s, this process of the dissolution and dispersal of production out of trade hands has intensified with the introduction of what we know as desktop publishing. The compositor is now almost extinct; the printer has become someone who runs presses to multiply from materials (disks, film) usually made elsewhere. But this pattern of drifting apart has its aspect of coming together, too. Thanks to the invention of a common page-description language (PostScript), out of the ruins of the old printing trade there has come the chance for designers to take command of these processes, as they haven't before been able to. Or not since, perhaps, the sixteenth century in Europe. This is true of both the areas I have distinguished: the design of typefaces and the overall configuration of text and image.

In the last ten years, some designers—those that are honest and serious—have admitted that, indeed, we never did quite know all the skills and subtleties of the compositor. So we have to think, examine, and articulate these things to ourselves, to our desktop-publishing programs, and, via templates and standard procedures, to the laypeople with whom we may be collaborating. It would be a delusion to pretend that designers were ever in possession of some higher wisdom that was taken from us by technological development. And, anyway, designers never really had much power. With computerization, the center of power moved from the printing trade to the designers of the software. But now, maybe, if we are lucky, these more primary designers, the software writers, will begin to realize the potential of their languages. Their problem is to resist the pressures to load applications with baffling, baroque excesses, and rather to design intelligent and intelligible features. Multiple Masters and TrueType GX have yet to prove themselves, but at least they are signs that we are truly over and out of the black hole of the 1970s and have a chance to enter new realms of sophistication and control.

We haven't reached these realms yet. Most of Latin-alphabet, desktop-publishing humanity still does not know what an *fi* ligature is and why it might be good to have this little thing in text. This, despite the fact that in taking care to search and replace ligatures there is only increased expenditure of time in production and no measurable gain for the reader. But the dot of an *i* is where the dear god is to be found. Small capitals and nonlining numerals remain a zone of confusion: look at how Canadian and British postcodes are typeset.

But then the setting of more than one line of text remains a dodgy business in all the desktop-publishing programs I have encountered. The space between words and between letters, where words get broken: there is no program that does it well, as if by magic. Even the best-set preferences result in text that has then to be checked over by a thinking, literate human being. And then there is the work of making up columns of text into pages. Some printers used to know, but hardly ever articulated this notion, that it was good to enable columns either to run short or to extend by a line or two, in order to configure lines and paragraphs in ways that made the best sense: avoiding headings cut off from the text that follows; or avoiding a short line (the *widow*) at the top of a page, which then looked more like a heading than the last line of a paragraph. You might think that all this is just the manners of another age and part of that dreaded "crystal goblet." I think it's more like basic visual syntax and semantics.

The realm of detail remains stubbornly out of reach of the theorizing and polemic that have surrounded recent typography. Ligatures and word breaks can't be grasped by big, single-tack ideas about the death of the human subject, the end of grand narratives, the terrors of the Enlightenment, the tyrannies of Western metaphysics. Such details are just too small, too mundane, too material, too much just a matter of keyboard layouts and pixels. The kind of theory that matters for word breaks is not poststructuralist semiotics, which hopes to describe pretty much everything in the universe, but rather what is useful here is the workaday grammar and etymology of a particular language. Where does it make sense to split words? According to sense or sound, or a bit of both? With some understanding of German, for example, you know why an *fl* ligature would be wrong in the word *Auflage,* and why it's good to break after *f,* or maybe, if pushed, between *a* and *g.*

One bad upshot of the craze for poststructuralist theory seems to be that we are getting classloads of postgraduate designers who might be well versed in Foucault, Barthes, and theories of discursive space, but who can't place a heading so that it belongs unambiguously to the text to which it refers or scale a picture when the scanner breaks down.

So there is still work for a typographer to do. It is modest work, but essential. This isn't a nostalgic view. "Golden ages" of printing lose their splendor when you come to ask just what was golden about those cramped workshops or those smudged pages. And I don't think that the troubled profession of the typographer ever really occupied the ground that some of us are now trying to lay claim to. It is rather that gaps have opened up to reveal ground that no one ever quite described before, that no one ever quite knew was there, and that it is important to try to be articulate about and to intervene in.

*Author's note: Some of the ideas here were prompted by an article by Paul Stiff, "Instructing the Printer: What Specification Tells About Typographic Designing," in* Typography Papers, *No. 1, 1996, pages 27– 44, a publication from the Department of Typography, University of Reading, England.*

*Originally published in Volume 12, Number 1, 1994.*

# TYPE IS DEAD: LONG LIVE TYPE
*Matthew Butterick*

Type designers tend to be a nervous lot, with reason. Especially in the United States, type design in the last ten years has been increasingly an undertaking for the brave, the masochistic, or the independently wealthy. Lack of copyright protection for type designs has resulted in unscrupulous companies profiting from cheap imitations, while the proliferation of desktop publishers has made fonts even more popular to pirate than QuarkXPress.

Now we are witnessing the emergence of a purely digital visual culture: users are taking their doses of typography on screen as well as on paper. Type and graphic designers alike are viewing this development with the proverbial cautious optimism. Typography is inexorably moving into the digital realm, going from design to output without pausing to rest on a sheet of paper. Should designers be excited or alarmed?

The ATypI conference is the largest annual gathering of type designers; the theme of last year's conference in Barcelona was "Into the Type Net." When I received the flier in the mail, I was slightly bemused ("type net"?) but curious, so I pressed on:

"The analog and linear alphabet is dead—long live digital text & type
in space & time! . . . [The 1995 conference] will cast an eye on the

present and future of interactive type and its relationship with the image in an expanding virtual-visual environment . . . ATypI welcomes people . . . who are interested to support communicative design aspects within the information society."

I still have no idea what this means. Even disregarding the linguistic kinks that may have cropped up in the translation from the original Spanish, phrases like "interactive type" and "virtual-visual environment" are vapid technobabble. But ATypI can't be blamed; this kind of terminology is endemic to the current discourse on digital design.

Something big is definitely happening, but most prognosticators of the digital future seem to be uncomfortable saying that life will be anything but bigger, better, and faster for everyone. It's clear that type designers and those who design with type will not be so fortunate. Ironically, current technology has made text more important than ever, but the same technology has conspired to further erode the value of quality typography.

The sole bit of good news is that text rules the digital frontier, because it is compact to load, easy to create, familiar to use, and compatible with all computing platforms. The popularity of the World Wide Web has shown that text is still a vital medium, and though it's less flashy than pictures, sound, and video, it offers the best bang for the bandwidth. And if text is alive and well, so should typography be: after all, there can be no visual representation of text without type, and the proliferation of text in a new medium would imply the necessity of new design solutions. More work for type designers, more work for typographers—the birth of a type renaissance! Right?

No. The jubilance that type makers should rightly feel has been cut by the grim realization of the workings of the software industry. Once, those who made type also controlled the means of production—in the days of hot metal, the choice of a Monotype versus a Linotype caster was similar to the choice of Macintosh versus Windows. Each platform had its strengths and foibles, but if you needed type, you chose one and stuck with it. A hot metal caster was a sort of operating system for type, and the matrices were the software that worked with it. This continued through the ages of phototypesetting and early digital typography, where proprietary systems meant proprietary fonts, and proprietary fonts meant type makers could still maintain control over font production and access.

But when type technology became commingled with personal computing technology, things changed. At that point, the ability to make and use type became available to anyone with a computer, along with the newfound ability to make speedy, accurate, and untraceable pirate copies. This was better for users of type, but much worse for type designers. Type has had to relinquish the power of its own proprietary barricades. Many of the improvements in type functionality introduced on computers have caused a decline in type designers' quality of life.

Moreover, the goals of interoperability and data exchange will continue to be antithetical to type's long-term aesthetic and economic viability.

For example, one brass ring for which Apple, Adobe, and others have groped recently is the portable digital document—a document that can be viewed and printed with its formatting intact, without needing the software that created it. These schemes have typically been riddled with unstable engineering and other difficulties. But let's take apart the problem: consider a page-layout document containing images and formatted text. Text is certainly portable, and formatting can be made into a series of tags; images can be converted to a variety of platform-independent, bitmap formats. All that's left are the fonts. The handiest thing would be to encapsulate the fonts into the document, but this would be tanta-mount to saving users the trouble of pirating the fonts themselves. Adobe's scheme at one point was to retain metric files of hundreds of typefaces in the software so that a reasonable facsimile could be built when the document was opened. Uncountable programmer-hours have doubtless been spent to preserve the type designer's livelihood, but the result is products that can't quite do what they claim. Surely more than one software company has thought, Why can't the fonts just be free so we can copy them?

Microsoft, with typical bravado, was the only company willing to act on that principle. Several years ago, Microsoft began to create its own type library. At first there were special font packs; then fonts showed up in other products. Now, it's rare that a box goes out the door without new typefaces in it. Microsoft is probably one of the largest publishers of typefaces in the world, and it has also built font embedding into its operating system for use in any sort of document. Nevertheless, users who are receiving dozens of free fonts may not see much point in paying for more.

Typographers who are wincing should stop reading now—that's nothing compared to the culture of the Internet. On the surface, Internet users look like the most fertile new group of type consumers: a giant new demographic suffering from an acute case of dreadful typography (Times and Courier are used almost exclusively). However, the language of Internet typography (HTML) allows for no explicit typeface choices, and only a handful of different sizes. Worse, much of the software that can be used for browsing the Internet is free. If users don't have to pay for an industrial-strength Web browser, why will they pay for a font, of all things? Microsoft has released Matthew Carter's Verdana, a type family commis-sioned expressly for use in Web browsers—and it's available from the company's Web site for free. Then there's the taste issue: I'm sure most graphic designers have had a client who insisted on a job being set only in Times, Palatino, or Courier. Now you have 15 million clients who feel the same way.

The undeterred typographer might still bravely withstand these slings and arrows and elect to create the consummate on-screen text typeface. Sadly, one's design choices at the level of the 12-point bitmap are limited to determin-ing how to render the curve of the lowercase *s*. It seems safe to speculate that there are no more than eight mutually distinguishable 12-point text faces, all of which had been discovered by 1985. It's a field with limited growth potential at best (Matthew Carter notwithstanding).

Some of the blame for the current dismal situation can be put with Apple, Adobe, Microsoft, Quark, and their ilk. All have had the opportunity to improve typography by enhancing software or hardware, but they have pursued it with little vigor. Certain developments (antialiased type) have been slow in coming, others (QuickDraw GX) have been overhyped, and others still (high-resolution displays) don't seem to be on anyone's task list. These improvements wouldn't just make typophiles happy; they would benefit anyone who has to experience type on a screen—i.e., anyone who owns a computer. Given the continuing importance of text to computers, it's surprising that type technology has been stagnating.

But the best consolation may be that print will never die. Part of the current anxiety seems to stem from the idea that print will disappear in the face of this putatively superior on-screen technology. It's not true. The experience of reading off an illuminated phosphor will never compare to thumbing through the Sunday *Times*. This isn't romantic atavism, it's a simple matter of a screen not being able to provide the density of information that the eye can efficiently comprehend. A printed text is also easier for us to navigate because we can manipulate it in a direct, physical, and familiar way.

Type, typography, and the printed word have been a phenomenal success for five hundred years, and there's no reason for that to change. Though the situation for on-screen type will improve, it will never evolve to such an extent that readers will stop wanting to read printed type. Sadly, the goal of preserving quality typography in the digital sphere is at odds with many trends in personal computing and the Internet. But the printed word is, and will remain, as irreplaceable to readers as it is to typographers.

*Originally published in Volume 14, Number 3, 1996.*

# FACTS AND ARTIFACTS

# WE ARE WHAT WE WRITE

*Moira Cullen*

All that mankind has done, thought, gained, or been; it is lying as in
magic preservation in the pages of books.
    —*Thomas Carlyle,* The Hero as a Man of Letters

There was a need," explains Ellen Mazur Thompson, the librarian at Maryland's College of Art and Design. "I sensed that the students who came
to me in search of resource materials on graphic design were really at a loss.
I assured them there must be something if only I could just find it." But her
search proved fruitless: no fundamental reference guide to graphic design in
America was available for public access. Armed with a Whitney Carnegie grant
and the cooperation of the AIGA, Thompson set out on an eighteen-month quest
compiling over 1,300 entries from "material printed for mass consumption
during the last three hundred years of the American experience." The result is a
bibliography, *American Graphic Design, a Guide to the Literature.*

Thompson's bibliography is not the first attempt to map out the textual
landmarks of graphic design. She joins other dedicated individuals, primarily
librarians, educators, and curators, who have been willing to devote endless time
and effort (with little or no financial reward) to build a body of knowledge.

Back in 1977, Hugo McCauley, assistant professor of art and design at
the University of Illinois, compiled one of the earliest computer-generated
design bibliographies. The first phase of an ambitious project involving twenty-
six design schools in the United States and Canada, McCauley's data bank was
extensive, including more than 1,700 listings from methodology, sociology, and
history to creativity and proxemics. Contributors received listings and updated
copies for free, while others were charged $25 "to support the project." Financial
contributions were welcomed, but the project never advanced beyond its initial
debut.

Two years later, the British librarian Anthony J. Coulson completed what
Thompson and others consider the pioneering work in the bibliography of design
literature, *A Bibliography of Design in Britain, 1851–1970.* Complete with time
line and over seven thousand listings (books, monographs, journals, and magazine
articles), Coulson's guide was amply funded by the British Design Council, which
promoted it as "the first authoritative collection of published sources for design
and art historians, students, designers, researchers, and collectors."

ICOGRADA, the International Council of Graphic Design Associations, published *Design History Bibliography* in 1987. Prepared by Victor Margolin, associate professor of design history at the University of Illinois in Chicago, the publication was a "working multilingual bibliography," a noble attempt to compile worldwide design literature in support of the teaching and research of design history. Margolin's focus was on product and graphic design; some six hundred titles in English, French, Italian, German, Spanish, Arabic, Danish, Dutch, Korean, and Swedish were included. Lacking a groundswell of response despite a modest promotion, ICOGRADA shelved plans for a second edition.

In the United States, 1987 was also the year that Ellen Lupton, then curator of the Herb Lubalin Study Center of Design and Typography at Cooper Union, wrote *Graphic Design Bibliography: History and Theory*, a "representative, not exhaustive" listing of over one hundred sources. Lupton concentrated on the theory rather than the practice of design, purposely excluding visual source books. Thompson, on the other hand, responding as a librarian to the students' need to locate visual materials, included seventy-four entries in her bibliography under Visual Resources.

All of which underscores the role the bibliographer plays in the selection process. "Choice making is important," says Katherine McCoy, co-chair of the Department of Design at Cranbrook Academy. "Authorship of the bibliography needs to be acknowledged. Personal biases can't help but be reflected."

Selective bibliographies also form the basis of many an academic curriculum. "*Which* schools read *what* is as interesting as what they read," says Meredith Davis, president of the Graphic Design Education Association (GDEA). Consider the choices reflected in the hand-typed bibliography prepared by Alvin Eisenmann, former dean of graphic design at Yale: Noam Chomsky's *Language and Mind*, Apollinaire's *Calligrammes,* and Lévi-Strauss's *Tristes Tropiques.*

"Idiosyncratic" is how McCoy refers to Cranbrook's bibliography, which she credits in part to her passion for hanging out in used-book stores. "I remember when the only book in 1967 was Josef Müller-Brockmann's *The Graphic Artist and His Design Problems.* You had to go to New York to find it." (Müller-Brockmann's book does not appear in Thompson's guide.) Today, Cranbrook's bibliography contains twenty-two categories in design and architecture, including a Communication Meanings section that deals with thought processes and conceptual navigation. According to McCoy, the bibliography is "well used as a studio tool" and is a core element of the curriculum.

Rhode Island School of Design (RISD) also cultivates an active bibliography, says Sharon Helmer Poggenpohl, adjunct professor at RISD and editor of *Visible Language*, an indexed quarterly "concerned with all that is involved with our being literate." Each graduate student is required to submit an annotated bibliography, on disk, listing all resources used to develop his or her thesis.

But, for individuals and institutions alike, building a bibliography is no easy task. Problems begin with design's interdisciplinary scope, the same quality that eludes definition. "Design does not signify a class of objects that can be pinned down like butterflies," writes Margolin, who is also coordinating editor of *Design Issues*, the semiannual journal devoted to design history, theory, and criticism published by the University of Illinois. "It is an activity that is constantly changing." He adds, "You can't cover everything."

Then there's the issue of preservation. Compared with other fields—art history and architecture, for example—graphic design arrived late on the scene in an attempt to document its origins. "In the late sixties, we didn't even realize we had a history," says McCoy, "let alone the desire or the wherewithal to record it." Resources are limited as well. Periodicals see themselves as information centers for their readers, yet editors bemoan the scarcity of time, staff, and finances necessary to keep records. *Communication Arts* (*CA*), in its thirty-sixth year of publication, has a cross-referenced subject index of its first twenty-three volumes. In 1981, *CA* began indexing the previous volume in its January/February issue, according to managing editor Anne Telford, who maintains an index of the last three years of articles and columns in her computer. *I.D.* magazine, on the other hand, has no formal bibliographic index of its thirty-nine years in print. "The service is invaluable, but we can't afford it," says editor Chee Pearlman. "On top of that, we have no space for preservation. Anything earlier than 1964, forget it—it's long since destroyed." Professional associations, citing the same lack of funds and staff, also lag in their attempts to track their own publications. Anyone who has tried locating previous articles in this very journal knows how maddening a blind search can be.

The real issue, however, is readership. Few would argue the need for design bibliographies, but is there a market? Just how broad and how deep does interest in design literature lie? Can it extend beyond the walls of academe? After all, the primary users appear to be students whose needs are often outer-directed—the last-minute attempt to footnote a required research paper or complete a rare written assignment. One hasn't the sense that design bibliographies are valued guides to enrich one's own appreciation of design, or that they are enjoyed for the pleasures of a written text—reading what designers think rather than looking at what they do.

"Designers don't read," says Rob Dewey, director of communications at the American Center for Design (ACD). "It's a cliché, but the average designer is not going out of his or her way to do research." (Several years ago, the ACD also took a stab at generating an annotated bibliographic index of design organization periodicals. It received a muted response.) A further complication is that graphic design resources are no longer just in book form but are generated electronically.

But if design bibliographies are to have wider relevance, they must serve as resources beyond scholarship. What is really lacking is a platform to support a greater need—developing an authentic design community, design's equivalent to more established fields such as art or architecture. We need a culture in which critics, journalists, curators, and historians interact with academics and design professionals, each contributing to and making vigorous use of a growing body of literature and reference material. Ironically, technology is paving the way.

Even as promises of an information superhighway hover on the horizon, several ambitious initiatives are being developed. Just as they have integrated themselves into the design process, computers will link designers electronically to massive amounts of resources. In the broadest sense, bibliographies may have come of age.

The GDEA plans to launch a project to develop an electronic bibliography compiled from graduate-level design schools across the country. According to Meredith Davis, the goal is to provide a service to upgrade the literature, to increase the quality of sources available as course material. As Davis says, "People just don't know where to find things." The bibliography will concentrate on areas of methodology, history, and critical theory and will be available in disk form for easy updating. There are also plans to develop a much-needed glossary of design terminology. (Perhaps we'll be able to speak the same design language, professionals and foreign students alike.) The target audience will be institutions and faculty, but no market will be excluded.

Rochester Institute of Technology (RIT), along with Cooper Union and the University of Illinois at Chicago, is assembling a National Graphic Design Archive (NGDA), an electronic network of images and text in which everything from designers' letters to flat work will be captured digitally on videodisk. Primary samples of complete designer archives are also being preserved and indexed. Barbara J. Hodik, professor of art history at RIT's School of Art and Design, says, "Nobody really gets that serious about looking at the real thing anymore. Everything is being viewed digitally, at least for reference. It shortens the search." Hodik conceived the project, which is funded by the NEA and is currently being developed by Roger Remington, RIT's professor of graphic design.

The design archives initiative, according to Dewey, is "one of the most meaningful things happening in the field. It's a sign that the design profession is coming into its own." The ACD, in its own vision for the year 2000, anticipates that the field will be more interested in and involved with advanced planning supplemented by analytical skills. Dewey explains that the ACD plans to make a meaningful contribution to the profession by developing an online database focusing on critical thinking, scholarship, and research. Its goal is to act as an information clearinghouse for the strategic use of design education in the broadest sense.

And meanwhile, an often overlooked English reference steadily builds a reputation on the shelves. Since its first issue in 1988, *The Design and Applied Arts Index* (*daai*) has grown into a comprehensive international index of approximately 270 current design and design-related journals. Published twice a year by Design Documentation in Robertshire, East Sussex (with funding from the Wolfson Foundation for Decorative and Propaganda Arts in Miami), *daai* lists news items;

conference and seminar reports; reviews of books, video, films and exhibitions; obituary notices; and illustrations, in addition to major articles in English, French, and German. *Daai* has been set up as a database (accessed largely by European users), and though it is not yet available online, the publication claims it "can respond to users' inquiries either by post, telephone, or fax. Using links we have established with design/craft organizations, journal publishers, libraries, archives, and museums, both in the United Kingdom and elsewhere, we are now prepared to offer a general information service to subscribers."

Each of these initiatives is complementary. Collectively, they are leading indicators of an uncharted potential for collaboration, both electronic and professional. Today, there may be a lack of writing on design, but as more associations adopt publishing strategies instead of the typical event-based membership model, the volume (and quality) of written material stands to increase. Just as the vitality and breadth of future electronic exchanges can be expected to transform the publications in which designers and the design community participate.

It is time to share the wealth. Design bibliographies may be the missing link—serving as both facilitators and documenters of a design culture in the making.

*Originally published in Volume 11, Number 3, 1993.*

# ON DESIGN EPHEMERA

*Roy R. Behrens*

Thinking of design ephemera, I am reminded of a nineteenth-century Italian connoisseur named Giovanni Morelli, who discovered a way to distinguish between forgeries and authentic paintings. His method consisted of focusing on insignificant details, an earlobe or a fingernail, because it was in those "material trifles," as he called them—which everyone, painters and critics, ignored—that the differences between the counterfeit and the genuine were most apparent.

Morelli's method was possibly known to Sir Arthur Conan Doyle because there is a passage in "The Boscombe Valley Mystery" in which Sherlock Holmes admits, "You know my method. It is founded upon the observation of trifles." In another story, Holmes demonstrates that method when, in contrast to Watson, he focuses on the peripheral fact that a family dog did not bark at an intruder during a burglary.

Sigmund Freud undoubtedly knew about the method, for—in the essay "The Moses of Michelangelo"—he compared it to psychoanalysis, which, like Morelli's method, attempts to discover "secret and concealed things from the unconsidered or unnoticed details, from the rubbish heap, as it were, of our observations."

In its own time, graphic design customarily ends up in the rubbish heap of society's observations, before it is actually thrown out in the trash. Of insufficient importance to save and too impermanent to last, a design *ephēmeron* (from the Greek *ephēmeros,* "lasting a day") is likely to function as a material trifle—a dog that didn't bark, as the detail that everyone tends to ignore.

At its point of origin, the raison d'être of design is to empower other things—products, concepts, opportunities—to function as a parcel (literal or metaphoric), a carrier, a container for something that's being conveyed. As the background component of commerce, it is made to embellish some other event, and it lacks the preponderance of the thing advertised. To paraphrase Morelli, it serves as the jowls and earlobes for a figure whose dominant features consist of the eyes and the mouth, the real organs of expression.

But later, displaced from its own time, taken out of cultural context, isolated and split off from the function for which it was made, design ephemera may give the appearance of heightened significance. Its change of appearance may be as pronounced as the magic produced by color swatches through "simultaneous contrast" when shifted from one background to another, as proven by Chevreul in the nineteenth century, Albers in the twentieth. Its visibility is redoubled, and as antique or artifact, it takes on the reserve and sanctity of an exotic objet d'art.

As design ephemera ages, if it survives physically, it often adopts the appearance of art. Widowed, timeworn, and no longer an operative functional thing, it begins to look oddly poetic, as Joseph Cornell so adroitly explored when he made glass-enshrouded shrines by juxtaposing dime-store ephemera: brass rings, bottles, corks, and balls.

Like all of us, Cornell was indebted to Marcel Duchamp, who discovered that commonplace functional things (snow shovels, urinals, bottle racks) can be recycled as artwork simply by lifting them out of the realm of industrial design and literally placing them on a pedestal; and to Max Ernst, who created "collage novels" from the detritus of popular illustration by the willful confusion of species and limbs.

"We do not make art," wrote Charles Simic in *Dime-Store Alchemy: The Art of Joseph Cornell* (Ecco Press, 1992), "we find it." And one place in which it is frequently found is the rubbish heap of design ephemera.

*Originally published in Volume 11, Number 3, 1993.*

# THE PERFECT FACE

*Richard Hollis*

Since the beginning of the century we have been in a state of continuous revolution.

— *Siegfried Giedion,* Mechanization Takes Command

iegfried Giedion is best known for his huge historical studies *Space, Time and Architecture* and *Mechanization Takes Command.* Giedion practiced as a typographer in Zurich in the 1930s, was a friend of Moholy-Nagy, and in his books acknowledged Herbert Bayer for his help with layout. So it's odd that in neither book does he talk about printing. For Giedion, writing before the middle of the century, perfectibility and the concept of progress are already illusions. He distinguishes two categories of historical fact.

The first are "transitory facts": like the ruling tastes of the nineteenth century in painting, architecture, and furniture that he describes, they are an outgrowth of fashion. On the other hand, there are "constituent facts": "marked by creative forces and invention: by accumulation and accretion, they form the core of historical growth." In identifying the most important typeface of the twentieth century, can we use Giedion's ideas, however simplistically, to prevent our launching into mere opinion?

First, what of Giedion's continuous (technical) revolutions? In the transfer of type image to paper, they have been surprisingly undramatic. Today's principal techniques were all present in 1900: lithography (though not for texts), the reproduction of images by halftone screen (although not in very large sizes), and mechanical typesetting. Mechanical typesetting brought about the need and opportunity to rethink the design of typefaces, mainly for printing directly from metal and onto a rougher surface than that used today. Type changed little, while most paper, apart from book wove and newsprint, became smoother, harder, and whiter. In the 1930s, "art" paper for reproducing halftones from letterpress blocks was brilliantly white and glazed. (Bodoni, despite its extreme variation of curves and hair-serif line widths, was considered the ideal typeface for this surface.) Gravure printing took the letterform image even further from what was on the design office drawing board. For the design of typefaces, the overwhelming technical revolution occurred in the last decades of the century; after filmsetting, type was no longer designed to be produced for casting as metal for relief (letterpress) printing. Nowadays, the transfer of a type designer's work via the disk is unmediated by the requirements of a type foundry, by the scrutiny of its drawing office, or by the demands of its punchcutters.

For designers, the continuous revolution has been most marked by this diminishing dependence on specialists in the graphic and printing trades. Electronic and digital techniques have made it possible for typographic designers not only to take over the work of the printer in assembling pages, of the process house in handling images, and of the typesetter in generating text, but also of the type designer, the most specialized skill of all.

Type designers revolutionized the work of typographic designers (whose profession, of course, didn't exist at the turn of the century), by adding bold versions to the normal text weight of typefaces. This provided a means of emphasis in addition to italics. As revolutions, the upheavals in typesetting methods have far outweighed the importance of new type designs. Setting metal type by hand or machine made mixing fonts difficult: the number of matrices available to the typecaster was limited, and few types had a common baseline. Type could not be spaced more closely than the metal allowed. With photosetting, these restrictions disappeared.

There is a paradox in Giedion's views on historical categories. Among the mysteries of print are both the persistence of the forms of the Roman alphabet and the consistent aesthetic attitudes to them over several centuries. A lay observer could easily be puzzled by the survival of serifs on recent typeface designs. Yet it is often suggested that type designs typify the period of their production. Adrian Frutiger, perhaps the best-known twentieth-century type designer, has claimed, "Type design endeavors to fall in line with contemporary industrial design, architecture, and landscape planning." Frutiger has illustrated Baskerville and Plantin next to an elegant horse-drawn open carriage and juxtaposed his own Univers with the French Caravelle airliner of the 1950s.

Is it this possibility, for a design to represent characteristics of its age, yet transcend them, which places typefaces in the category of constituent facts? The types that carry a heavy burden of contemporaneity would seem inevitably consigned to the transitory group. (And here we must distinguish true type designs intended for continuous text from alphabets of lettering, such as Cassandre's Bifur and the Italian Eurostile.)

These transitory typefaces, from the graphic designer's point of view, are most useful when they are new: they associate their message with contemporary attitudes. They will always be there, ready to be reclaimed from the dustbin of history. The contemporary will have become retro, representative of its period.

As constituent facts, we can classify the most obvious pre-twentieth-century designs: Bembo, Garamond, Plantin, and Baskerville; Bodoni and Walbaum; Century. Here we come to the difficulty of "display" typefaces, or those not designed for extended text setting; first the Clarendons, and then the grotesques, which would include Franklin and News Gothic and the European jobbing (Akzidenz) grotesques.

Grotesques raise difficult issues, even political questions. Grotesques date from the nineteenth century, yet they dominated the visual revolutions of central Europe from the 1920s on. The most obviously twentieth-century typefaces, the geometrical monoline sans types such as Kabel (Cable), Erbar, and Futura of the 1920s, were rarely adopted by the uncompromising avant-garde of the time. There is no evidence to suggest that there was a consciously "workerist" intention in modernist designers' use of nineteenth-century grotesques meant for advertisements. But the machine aesthetic of the monoline sans, which in France associated its forms with ocean liners and luxury motor cars, was a far cry from the utopian aim of using industrial production to provide housing and make well-designed domestic goods cheaply available. Linked to chic, with consequent elitist overtones, the monoline sans seems to belong with the transitory.

The questionable readability of sans in text has been responsible for the surviving production of serif types. But the variables of intercharacter, interword, and interline spacing that affect readability also affect the appearance of the type itself, whose character fit had been assured when type was generated as metal. The typographic designer can now manipulate typeforms on the screen to the margins of illegibility. Digitization has taken away many of the technical considerations. What you see is what you get when it is printed. The image of the letterform sits there on the surface, without ink spread, without indenting the paper.

Those who believe, like Giedion, that commercial and technical pressures decide historical significance will be obliged to choose Univers, if only for the richness of its reference. Its design acknowledges the existence of the nineteenth-century grotesque, but gives it an optical refinement that makes it suitable for text. Its humanistic, calligraphic references point back in history and challenge contemporary designs of the period, particularly Helvetica, which refined the grotesque's form.

Univers was aptly named. Its design can be used to demonstrate a particularly Cartesian, and therefore French, logic in the organization of its different weights and widths (compared with the irregular budding and flowering of, say, Century's offshoots).

It nevertheless takes into account national languages. We have to consider not only the period to which a typeface belongs, but the influence of its country of origin. Apart, obviously, from black letter or Cyrillic, there is no clear national association with a letterform. But language has a bearing on this: the frequency of capital letters in German; the accents in languages derived from Latin; repeated combinations of certain letters in any language—these all affect the typeface's visual rhythm. The Swiss, without a single national language, are especially sensitive to these nuances.

Univers bridged several revolutions in technology. It can even be said that its design expresses them. Belonging to the moment when type generation was moving from inked-metal letterpress to photographic processes, it was designed as drawn letters to allow for optical or chemical distortion—particularly the filling in of acute angles, either in the photographic process or in the printing. It was made by mechanical punchcutting for metal type, used for Monotype and Linotype, for every form of film and photosetting matrix, for strike-on typewriter composers, and for digital systems. As a face for designers, it became the standby for the new wave (partly because it was widely available). But it was also the standard face to give an up-to-date look. In this way, Univers exemplifies the significant changes of the middle of the century. It is the only twentieth-century typeface that can safely be categorized with Giedion's "constituent facts."

*Originally published in Volume 14, Number 3, 1996.*

# IS THERE A CANON OF GRAPHIC DESIGN HISTORY?
*Martha Scotford*

**A** *canon,* defined by the *American Heritage Dictionary* as it might relate to graphic design, is a basis for judgment; a standard; a criterion; an authoritative list (as of the works of an author or designer). The word was originally used to designate the books of the Bible officially recognized by the Church. The concept of *canon* is under debate right now in literary/educational circles, as its existence is alleged to produce a culturally narrow and elitist university curriculum, among other cultural problems.

Having followed the discussion about the problems arising from the study of literature produced mainly by Western white males, it occurred to me that the study of graphic design history, coming out of its infancy, may be producing its own canon, perhaps unintentionally and unconsciously. What would such a canon consist of? Are there designers and works that are used to represent whole periods, styles, and theories in graphic design history? Are some designers' works more revered than others? Why? Judgments are implied when certain designers and works become better known than others; is this process wholly legitimate and deserved? What is it based on? What problems will it cause for the future study of graphic design history?

## PREMISE

I want to make it very clear at the outset that in suggesting a canon here, I do not wish to perpetuate one; only to show one may exist for the purpose of discussion. Given what I believe is its unintentional nature, it may be that there are "mistakes": this could be *a* canon, but not *the* canon of graphic design. It could very well be that some designers and their work do not belong here or that others have been overlooked.

If a canon of graphic design exists, or is developing, how can this be proved? The specific period I am discussing here, modern graphic design, is broadly dated as beginning in 1850. Given the visual nature of the subject, it is most strongly established and communicated in a visual way, i.e., by reproduction, especially in books. Exhibitions and poster reproductions could also be studied, but books seem the most widely available and least ephemeral source at present to explore the presence of a canon.

## METHOD

Five books were chosen for the study; these represent the best known general historical surveys of the past twenty years. The following is a description, alphabetical by author, of each volume and explains the criteria cited by the authors (with page reference noted) used for the inclusion of design works in each of the volumes. It also includes the limitations, if any, of each for the purposes of this study.

1. James Craig and Bruce Barton, *Thirty Centuries of Graphic Design* (Watson-Guptill Publications, New York, 1987), 224 pages; 10 pages for study period; 400 black-and-white illustrations. The subtitle, "An Illustrated Survey," accurately describes the prolific use of reproductions over text. The text is more in outline form than prose, and is often in the form of timelines, lists, and technical sidebars. The book starts with prehistory and includes more discussion and reproductions of the fine art concurrent with graphic design than do the other books in this study. "Designers and illustrators have been carefully selected to show diversity and to create a feel for a specific period." (Page 9.)

2. Alan Fern and Mildred Constantine, *Word and Image* (Museum of Modern Art, New York, 1968), 160 pages; 138 pages devoted to study period; 211 illustrations, 30 in full color. The most limited resource, in subject matter, for this study because it is restricted to posters and to those in the MoMA collection. However, it is critical because posters, collected and saved, have always been one of the most prominent and important media in graphic design and its history. In addition, this particular collection is large and well regarded. It must be accepted that there have been judgments at all levels: what was selected for the collection and then what was chosen for inclusion in the book (about 10 percent of the collection). Critical selection is what makes a canon. The preface to the books states that works for the collection have been "selected primarily for their aesthetic quality, but also include work of mainly historical or social significance." (Constantine, page 6.)

In his essay's introduction, Fern states that the book "is a brief history of the modern poster (and its close typographical relatives) as an art form . . . I have limited my investigations to those designers who have approached the poster as a means of expression as well as communication, and have explored graphic design and typography as serious creative media." (Page 11.)

3. Steven Heller and Seymour Chwast, *Graphic Style: From Victorian to Postmodern* (Harry N. Abrams, New York, 1988), 238 pages; 233 for study period;

over 700 illustrations, 225 in color. This is the most recent publication and covers exactly the period under discussion. The book is a survey like the others, but makes no attempt at scholarly analysis. Rather, it "is primarily concerned with the images, not the image maker . . . we consistently emphasize the formal, emblematic visual characteristics of a design period . . . we are tracing nothing less than the evolution of the popular tastes of the period." (Page 12.)

This is the only volume among the five to concentrate on visual form. It is notable for its many anonymous pieces and for the breadth of its visual offerings.

4. Philip B. Meggs, *A History of Graphic Design* (Van Nostrand Reinhold, New York, 1983), 511 pages; 335 pages on study period; over 1,000 illustrations, all black-and-white. The first survey published in the United States, this book appeared just as many design programs were incorporating graphic design history into their curricula. It has become the textbook for such courses and the standard reference for design professionals. The author expresses the necessity for the understanding of the past so "we will be better able to continue a cultural legacy of beautiful form and effective communication." (Page xi.) The survey begins with the invention of writing after the pictograph and petroglyphs of prehistoric times.

5. Josef Müller-Brockmann, *A History of Visual Communication* (Niggli/Teufen, Switzerland, 1971), 334 pages; 214 for study period; 570 illustrations, 6 in color. The only European publication among the five, this was the first historical survey of the subject to be published. It explores the wide scope of the field that its well-known author/designer considers more accurately termed *visual communication* than *graphic design.* He states that the survey is not complete, but he has "concentrated on those aspects of particular interest to me: factual advertising, experiments which influence our thinking, and artistic works which set the stylistic trend." (Page 6.) The book begins its discussion with prehistoric cave paintings and early writing forms.

### CRITERIA FOR ANALYSIS

Having selected these books for study, what are the criteria for tabulating what is published in them? One, of course, is the visual imprint—how certain works and designers are made more memorable than others by differences controlled by size, color, and repetition. A caveat is in order: I have no pretensions to being a social scientist and have developed the tabulation system here as a way to prove relative rather than absolute presence of designers and works. I have been as accurate as possible with the tabulation, and the numerical interpretation (using the median and setting the categories) is governed by my desire to be inclusive. It is hoped that no one will waste time recounting the numbers. That is not the point.

The study began with the creation of a list (alphabetical by author), tabulating each reproduction of a design work and noting whether that reproduction is black-and-white or color, and its relative size to other work in the book. In general, small is any size up to one-quarter page; medium is one third to two thirds of a page; large is two thirds to full page. Once this list of 286 designers/partners was compiled for each book, and the information from all books was combined, the list was edited to cull a list of all the designers (205) who were represented at least twice among the five books: either a single work reproduced in two different books, or two different works shown in one or two books. The list was then studied to discover what patterns of appearance might exist among the designers and the works that could prove a canon existed. It could then describe what it contained. Once this tabulation was complete, these findings were broken down even further to study other criteria for each designer:

1. Total number of individual works reproduced.
2. Total number of all works reproduced.
3. Number of repeats (#2 minus #1).
4. Total number of large reproductions.
5. Total number of medium reproductions.
6. Number of large and medium reproductions (#4 plus #5).
7. Total number of color reproductions.
8. Total number of large reproductions in color.
9. Total number of single works reproduced four times (four books).
10. Total number of single works reproduced three times.
11. Total number of single works reproduced twice in color.
12. Country of birth/significant practice.
13. Gender.
14. Born before 1900.
15. Born 1900–1919.
16. Born 1920–1929.
17. Born 1930–1939.
18. Born after 1940.
19. Deceased.

From the edited list of 205 designers, a smaller list (63) was made of designers/partners who had a significant appearance in at least one category of the first eleven. *Significant* was defined as having a number two-below the median for that category or higher. The results of this operation were studied and the absolute lack of women was duly noted. I decided to include on the list those women designers (6 out of 14) having the highest frequency of reproduced works. As well, a very few other well-known designers were allowed, whose numbers were just below the cutoff point and were interesting in relation to the others. I fully realize this might be a canon trap in itself; my reasoning is that one instinctively looks for certain designers and would want to see these numbers for comparison. I think these inclusions strengthen the example.

## DISCOVERING THE CANON

The table on the opposite page gives the corresponding numbers for the sixty-three designers/partners and each criteria. These are not scores or ratings; this is not a contest. These numbers reveal the relative weight/importance that these specific five books have placed on certain designers and works.

The numbers in bold are those that are considered significant for the final cut of the list; these fall at or above the median for each category. This again seems the broadest way to include individuals. You will notice a range in the amount of bold numbers among the designers. There are eleven categories; it was decided that if a designer had bold numbers in five or more categories (that is, a significant showing in eleven criteria), that designer had been consistently "featured" by the majority of the books and could be considered part of the canon of graphic design. The table here produces a canon of eight designers (in alphabetical order): Herbert Bayer, A. M. Cassandre, El Lissitzky, Herbert Matter, László Moholy-Nagy, Josef Müller-Brockmann, Henri de Toulouse-Lautrec, and Piet Zwart.

## INTERPRETING THE CANON

What do we notice about this group? First, and more about this later, the canon is all male. They were all born before 1920, several before 1900, and all but one (Müller-Brockmann) are deceased. They are all native Europeans: two are from Eastern Europe (Lissitzky and Moholy-Nagy; Cassandre was born in Russia to French parents, but left Russia to attend school); two are French (Cassandre and Toulouse-Lautrec); two are Swiss (Müller-Brockmann and Matter); one is Austrian (Bayer); and one is Dutch (Zwart).

Are there surprises here? Perhaps the only surprise is Toulouse-Lautrec, who, though considering him important to poster history, most would not expect to make the graphic design canon. One should question the inclusion of Müller-Brockmann because he is the author of one of the books; however, records seem to indicate he has been approximately as generous to himself as was Meggs.

More surprises in the inclusion area: chauvinistically, we might murmur, "What, no Americans?" And there are several poster "masters"—you can fill in your favorites—who might be expected on the list. Each period/style has its heroes, but, across the broad survey period, it is difficult for these individuals to stand out consistently. There are also several designers who have very respectable showings in the category of "number of reproductions," but who have not been set apart by size or color of such.

A possible explanation for some of these exclusions may be the nature of the work. For instance, Armin Hofmann's revered posters are originally in black and white, so featuring him by a color category is difficult. (This is one example of the possible disservice to individual designers by the criteria used for this list.) Another designer in a similar situation is William Morris. He worked as a graphic designer primarily in book design; books are mostly printed in black and white.

| DESIGNER | Total # individual works reproduced | Total # works reproduced | Total # repeats | Total # large | Total # medium | Large & Medium | Total # in color | Total# large & in color | Total # × 4 | Total# × 3 | Total# × 2 and in color | Born before 1900 | Born 1900–1919 | Born 1920–1929 | Born 1930–1939 | Born 1940 | Deceased | Country of birth/significant practice |
|---|---|---|---|---|---|---|---|---|---|---|---|---|---|---|---|---|---|---|
| *MEDIAN* | *18* | *23* | *5* | *3* | *8* | *11* | *3* | *1* | *1* | *2* | *1* | | | | | | | |
| Baumberger | 4 | 4 | 0 | 3 | 1 | 4 | 1 | *1* | 0 | 0 | 0 | • | | | | | • | Switzerland |
| **Bayer** | **30** | **40** | **10** | **4** | **17** | **21** | **0** | **0** | **2** | **1** | **0** | | • | | | | • | **Austria/Germany** |
| Beardsley | 16 | 16 | 0 | 1 | 3 | 4 | 1 | 0 | 0 | 0 | 0 | • | | | | | • | Great Britian |
| Beggarstaff | 5 | 8 | *3* | 3 | 2 | 5 | 0 | 0 | 0 | 1 | 0 | • | | | | | • | Great Britian |
| Behrens | 11 | 17 | *6* | 1 | 6 | 7 | 0 | 0 | *1* | 0 | 0 | • | | | | | • | Germany |
| Bernhard | 9 | 12 | 3 | 2 | 2 | 4 | *3* | 1 | 0 | 1 | *1* | • | | | | | • | Germany |
| Bill | 15 | 19 | 4 | *3* | *9* | 12 | 0 | 0 | 0 | 1 | 0 | | • | | | | ? | Switzerland |
| Binder | 5 | 9 | 4 | 0 | 2 | 2 | 0 | 0 | *1* | 0 | 0 | • | | | | | • | Austria |
| Bonnard | 3 | 6 | 3 | 1 | 4 | 5 | 1 | 0 | 0 | 1 | 0 | • | | | | | • | France |
| Bradley | *18* | 19 | 1 | 0 | 6 | 6 | 1 | 0 | 0 | 0 | 0 | • | | | | | • | United States |
| Brodovitch | 14 | 15 | 1 | 0 | 5 | 5 | 1 | 0 | 0 | 0 | 0 | • | | | | | • | Russia/France/U.S. |
| Carlu | 5 | 9 | 4 | 2 | 3 | 5 | 2 | *1* | *1* | 0 | 0 | | • | | | | • | France |
| Casey* | 4 | 4 | 0 | 0 | 2 | 2 | 0 | 0 | 0 | 1 | 0 | | | • | | | • | United States |
| **Cassandre** | **19** | **27** | **8** | **6** | **12** | **18** | **7** | **2** | **0** | **3** | **1** | | • | | | | • | **Russia/France** |
| Cheret | 11 | 15 | 4 | 1 | 7 | 8 | 2 | 0 | 0 | 2 | 0 | • | | | | | • | France |
| Chermayeff & Geismar | 15 | 15 | 0 | 0 | 5 | 5 | 0 | 0 | 0 | 0 | 0 | | | | • | | | Great Britain/U.S. |
| Erdt | 2 | 4 | 2 | 1 | 1 | 2 | 1 | 0 | 0 | 1 | 0 | • | | | | | • | Germany |
| Glaser | 11 | 12 | 1 | 1 | 1 | 2 | 0 | 0 | 0 | 0 | 0 | | | • | | | | United States |
| Golden | 5 | 7 | 2 | 0 | 2 | 2 | 0 | 0 | 0 | 1 | 0 | | • | | | | • | United States |
| Grasset | 8 | 10 | 2 | 0 | 3 | 3 | 0 | 0 | 0 | 1 | 0 | • | | | | | • | France |
| Greiman* | 8 | 9 | 1 | 1 | 2 | 3 | 0 | 0 | 0 | 0 | 0 | | | | | • | | United States |
| Heartfield | *19* | 19 | 0 | 0 | 5 | 5 | 2 | 0 | 0 | 0 | 0 | • | | | | | • | Germany |
| Hofmann | 11 | 12 | 1 | 1 | 3 | 4 | 2 | 0 | 0 | 0 | 0 | | | • | | | | Switzerland |
| Hohlwein | 12 | 17 | 5 | 2 | *10* | 12 | *3* | 0 | 0 | 1 | 0 | • | | | | | • | Germany |
| Huber | 7 | 1 | 2 | 2 | 4 | 0 | 0 | 0 | 0 | 0 | 0 | | • | | | | | Switzerland/Italy |
| Huszar | 7 | 10 | 3 | 0 | 4 | 4 | 1 | 0 | 0 | 1 | 0 | • | | | | | • | Netherlands |
| Kamekura | 10 | 12 | 2 | 1 | 2 | 3 | 0 | 0 | 0 | 1 | 0 | | • | | | | | Japan |
| Kauffer | 16 | 20 | 4 | 4 | 4 | 8 | 5 | *2* | 0 | 0 | 0 | • | | | | | • | U.S./Great Britain |
| **Lissitzky** | **39** | **49** | **10** | **6** | **17** | **23** | **4** | **3** | **1** | **4** | **1** | • | | | | | • | **Russia/Germany** |
| Lubalin | *21* | 21 | 0 | 0 | 5 | 5 | 0 | 0 | 0 | 0 | 0 | | • | | | | • | United States |
| Macintosh | 5 | 9 | 4 | 0 | 8 | 8 | 2 | 0 | 0 | 1 | 0 | • | | | | | • | Great Britain |
| Marinetti | 6 | 10 | 4 | 0 | 2 | 2 | 0 | 0 | 0 | 1 | 0 | • | | | | | • | Italy |
| **Matter** | **16** | **25** | **9** | **4** | **9** | **13** | **3** | **1** | **1** | **1** | **0** | | • | | | | • | **Switzerland/U.S.** |
| **Moholy-Nagy** | **18** | **23** | **5** | **1** | **11** | **12** | **2** | **1** | **0** | **1** | **0** | • | | | | | • | **Hungary/Germany/US** |
| Morris | 9 | 13 | 4 | *3* | 3 | 6 | 0 | 0 | 0 | 0 | 0 | • | | | | | • | Great Britain |
| Moscoso | 5 | 6 | 1 | 0 | 3 | 3 | 4 | 0 | 0 | 0 | 0 | | | | • | | • | United States |
| Moser | 16 | 7 | 0 | 7 | 7 | 2 | 0 | *1* | 1 | 0 | 0 | • | | | | | • | Austria |
| Mucha | 12 | 12 | 0 | 1 | 5 | 6 | 2 | 0 | 0 | 1 | 0 | • | | | | | • | Czechoslovakia/France |
| **Müller-Brockmann** | **14** | **23** | **9** | **3** | **12** | **15** | **4** | **1** | **0** | **3** | **1** | | • | | | | | **Switzerland** |
| Neuberg | 7 | 7 | 0 | 2 | 2 | 4 | 1 | *1* | 0 | 0 | 0 | | • | | | | ? | Switzerland |
| Philips | 5 | 5 | 0 | 1 | 0 | 1 | *5* | *1* | 0 | 0 | 0 | • | | | | | • | United States |
| Rand | *24* | 28 | 4 | 2 | 7 | 9 | 0 | 0 | 0 | 0 | 0 | | • | | | | | United States |
| Ray | 5 | 3 | 2 | 0 | 4 | 4 | 0 | 0 | 0 | 1 | 0 | • | | | | | • | U.S./France |
| Rodchenko | *18* | 18 | 0 | 1 | 7 | 8 | *5* | 0 | 0 | 0 | 0 | • | | | | | • | Russia |
| Roller | 6 | 8 | 2 | 0 | 3 | 3 | 1 | 0 | 0 | 1 | 0 | • | | | | | • | Austria |
| Rudin* | 5 | 5 | 0 | 2 | 4 | 5 | 0 | 0 | 0 | 0 | 0 | | | • | | | | Switzerland |
| Schlemmer | 3 | 5 | 2 | 0 | 2 | 2 | 0 | 0 | 0 | 1 | 0 | • | | | | | • | Germany |
| Schuitema | 7 | 7 | 0 | 2 | 3 | 5 | 0 | 0 | 0 | 0 | 0 | • | | | | | • | Netherlands |
| Schmidt | 8 | 13 | *5* | 0 | 7 | 7 | 0 | 0 | *1* | 0 | 0 | • | | | | | • | Germany |
| Schultz-Neu | 1 | 3 | 2 | 0 | 2 | 2 | 1 | 0 | 0 | 1 | 0 | • | | | | | • | Germany |
| Schwitters | 11 | 13 | 2 | 2 | 2 | 4 | *3* | 1 | 0 | 0 | 0 | • | | | | | • | Germany |
| Sutnar | *23* | 25 | 2 | 0 | 7 | 7 | 0 | 0 | 0 | 0 | 0 | • | | | | | • | Czechoslovakia/U.S. |
| Thompson | 10 | 10 | 0 | 3 | 5 | 5 | 1 | 0 | 0 | 0 | 0 | | • | | | | • | United States |
| Tissi* | 5 | 6 | 1 | 0 | 0 | 0 | 1 | 0 | 0 | 0 | 0 | | | | | • | | Switzerland |
| **Toulouse-Lautrec** | **11** | **17** | *6* | **2** | **12** | **14** | **5** | **2** | **0** | **0** | **1** | • | | | | | • | **France** |
| Tschichold | *20* | 20 | 4 | 2 | *8* | 10 | 1 | *1* | 0 | 1 | 0 | | • | | | | • | Germany/Switzerland |
| van de Velde | 6 | 9 | 3 | 0 | 5 | 5 | 1 | 0 | *1* | 0 | 0 | • | | | | | • | Belgium |
| VanDoesberg | 9 | 12 | 3 | 1 | 3 | 4 | *4* | *1* | 0 | 1 | 0 | • | | | | | • | Netherlands |
| Vivarelli | 7 | 10 | 3 | 1 | 6 | 7 | 0 | 0 | *1* | 0 | 0 | | • | | | | ? | Switzerland |
| Weingart | 14 | 14 | 0 | 0 | 3 | 3 | 2 | 0 | 0 | 0 | 0 | | | | | • | | Switzerland |
| Wyman & Terr | 7 | 8 | 1 | *3* | 5 | 8 | 0 | 0 | 0 | 0 | 0 | | | | • | | | United States |
| Yokoo | 7 | 8 | 1 | 1 | 2 | 3 | *4* | *1* | 0 | 0 | 0 | | | | • | | | Japan |
| **Zwart** | **21** | **29** | *8* | **1** | **14** | **15** | **0** | **0** | **0** | **1** | **0** | • | | | | | • | **Netherlands** |

**boldface = Canon**    *Female    (Median) numbers in italic*

Other designers, working mainly with typography, are using smaller formats that are seldom reproduced in a large format.

One case struck me as a serious misrepresentation of the designer's work, not in the number of reproductions, but the nature of them. Cheret's posters were and are important for their pioneering use of color, both technically in historical terms and aesthetically for the richness of the effects he achieved in lithography. Yet, these five books present only two of his works in color.

Interestingly, after the initial curiosity of discovering the canon's identity, the rest of the list shows how different designers are represented in the books, and brings to mind those designers who have not made the edited (and amended) list of sixty-three. Here, in my opinion, are the more intriguing cases of inclusion and exclusion.

The most obvious distinction, about which I do not intend to get polemical, is that of gender. There are no women in this canon. There are six women represented on the edited/amended list, four of them independent designers. (Margaret and Frances McDonald were part of the Mackintosh group and had less to do with graphics than other design formats.) The numbers for the independent four indicate they are poorly represented in all categories. There may be explanations, but not many excuses: the women are all younger than the men (two of the women born in the 1920s, one in the 1930s, one in the 1940s) and therefore have had shorter careers (less production is not always a correlation). But even comparing the two oldest, Casey and Rudin, with male designers of their generation, Glaser and Hofmann, produces a serious discrepancy. And the youngest woman, Greiman, is reproduced more frequently than the rest, but not featured as well as the second youngest, Tissi. Once we have passed into the post–World War II generation, there are many more female designers from which to choose, but this option has not been exercised. Possibly, there are problems with critical distance, yet the contributions of Muriel Cooper, Barbara Stauffacher Soloman, and Sheila Levrant de Bretteville (among others) have been recognized elsewhere.

As stated before, I believe the canon that exists was unintentionally created. That is, each book in the study is an individual set of decisions. But what were all those decisions based on? Aesthetics? Economics? And who made the decisions? Authors? Publishers? Book designers? Clive Dilnot pointed to this problem in 1984, before several of the books used for this study were published: "At present, there is no real discipline of design criticism, but a canonical list of 'important' design and designers is rapidly being established, despite that the critical arguments for their inclusion in such a list remain almost unstated. We are seeing this sharp differentiation into 'important' and 'unimportant' design works, which is tending to exclude the unimportant works from the definition of design and to restrict the material we actually discuss."[1]

Each book is a different and separate case, and no specific research has been done by me on this aspect. But one anecdotal piece of evidence leads me to suspect the general logic I would otherwise credit to the authors: the relative and real sizes of the reproductions in each book are related to the design format of that book. One assumes the authors of each are selecting the pieces to be reproduced, and that they have some reasonable idea of what they consider more or less important for their particular presentation—and would seek to express this by size and color. However, Phil Meggs has told me that the publisher's designer did the layouts for his book and, as that particular inexperienced designer was not a historian, the design works were used to fill six pages as needed. For purposes of the canon, this is the reality that the reader finds, assuming there are few other resources for the beginning graphic design student.

There may be some other practical issues affecting the canon. The availability of works for reproduction is affected by several factors. Some works that a conscientious author would want to show are not available due to collection restrictions, or the cost of permission is prohibitive. There may be copyright restrictions. In many cases, where no source is given for the work, it is from a private collection that may also be that of the author. How does this affect selection? In only one area might it be salutary: the increased inclusion of anonymous work.

What about color? Two of the five books have no color reproductions at all; one (Müller-Brockmann) has very few. The decision is mainly about economics, the trade-off being the ability to print more black-and-white illustrations rather than fewer in black and white plus a few in full color. A cursory inspection of *Word and Image* shows that the appearance of a poster in color may have more to do with its location relative to page imposition than with aesthetics or critical importance. Looking through *Graphic Style* also reveals that specific pages in each signature are available for color; it is hard to assess how much this dictates to the authors and how much they will work within this production limitation. *The History of Visual Communication*, with so few reproductions in color (only six), may be the only book to express an accurate opinion with color.

Does this dismiss color as a criteria? Yes and no. Since it is my belief that this canon and the list it generates are unconsciously created, we need not be concerned with the lack of control on the author's part over color, but we do need to deal with the reality of the reader. Not knowing and/or not concerned about bookmaking, the reader may naturally assume color has significance and will pay more attention to and remember works shown in color. If we consider color a noncategory, given this discussion, what happens to the canon if color is removed as a criterion? Left with eight criteria (the median then becomes four), are there significant changes? No, the eight designers remain and no one is added. The color categories remain.

As I have mentioned, many designers' works have been reproduced in healthy numbers; that is, the books have provided a reasonably broad presentation of the possible designer pool (exceptions as noted). Some designers you might have expected in the canon have a strong presence in the books, based on frequency of appearance: Beardsley, Bill, Bradley, Brodovitch, Chermayeff and

Geismar, Heartfield, Hohlwein, Kauffer, Lubalin, Rand, Rodchenko, Sutnar, Tschichold, and Weingart. If this group is added to the Canon Eight, we get a much broader selection by geography/nationality and by generation (but still no women).

You will undoubtedly have thought of some designers you consider important and will have attempted to find them on the list here. Lustig and Danziger are two that come to mind. They both have considerable western U.S. connections. Is there bias for the East Coast in this list? De Harak and Vignelli are two others who do not appear on the final list. It is true that it takes time for judgments of historical and contemporary importance of individual designers to be made. This is the most obvious reason we see so few postwar generation designers represented: careers are not long enough yet; the time-distance is not sufficient, and there are so many more to choose among than in the case of earlier generation designers. The same cannot be said for the generation born in the twenties and thirties; they are quite sparse on the list here and have certainly developed their work/careers sufficiently for us to assess it.

The canon and the list are Western biased (First and Second worlds). Some of the books have sought to partially redress the imbalance with some work from the Far East and Third World nations. Japan, as the Eastern nation with the most highly developed (in a Western sense) graphic design, is represented by two designers: Kamakura, of the first generation to adapt Western/Swiss design, and Yokoo, much younger and influential here in the early seventies. They are better represented than any of the women.

Other questions and comparisons will occur to you. Feel free to use the table to satisfy your curiosity. There are even some silly discoveries: accounting for variations among languages, the most popular name for a designer is William (eight); the second most popular is John, and the third is a tie between Herbert and Henry. For national chauvinists, looking at geographical distribution and birthplace, we find the U.S. with thirteen, Switzerland with eleven, and Germany with ten. Consider population size.

## PROBLEMS FOR THE FUTURE

Is the existence of a canon a problem? Is this canon a problem? A canon creates heroes, superstars, and iconographies. In singling out individual designers and works, we may lose sight of the range of communication, expression, concepts, techniques, and formats that make up the wealth of graphic design history. As we attempt to become more objective and critical, it will also be harder to assess the "stars."

The existence of a graphic design canon, so early in the development of graphic design history and criticism, may focus too much attention and research in certain areas, to the exclusion of others equally significant. A canon reduces a lot of material (designers, works, facts, biographies, influences, etc.) to a smaller and perhaps more manageable package. Fewer names and works may make it easier to teach and learn and even to imitate, but reduces the rich, complex, and interrelated history that truly exists. If we narrow the field now, it will take much longer and be much more difficult to properly study and understand our cultural and professional heritage. For students new to the study of graphic design, a canon creates the impression that they need go no further; the best is known, the rest is not worth knowing. This is unfair, dangerous, and shortsighted.

The existence of a canon is the result of a natural reliance on art history (and on the example of architectural history) as a model for studying graphic design history. There are other ways of looking at, and exploring, graphic design history. These may well result in other ways of understanding and categorizing design works: by explicit and/or implicit content, by communication intent, by communication concept, by audience, by visual/verbal language, etc. The master/masterpiece approach also dismisses the existence (and possible importance) of anonymous works. How can the study of ephemera ignore the significance and influence of this category of works? Graphic design work will always, and finally, reveal its cultural origins. These origins need not be a particular person to be appreciated and understood; the origins can well be a specific time and place and people. With a perspective closer to *cultural* history than to *art* history (with its implied elitist flavor), we might come closer to a realistic and meaningful evaluation of our design cultural heritage.

Whether we agree that there should be a canon or not, I submit one exists and is being created, and that this process will continue at an increased pace as graphic design history develops further through publications, exhibitions, scholarship, and collections. We need to evaluate and control the process; if we need a canon, if we really need to label and separate, we need to assess better what canon exists and to amend it to make it intentional, conscious, responsible, and truly meaningful for all.

*Note*

1. Dilnot, Clive, "The State of Design History, Part II: Problem and Possibilities," *Design Issues* vol. 1, no. 2, Fall 1984.

*Originally published in Volume 9, Number 2, 1991.*

# IS A DESIGN HISTORY CANON REALLY DANGEROUS?

*Philip B. Meggs*

**M**artha Scotford's article "Is There a Canon of Graphic Design History?" makes fascinating use of statistical data. By studying the number, size, and black-and-white versus color reproduction of works by 205 designers, included in more than one of five design history books, she suggests that a canon may be emerging and warns of its dangers.

Significant philosophical and cultural differences exist between the authors of these books. Josef Müller-Brockmann (*A History of Visual Communication*, 1971) is a Swiss modernist whose life and work centers upon constructivism and geometric purism, while Steven Heller (*Graphic Style: From Victorian to Postmodern*, 1988) is a New York art director with a strong interest in illustration, political statement, and expressionism. As one might expect, the designers and works selected by these authors are vastly different. Müller-Brockmann's book focuses upon Central Europeans who immigrated to America (Bayer, Burtin, Moholy-Nagy, and Matter), while Heller's book includes over eighty Americans.

William Morris, who played key roles in defining the late nineteenth-century design agenda, has faded with the passage of time, while the history of the late twentieth-century is still being formed. Contemporary designers whose work might lead to their being singled out as major design forces are still evolving. Anthropologist Edmund Carpenter observed that he didn't know who discovered water, but it sure wasn't the fish. This quip crystallizes our difficulties in recording history as it is being made; the most ubiquitous works might actually be highly significant to the next generation of designers and design historians, but overlooked today as contemporary design critics respond to the shock of the new.

I doubt that indexes such as the size, position, and color of reproductions in books mean anything, because factors other than the insignificance of the work influence these decisions. In Müller-Brockmann's book, a rigorous three-column grid on a horizontal page becomes a governing force. Heller told me that there were things in his book he wanted to accomplish editorially that conflicted with things designer Seymour Chwast wished to do with the layout: Heller's editorial desires prevailed on some spreads; Chwast's layout concepts prevailed on others.

A striking example of pictorial layout not conforming to historical importance is found in the first edition of my book *A History of Graphic Design*. The publisher's staff designer actually took 218 line images provided by the author and pasted the originals directly onto the mechanicals. He did not resize them to conform to the format grid or express the relative importance of the works. This resulted in awkward layouts and imposed an arbitrary hierarchy with simple line work such as logos and type specimens becoming very large, while complex and important works were reproduced very small. Any attempt to assign significance to the size of works after such a capricious process will be grossly distorted.

The dangers of a canon should be acknowledged; however, there are risks in repudiating canonical figures whose philosophies or works had seminal or pivotal impact upon the evolution of graphic design. To repudiate seminal works or designers to avoid a canon—with this repudiation based on nationalistic, ethnic, political, or gender issues separate from the evolution of graphic design and its cultural role—is an equal danger. Until the fledgling design history movement evolves more cohesive methodologies and criteria, picture counts and reproduction size may provide, not a canon, but a popularity contest.

By making her tabulation and calling attention to the potential dangers of a canon, Scotford has provided a great service to the design profession and the evolution of design history research. Elitism and exclusion pose serious hazards within a democratic and pluralistic culture. If design history and design education embrace a canon, this could lead to a design profession that responded to its own internal criteria instead of evolving in creative interaction with the needs of society, shifts in the cultural milieu, and technological innovations. Graphic design often provides an important voice for cultural segments, as evidenced by the sixties psychedelic poster and recent Soviet graphics supporting glasnost and perestroika. The potential for women, minorities, and younger generations to have graphic statements to support their causes and help define their experiences could be seriously undermined.

*Originally published in Volume 9, Number 3, 1991.*

# LOVE, MONEY, POWER

# THE GENDERED SELF

*Janet Fairbairn*

**W**hat inspires us to become artists? Is it education, cultural construction, demographics, environment, mentors, personal tragedies, accomplishments, travel, and/or art movements? We take for granted the importance of education and culture in an artist's life, but art originates in the deepest recesses of a human being—the mysterious place of one's soul.

We cannot understand everything that is happening within and around us in the production of a work of art. We have to allow something that is beyond us to happen. The process includes all the relationships and experiences we have had, all the images we have seen, all the sounds we have heard, all the feelings we have felt, all the losses we have grieved.

Not only do women differ from men, we also differ among ourselves in areas of sexual preference, religion, age, race, ethnicity, marital status, physical strength, personal appearance, and goals. Feminism should not seek to treat women the same as men, but allow them access to the same opportunities enjoyed by men.

A designer may express a personal bias or political view through his or her work. Women designers can bring their gender into the public and professional spheres of design. I began seriously contemplating the issue of gender difference while researching an independent project, "The Gendered Self in Design: Interviews with Fifteen Women," during my final year as a graduate student in graphic design at Yale University in 1991. I sought to advance my understanding of the appetency, initiative, and ability of women to invest a self-image in their artwork.

I chose these women for their strong design ability, not for their feminist stance or opposition to it. I sought a substantial range in age, background, education, locale, and prominence. I included women with varied cultural and educational backgrounds and women with experience outside the field of graphic design. I asked all of them how design, cultural traditions, education, art movements, mentors, regional areas, the feminist movement, and their own response to art and art making influence their design.

The women I interviewed discussed many theories and shared their ideas and experiences. I discovered how some achieve fulfillment, continue to grow within the field of graphic design, and include a sense of self in their work. In many of the interview responses, I found confusion about the meaning of feminism. Often the respondent had a desire to support feminism, but rejected or feared the attitude she associated with feminism.

"To me it is all politics: what I do for a living, who I do it with, and the choices I make are dictated by the values that I feel are essential. I feel that this partly comes from my generation (and perhaps also as a kind of sixties liberal-Catholic idealism that I was indoctrinated into during grade school). The other thing I would emphasize is that I came of age intellectually when postmodern theory was really breaking. Therefore, I cannot be a pure modernist. I'm fascinated by modernism, but to me it's history. I do seek to understand everything in terms of time and history. I can't believe in universals, or timelessness, and I tend to reject all design theories based on generalizations that obliterate the specifics of gender, or race, or class, or nationality, or even the time that the design is produced. All this influences the way I think about design, the way I understand it, and the way I teach it, and it has a lot to do with starting to read in my field in the mid-seventies. . . . I would say it's more obvious in my teaching. I try, as best that I can, to nurture students and make sure that women, in particular, feel there is a place for them in the world. . . . I am less conscious of my gender in my own studio than I am in school."

*—Lorraine Wild*

"All of it is autobiographical, in some aspect, but almost all of it deals with self or gender or the underlying patriarchal culture. . . . My work revolves around issues of self, having a female voice, and female anger. . . . But feminism and critical theory have changed education enormously in the last ten years. It is really gratifying to see it. Whether people resist it or not, change has occurred and can't be denied. Students often resist anything labeled *feminist*. When they began to realize that it's really about taking control of their own lives and understanding the implications of that kind of empowerment, the light goes on and it's a whole new ball game."

*—Barbara DeGenevieve (photographer, educator)**

"A design that reveals the self is motivated by the desire to find others who feel the same way about an aesthetic or an idea."

*—Laurie Haycock Makela*

"I just think of the problem at hand, and I solve it in what I consider an appropriate way. . . . There is emotion, there must be. I've always thought of design as being a creative act itself, creating something with a lot of emotion and excitement. I don't see that you can pin it down with any equation."

*—Jacqueline Casey*

"Self-image can mean a variety of things. Any motif that a designer feels is characteristic of herself and/or visually revealing of her personal feelings can be perceived as self-image. I am amused by the comments I receive from those who see my greetings posters. Often I am told the pictures of me don't look anything like me. Since I am trying to portray my inner self, I feel the posters should do more than merely capture my physical appearance. . . . I am motivated by a need to make visual statements about those things that affect my day-to-day life."

—*Mary Melilli*

"It is not even my sense of self. It is not like I am trying to put myself in my work. I have no choice, that is all it is. Myself, mediated by the culture I live in. . . . All my work is about gender and power, all of it. I don't have to change it or make it come out a certain way, or work subversively. That's my work."

—*Barbara Kruger (artist)\**

"That is assuming that I do include a sense of self in my work. I don't express myself in what I do. In fact, most of the time I try to suppress my personality, my ego, and my sense of self, to more clearly pay attention to my client's personality."

—*Sylvia Harris*

"I know that there is something of me in all that I do; there is most likely a coded self in the work that all designers do. Looking at my work, I see themes and forms recur, making me more conscious of what that 'me' is. It would be perilously essentialist to claim that the self I find in my work is totally framed by gender. What is perhaps more accurate is that aspects of myself that I now recognize reappear and have become signs to me of issues I am working out in the work I do."

—*Sheila Levrant de Bretteville*

"I don't even think of myself as a female designer. I don't see how my being female gets into the picture . . . being a woman is not a conscious identity that enters my work. . . . If my voice comes through in the work and a client sees it as the fulfillment of a need for them, then I have achieved the best possible solution. What I am striving to produce is a design that satisfies both my needs and my client's. The first question I always ask myself is, How do I respond to the client's needs and address my own too?"

—*Lucille Tenazas*

"I can't imagine doing design without having a personal agenda. I think solving the problem is one part of the problem, but I think having other kinds of ongoing personal underpinnings is really important to the work. For me, it is like work that is lacking a soul. That doesn't mean that every job has to have the color pink. I am very interested in universal symbols, color systems, and mythologies. I try to impart a certain part of my understanding of that—and things that could be called collective understandings, into the work. . . . I don't think it's so much my age that influences it, but it's age in general, the time in which you were born, that I think is very influential ultimately in your work. . . . I think the age during which I was born put me in a position as a designer—I'm this 'bridge generation' between really embracing and being creative with technology, and being still grounded to the traditional disciplines of graphic design."

*—April Greiman*

"That would be all the work because, in any problem given, I translate what the client's need is. Then, I also turn it into an element that is not only functional, but aesthetically pleasing. I think that is the ultimate goal. That is part of myself no matter what I do. I always have that aesthetic need."

*—Ine Wijtvliet*

"I really dislike talking about what I do—I'm very factual when I talk about it. I do this for this reason: what you're trying to do in a way is have me sum up what my work is like. I don't like doing it. I think it's very damaging to the work. It's like you're confusing words with what the form is."

*—Maya Lin (architect, sculptor)\**

"It has always been my whole life. I have always had the good fortune or the curse not to be able to separate myself from the work."

*—Deborah Sussman*

"Either I asked for the assignment or I turned it into the direction that was of personal interest to me. Otherwise, in some way, anything I do—and I always try to be authentic in everything I do—has a piece of myself, if I want it to or not. If I design something, and it has to do with an issue I care about, then it has to carry a piece of me; there is no other way."

*—Inge Druckery*

"I don't see how anybody can help it. I think there is a range of
objectification that was enabled by any stylistic language of design. The
Swiss/German/American development of modularity and grid stuff
allows a lot of people to express in a relatively expressive genre. Certain
designers, though, tend to infuse even the most rigid formalism with
their own personality—whether it is themselves or not, I don't know. . . .
I don't think anybody can avoid being idiosyncratic in some fashion. . . .
I think everybody has a hidden agenda when they work for hire."

—*Muriel Cooper*

When I asked women about the female sense of self in their work, their
responses would often go beyond the realm of graphic design. The question
provoked them to comment on philosophy or to relive past struggles in their
private and professional lives. Some accepted gender differences, some criticized
the notion of difference, and some attempted to go beyond difference. The vigor
of the responses shows that the question of gender difference challenges us to
think about our lives in ways we may not have considered.

*\* These individuals do not make their living in graphic design.*
*Originally published in Volume 10, Number 1, 1992.*

# KEEPING THE WORLD SAFE FROM HYPOCRISY

*George Lois*

I have turned down a couple of thousand appearances at design conferences. But
I came to "Love, Money, and Power" because I like its themes.

Love. Anybody who doesn't love being a designer, doesn't love putting
ideas down that might change the world, and who doesn't have the talent to
do it, shouldn't be in the business. Love is what pushes us all.

Money. If you go into this business looking to make money, you're in big
trouble. It's not that you can't make a ton of money. But anybody who comes into
the business trying to make money is a bum.

Power. The ability to effect change.

I find these three themes very exciting. In a sense, it's the story of my life.

I have done some political campaigns. I wish I had done more. I wish I
had done every campaign against Nixon, Reagan, and Bush. But the Democratic
party is scared of me, and maybe I don't blame them, because I think I know how
I can make any Democrat win.

I did the campaign for Bobby Kennedy in New York in 1964—a tough, tough campaign. Bobby was a carpetbagger. Bobby was going to get beat. He was running against a real Republican stiff, Senator Kenneth Keating. We did a campaign that busted through, but it was down to the wire.

It came down to the last week, when Bobby Kennedy let me run a twenty-second commercial: it said, "Think about it. When you go into the voting booth, which of the two men running for the Senate would make a great United States Senator?" White type on a black background, nothing else happening. And it went off. Everybody in New York understood, especially the Democrats who were going to vote against Kennedy because they thought he was a snotty kid. They realized what you basically have to do is vote for somebody who has a chance to be great.

Around 1976, I read a book by Ruben "Hurricane" Carter, a great fighter, who was about to fight for the middleweight championship. It was called *The Sixteenth Round*. A beautiful book; an incredibly intelligent man. He was in jail for a sentence of three hundred years for robbery and the killings of three white men—in the fascist state of New Jersey.

I was absolutely positive that "Hurricane" was innocent. I ran a small ad on page two of the daily *New York Times*, "From Ruben 'Hurricane' Carter, #01424567777," talking about the fact that he was innocent. That afternoon, I started to organize the committee, run by Muhammad Ali, Burt Reynolds, and supported by thousands of people in America, to try to get Carter out of jail. We raised hell. We had marches of 20,000 people to the State House. I got Bob Dylan to write a song called "Hurricane."

We got Carter a new trial. He was reframed. Got another trial. The State Supreme Court of New Jersey threw it out, citing the viciousness of his jailing.

There are ways that designers and advertising people can get important things done.

My work has always been a mixture of words and pictures. My job is to get words on people's tongues. I want them to say, "When you've got it, flaunt it." And then I want the image of Salvador Dali sitting next to Whitey Ford as he describes how to throw a curveball. I want an image in their minds of Sonny Liston listening to Warhol as he explains the significance of a Campbell's Soup can. But I want them to say, "When you've got it, flaunt it."

My job, when I did a cover for *Esquire*, was to sell the hell out of the magazine. I chose to make statements about what content might be about, not always what it was about.

My salvation in life was to work for myself, set my own rules for the kind of clients I wanted to work for, throw them out on their ass if they pissed me off, and create an atmosphere around me where no account, marketing, or financial person could tell me what the hell to do. We all have to search for that power, find that power so that we allow ourselves to get the best out of ourselves.

The search for that power is something that many of us spend our whole lives looking for, and are frustrated all our lives. It's the only fight, because if you have talent, and you really think that you have something to give, not getting it out is a terrible thing.

You don't want to be in this business to make money. You want to be in this business to be able to get that talent out. You'll make enough money to eat. The important thing is that you have power to change things, and that you must have the power to be allowed to try to make those changes.

*Originally published in Volume 9, Number 4, 1992.*

# THE WORLD ACCORDING TO DISNEY

*Tony Hendra*

I n today's sermon I want to take as my text a familiar quotation from the Book of Genesis, 1:2: "Darkness was upon the face of the deep and the Spirit of God moved upon the Walter. . . ."

In thinking about the power and influence of the Disney Corporation, standard descriptions are unsatisfactory. Obviously it is not just: (a) a studio with a large inventory of family entertainment (although it is that); nor is it (b) a multimillion dollar corporation with global brand names (although it is that); nor is it (c) a political organization—fascists with black ears instead of black shirts.

Although the colors of its central symbol, Mickey Mouse, are black, white, and red—the same as those of the Nazi swastika. And in the late thirties and early forties, Mickey's famous yellow feet were brown—the color of Hitler's shirts.

No, Disney isn't just a studio, or just a corporation, or just a political party. It's all these things and more. It's a religion. If we examine Disney's work, we find evidence of religious intent. We're going to be referring to this religion as "Disneyism," or the "Church of the Holy Rodent."

Our methodology will be to point out similarities between the Church of the Holy Rodent and Catholicism, it being numerically the largest religion in the U.S. and also because I was once a Benedictine monk.

Okay. Let's start at the top: Mickey Mouse. The crucial question, Is Mickey divine? The answer, Absolutely. Comparing Mickey to Christ, we find Mickey comes out ahead in several categories.

Christ has one halo. Mickey has two. We call them ears, but no mouse ever had ears like that. Those are halos. Second, unlike Christ's, Mickey's crucifixion pose is happy. This guy's off the cross. No depressing nails or blood. But never doubt that Mickey has been crucified. Check out his sacred little hands and what do we see? Bang in the center—stigmata!

Even though all Disney characters have identical hands, only Mickey has stigmata. What they all have, though, is three fingers.

This brings us to the crucial question of the Trinity. There are three principals: Mickey, Donald Duck, and Goofy. It is worth noting that many other characters come in threes: the Three Little Pigs, or Donald's three nephews— Saint Hugh, Saint Lou, and Saint Dew. With the top three, though, Disney's religious intent is quite clear. Mickey, Donald, and Goofy are, while distinct persons, all of the same spirit. The classic formulation of the Holy Trinity.

Mickey is a goof, but the leader. He's an aloof goof. Donald is a goof too, but he lives in the world. He's involved with more mundane things like cars and hammers. He's an uncouth goof. Goofy though, is pure goof, the spirit of goofiness, a Sufi goof.

So the Church of the Holy Rodent has a clear Trinity: God the Vermin, God the Duck, and God the Holy Goof. The more pagan among you might want to throw in the King of the Underworld, Pluto. Note too that all three persons of the Trinity are male. Which brings us to Minnie.

From a spiritual standpoint, Minnie is a bit of a loose cannon—and I don't mean that ecclesiastically. She has a tendency to flirt, for instance. I think Minnie had a past. Then she met Mickey. She reformed. She became a new woman, a born-again rodent. Minnie Magdalen.

Turning from symbols to motifs, we find still more evidence. The opening scene of *Bambi* is a thinly disguised version of the Nativity: animals rush about yelling, "The Prince is born! The Prince is born," then they gather around Bambi's mother to watch the Christ child—the Bambino—make his first move. When Bambi's mother is shot, the Great Stag—God the Father—intones to Bambi: "Come my son."

The theme of resurrection is even more pronounced. Take Snow White— please.

Snow White dies. She is without question dead. A victim of aggravated homicide. The dwarfs cry and frankly, so do I. Then along comes the power of love and, hallelujah, without explanation, she's resurrected!

Ditto Sleeping Beauty. Falls asleep for a hundred years. Symbolic death. Kiss. Boom, Easter Bunny!

Then there's the capper. Pinocchio. Not only does this guy go through the torment of Jonah in the belly of the whale, he dies and rises again in a transfigured form—as a *real boy*! And on top of all this, his father's a carpenter!

Pinocchio's story recalls the opening of the Gospel According to St. John: "In the beginning was the wood, and the wood became flesh." I'd also like to point out that the initials of Pinocchio's conscience, Jiminy Cricket, are J. C.

Beyond textual clues, the fact is that Disneyism as an organization, as a historical force, as a body of art, and as a body of implicit and explicit values, operates as a religion. Let's compare its major operational characteristics with those of Catholicism, and you'll see what I mean. Like Catholicism, the Church of the Holy Rodent: (a) interprets old myths and invents new ones, (b) delineates moral behavior in minute detail and describes the punishments for ignoring them, (c) presents an idealized version of reality, (d) encourages pilgrimages to major shrines, and (e) hates sex.

Obviously, I'm going to deal with the last of these first because it's the most fun. Like all great Western religions, Disneyism deplores sex. No Disney character from Steamboat Willie to Mary Poppins has ever had sex. All births in Disney are virgin births: Mrs. Bambi, Mrs. Dumbo, and Geppetto. No sex.

Here's an impossible image: Sleeping Beauty wakes at the Prince's kiss, reaches out sensuously, and unbuttons his fly. Never happen. Disney princes don't have flies. No fly on Prince Charming. Zippidy-doo-dah in the fly department.

Precisely because of this asexual approach, Disney's saints have been a tremendous turn on for some people. One classic was Wally Wood's Disneyland memorial orgy, which appeared in the *Realist* not long after Walt Disney's death. Disney tried to get this one suppressed, but since the *Realist* and its editor, Paul Krassner, had no offices and no money, there wasn't much to threaten them with. Krassner, however, was not invited to do a rewrite of *The Love Bug.* Disney was much more successful with the folks called The Air Pirates, a small underground comic group in San Francisco.

Disney sued The Air Pirates for $700,000—the equivalent nowadays of ten times that much—and threw the book at them. Copyright infringement, unfair business competition, the works. The Air Pirates were tiny, but they were a viable business and they had distribution. They went to court, lost, and were ruined. Judges agree that Disney images are sacred. They have special privileges that supersede constitutional rights.

Obviously, Disneyism reinterprets old myths, fairy tales for example, but the invention of new ones is fascinating. Take the emergence of Mickey Mouse as a national icon. In 1935, a mere six years after his creation, the *New York Times,* in all seriousness, called Mickey Mouse "the best known and most popular international figure of his day." Hitler and Stalin, of course, didn't agree. The result was World War II. But, ironically, it was World War II that established Mickey (and the rest of the Trinity) as the national and international icons of the U.S.; just as the Virgin or the Cross had been borne into battle in previous crusades, the sacred image of Mickey or Donald or Goofy graced fighters, bombs, shells, tanks, and submarines in the crusade against fascism. Mickey played into another characteristic of great nations at war. However inevitable their victory, they like to see themselves as the underdogs. Mickey, like Christ, is the ultimate underdog. (Donald, of course, was an underduck.)

The Church of the Holy Rodent delineates moral behavior in minute detail and describes the punishments for ignoring the rules. This one is self-evident. From the first days of the Mickey Mouse monastery, Disneyism has been unswerving in its dedication to what are called traditional American values. No sex we know about. But lying and smoking are out, too (see *Pinocchio*). *Snow White* tells us not to trust poor people, especially when they're selling fruit. *Dumbo* tells us that diversity can be overcome by an act of will; *Cinderella*, that ugly people are evil and beautiful ones good. *Song of the South* tells us that African-Americans are born storytellers; *Peter Pan*, that you can stay young forever, if you have access to fairy dust. These are all American values.

Disneyism presents an idealized version of reality. This one seems obvious, but there's more going on than meets the eye, literally. Like Catholicism, Disney insists there's something spiritual going on beneath the surface of the natural world. "Disneyology" says that beneath the outward details of the natural world—which includes planes, cars, trees, chairs, but especially animals—there is intense humanity. Planes, cars, trees, chairs, but especially animals, are much kinder, gentler human beings than human beings. Back to *Bambi* for a moment. In the world of *Bambi*, the only evil is man. All the animals are not only unbearably cute, but irredeemably nice. "If you can't say anything nice, don't say anything at all." In the real world, of course, the kindly old owl who is Thumper's friend is a predator. A routine part of any kindly old owl's life is to hunt Thumpers down, rip open their bellies, and eat them raw—starting with those big cute eyes. But, in *Bambi*, the animals are not only better than real animals, they're infinitely nicer than people. *Bambi*'s message is this: if you were a better human being, you'd be a deer.

A personal note here. While researching this lecture, I came across a fascinating quote from a guy named Frank Thomas, one of Disney's favorite animators. Frank said that he used to tell his trainees: "An absence of line makes cartoon characters softer and more appealing. When drawing cartoon animals, think of Doctor Dentons." This image was familiar to me. I realized it was very close to the idea I had as a child of what my *soul* looked like. A sort of disembodied Doctor Dentons floating around inside me.

What we've dealt with up to this point is the animation of Disney, his most unique and sacred work. But there's much more to Disney, historically, than that. Just like Catholicism, the Church of the Holy Rodent has passed through three great historical stages: the formative or inspirational stage, characterized by great purity, energy, and growth; the "Middle Ages," an era of established authority, when the church became didactic and authoritarian, expanding its influence into all aspects of human life; and crass, naked commercialism.

The first stage we've dealt with. The second is represented by the huge expansion of Disneyism after World War II and through the fifties and early sixties into nature films, live-action features, television preeminence, and educational programs. I think it's uncontested that during this time Disneyism was the bastion of traditional American family values. *Walt Disney Presents* was as much a part of Sunday as going to church, and all the family had to watch. Even Dad.

Two interesting points, relevant to our thesis. Artistically, the first stage of Catholicism was marked by iconoclastic nonrepresentational art. Ditto Disneyism. In its second stage, Catholic artists, while still using approved themes, became more and more fascinated by realism. Ditto Disneyism.

Now, instead of virgins like Snow White and Bambi's mother, we get virgins like Mary Poppins and Davy Crockett. It's the difference between an eleventh-century Romanesque Madonna and a Madonna by Raphael. This period also sees the establishment of Disneyism's first religious order—the Mouseketeers. These were the Jesuits of Disneyism. Fierce, chirpy, cheery apostles of neatness and niceness.

It is interesting that when Annette Funicello developed breasts, she was expelled from the order. The Disney archives actually say Annette left because she "outgrew her role." By the way, there are persistent rumors that Walt, who was a man untroubled by the slightest sexual urge, had the hots for Annette. This never happened before or after; so there perhaps we have the basis for Martin Scorsese's first animated feature, *The Last Temptation of Mickey.*

But the great achievement in Disney's second stage was the establishment of its first two shrines: Disneyland and Walt Disney World. These shrines are tended by large religious communities, who live by strict "Disneyite" principles. Some even model themselves slavishly on the Holy Family. As usual, Disneyism beats out Catholicism. At Catholic shrines you are required either to do abject penance, or to be horribly crippled.

Another fascinating comparison: Walt Disney World has a deal with the state of Florida that suspends all Florida's laws and taxes within its boundaries. Disney World is entitled to its own police force, municipal services, and standards. It can make its own laws and pays no taxes to the state. This is exactly the same deal the Vatican has with the Italian government.

One last thought about Walt. If you're still not convinced that Disneyism is a religion, consider the case of its founder. It's not unsubstantiated that when he died, Walt Disney was cryogenically frozen. Like Snow White, Walt's out there somewhere in the desert, lying on a slab, surrounded by bluebirds, waiting for a Prince Charming to come along and kiss him on the lips. The founder of the Church of the Holy Rodent believed in his own resurrection, and when that happens—watch out Annette!

Where does Disneyism stand today? After Walter fell asleep, the Church of the Holy Rodent went through a period of stagnation, and then reformation. Once again, just like Catholicism. In the early eighties, a new hard-charging, more secular-minded clergy emerged, led by Bishop Michael Eisner, later to become Pope Michael, or, as he's now known, Pope Mickey. He is assisted by his inseparable companion Cardinal Jeff Katzenberg. These two inaugurated a period of great secularization. Just like the post-Reformation church, these prelates were willing to work with worldly interests—even people who actually engaged in sex—provided they turned a profit.

But the most significant parallel with post-Reformation Catholicism is Disney's tremendous interest in foreign missions. Now Disneyism will be exported wholesale to such places as Japan and France, to convert the ignorant heathens.

There's obviously tremendous potential growth in this area. We can easily imagine Disneyism not only proselytizing foreign countries, but—just as it has in America—reinterpreting their histories.

Those of you who follow such matters know that things are not going well right now for the Church of the Holy Rodent. There's a reason for this. The hard-eyed men at the top have, I think, lost sight of the great moral vision of their founder. Instead of movies like *Snow White* and *Mary Poppins,* they make *Pretty Woman.* They've sold Mickey for thirty pieces of silver. I have a solution for their problems, and it's one which would appeal to Walt if he were alive, or will when he comes back.

I suggest the fusion of these two great religions, Disneyism and Catholicism. Romanism and Rodentism. Each could give the other something it needs. Catholicism would give Disney tradition, a connection with the historical Christ, and some great sets and costumes. Disney could bring to Catholicism what it most lacks: warmth, cheeriness, chirpiness, modern sanctity.

Disneyism could make Christ *cute.*

*Originally published in Volume 9, Number 4, 1992.*

# ABSOLUTE INDIVIDUALS
*Moira Cullen*

I am thinking about desire. Not all desire, mind you, but a drive unique to human beings (as far as I know) to change the course and context of an individual's path in life. What is this yearning? Explain this intimate, irrepressible urge to loose oneself from the bonds of origin, leap bounds of convention, challenge habit and expectation, forsake the familiar, and step out from the fold. Describe the lure of a life lived out-of-center, on frontiers that reach the rim. Tell me of the mystery and madness of dancing on the ledge.

Curiosity prompted me in a pursuit of the personal: eccentrics, quite frankly, those individuals whose choices and practice placed them outside the epicenters of design. Forgoing the usual suspects (the Kalmans, Friedman, Greiman, VanderLans, and Licko) or even their progenitors (Cassandre, Lionni,

Rand, Bayer, and Bass) for perhaps their progeny, I sought a new breed of explorer. I harbored no plans to stalk the Howard Hughes of Helvetica; no late-night prowls for stylistic weirdos. Personal history—the path, not the product—was my goal. However, the prospect of unearthing untold designer deviance, past and present, beckoned a momentary intrigue.

Who knew what quirks, habits, markings, or strange predilections lay beneath composed grids of normalcy or behind that mild-mannered postmodernist? Who were these designers? What did they eat, smoke, drink, and drive? Did they dress all in black or matching Pantones, neglect their pets? Were they known to keep odd hours, exhibit bizarre visual or spatial tics, have recurrent dreams of fantasy fonts? Did they pace uncontrollably, doodle suspiciously, indulge in excessively intimate or prolonged relationships with the tools of their trade?

"Tell me," I began, "are you eccentric?" Cradling the phone, I mouthed a riff of Jimi Hendrix while my words made their way from Manhattan to Minneapolis. A pause. And then P. Scott Makela's slightly garbled reply. "Definitely. Well, it's eccentric if you're not a good employee, don't you think?" I could all but hear a grin.

Makela, the outré designer/typographer/writer/musician known for lush, layered graphics for the likes of the Minneapolis College of Art and Design, the Walker Art Center, Nike, and Cranbrook Academy of Art, is most visible among a daring new breed of digital darlings. "Essentially, I'm a working-class designer dealing in propaganda and research and development.

"Most designers are more anal; for them, precision rules. I come from a background where emotion and passion are everything: food, sex (I've always thought graphic design lacked a certain sexiness), the intensity I felt as a teenager when I rejected a strict Catholic upbringing and accepted Jesus Christ. Time mellowed me out, that and art school and cigarettes, but I can still recall an image of the Apostles with flames above their heads."

He talks of his past: dyslexia, a speech impediment ("From the beginning I had a hard time making myself understood"), shadowy streaks of mental illness that run through his blue-collar family ("I slide in between wellness and hallucination, visions come to me and I use them to power the work").

He recites former incarnations: dock boy, insurance salesman, existential student with a degree in political science and economics from the University of Minnesota that left him at "a dead-end Marxist, idealistic end point," playing music in a heavy-duty postpunk band called Kindergarten. Wanting to become an art director (the urge emerged to fill the void), he signed up for the commercial art program (these were precomputer days) at the local vocational school. When the waiting list was too long, he got a "hard-core, Basel-style, theory-based, design education" and a BFA from a "real" art college (Minneapolis College of Art and Design) instead.

Fresh out of school, he went west (these were the heady days of "California style"). He worked, taught design at Cal Arts and Otis Parsons. Five years later, in a state of "post-Olympics exhaustion," he had gone through a divorce, turned down a major job offer with a large, prestigious firm, left L.A., and gone back to school at Cranbrook. "Grad school was not about cachet," he confides. "I wanted to investigate my own agenda, to add a muscularity to the work I was seeing."

Makela has come full circle. A self-proclaimed "outsider" in his home-town of Minneapolis, he operates Words and Pictures for Business and Culture, a lean design machine (Makela plus a writer and an assistant or two ensure there's never a "B squad") out of a studio attached to the house he shares with wife Laurie Haycock Makela (design director of the Walker Art Center), daughter Carmela of font fame ("the most powerful little girl I've ever met"), and the family dog. "The only time I'm separated from them is when I'm on the road" (Japan, Sweden, Brazil, Norway, Amsterdam, and L.A. in the first half of this year alone). "With FedEx, modems, airline tickets, and the right Powerbook, I can work anywhere, and when I land there's a studio waiting for me."

Did the birth of his daughter soften him up? On the contrary: "She chugs ahead like an engine and makes me look at everything. She reminds me I should be digging, digging for deep cultural scratchings. . . .

"You see, I believe everyone should destroy themselves frequently . . . I shed my own skin once every three or four years . . . always moving forward . . . on the lookout for new ideas . . . building myself up again every day. . . . I'm driven to work, communicate, produce . . . instinctively, I don't know why . . . I can't put language to it . . . it's some kind of guiding light . . . a torch under my ass . . . I'm hallucinating this beautiful vision of the future ahead of me. . . ."

The future calls (by the name of Carmela). "Hey, it's time to go." Makela signs off and hops in the van, another suburban dad picking up his daughter at day care.

I step ashore in Sausalito. Behind me, a fog rolls over the San Francisco shore. Someone was here to meet me, and as the lone traveler in black on a ferry full of plaid and pastel tourists, I would be easy to spot.

We greet, eye each other askance (two strangers in design), hop in a '67 VW, and zip through town to a white cottage on the hill. Bougainvillea splashes fuchsia over the door. "This is it," she says, pulling the brake with a jerk. I had arrived at the studio of Patricia McShane and Erik Adigard Design, known to the world as M.A.D.

No sooner had she parked the car and brewed a pot of espresso than McShane disappeared into the front studio, silent save for the random *click click* of a mouse, to be with her work (an alternative educational CD-ROM on teenage dating skills). So Adigard and I sat on the deck overlooking the bay, dappled with boats in a dazzling sun, and he told me the story of M.A.D.

"An uncontrollable drive, a madness to create" brought Adigard and

McShane together to form M.A.D. in 1989. Both had been art-school dropouts, he from Paris, she from San Francisco State, when they met several years before in the graphic design program at California College of Arts and Crafts (CCAC). He is driven by theory and concept, she by process and craft; she is hooked on the computer, he is not. As M.A.D., they work independently, together, and have no plans to grow.

Adigard recalled dizzy days of Paris in the seventies. "Deconstruction, doing surgery on every sentence helped confuse me. I thought I would never get out of that world. It was so Cartesian, everyone had a role; if you got good grades you couldn't be an artist because you would starve. In a way, it is easier knowing exactly where your place is. When you start to look between the blacks and whites and grays, it becomes difficult. But I found confusion is much more interesting than clarity."

A journal he kept in his twenties (he comes from a family of writers) and interviews with his friends about why they did what they did convinced him that design was his calling. "I was uncomfortable with writing but had the same thirst. I began to think of graphic design as another form of journalism." Years later, on a tip from McShane's boyfriend (with a warning that he might be meeting a bunch of losers), Adigard walked in on the production of the first issue of *Wired* and has turned heads ever since with searing visual essays that set up context and content in a sequence of full-color, full-bleed spreads.

As for McShane (she agreed to speak later, long distance, by phone), she began designing at age five. "It started with this little padded bed I made for my doll, then doll clothes. Soon I was making real clothes, jewelry, purses, hats for my mother's friends that sold in stores in the Bay Area. These were one-of-a-kind pieces. I was an artist even then."

But she, too, was drifting until 1984, when a friend suggested that she attend the Stanford Design Conference. She went, was "smitten," and one month later (after a conversation with a dean convinced her that graphic, not industrial, design was the future) had enrolled at CCAC and was "playing around with typography" on one of the very first Apple Macs (courtesy of her computer engineer boyfriend). "It was a blast."

The chocolate-dipped biscotti has melted in the brilliant sun. I ask Adigard where he sees M.A.D. now that digital design has become the new radical chic. "Definitely outside the center, on the edge." Despite mass culture's craving/quest for the forever young and the forever new that can flatten the edge into mainstream mush?

He frowns. "But the edge is always a center. How do you escape that position? Maybe the new position is not in graphic design anymore, maybe it's in journalism, online art, whatever. At the risk of losing money or clients, I/we will continue to go out on the rim to find the core of things. For me, I will always try to stay in a slight state of confusion."

Post Tool. The name is visible from the freeway, written large on a sign above the warehouse (a chain of northern California hardware stores) that houses the second-floor studio (formerly a Chinese sweatshop) of Gigi Biederman and David Karam, a.k.a. Post Tool Design.

Shameless appropriation? A stroke of marketing genius? Karam and Biederman, two twenty-something San Francisco designers (whose paths also crossed at CCAC), explained the name and other choices during a three-way phone call to Palo Alto, where the two were busy working on an eighty-page, eight-color brochure for FrogDesign.

"Post Tool is a rebellion against being used as production tools by other designers. Sure, we took the name; it fit and there was all that free advertising." What (if anything) does Post Tool Design have in common with their retail namesake? "Well, we do use postmodern design tools." No legal problems so far, but "we do get a lot of phone calls from people needing power-tool attachments."

"Eccentric? We don't even consider ourselves graphic designers. We claim a broader definition. More and more, we're working in fine art, blending art and technology, exploring new means of expression" (a new age video for Steelcase, an interactive CD-ROM and logos for Lollapalooza '94, a promotional disk for Warner Records band Lush). "It suits us."

"Frankly, together we're one complete brain," says Biederman, the artist, who comes from Colorado by way of Skidmore College (fine arts and art history) and Parsons in Paris, where she studied graphics and environmental design (her father was one of the original Levittown architects). For her, "Design was a livelihood compromise."

Karam, on the other hand, designed his first interactive computer game (a text/graphics/sound adventure called Preserve) at sixteen, long before he accepted a flute scholarship to the University of Texas, where he majored in computer science and was a color guard in the marching band. Soon he was in California, working for Wells Fargo Bank, where *computer* signified *design* ("Hey, he knows the Mac, he must be a graphic designer"), cranking out in-house corporate communications for the company's 30,000 employees. Later, when Karam decided he might do well to take a graphic design class (or two), the bank funded his attendance at CCAC. Two years later he was teaching (at the invitation of the dean, Michael Vanderbyl), and continues to teach in CCAC's computer design tools department.

This postmodern tool, what's it good for? "As an explorative device for a quick exchange of ideas," says Biederman. "Some of David's and my best experiences have been sitting side by side in front of the computer." "It's fascinating to read the marks," Karam adds. "You can even trace another designer's process, see the points where the designer or the computer made the decision. It's like having a dialogue with a lot of people, some of whom we know, some we'll never have contact with."

Post Tool is just fifteen months old (the pair had been working together for more than two years under a different name) and intends to stay small ("Well,

I'd like a bookkeeper," admits Biederman), preferring instead to collaborate with other designers, videographers, and musicians like GraviTech, their local San Francisco faves. "The sound part is an important piece."

The next goal? Color Powerbooks. One idea is to travel and work as roving "technomads," armed with digital cameras and portable recorders to catalog the visual language created inadvertently through products, textbooks, advertising—way cool.

"Referencing different eras, that's our vocabulary. Vernaculars, that's the communication."

It's a late-night (New York time) phone call. Rex Ray speaks from his studio in the heart of San Francisco's nightclub district south of Market Street. "I come from an underground alternative culture," says Ray, a German-born, one-time Army brat, painter, video and performance artist, and self-taught graphic designer. His connection to design began in the early eighties at the start of a ten-year collaboration with the Residents, a local cult band known for its "naive, drug-soaked deconstruction of pop music." (Nearly ten years later, Ray designed the package for Voyager's CD-ROM release of the Resident's *Freak Show*).

"I have a deep lust for the art of the last hundred years, but as an artist I realized immediately that the way to reach a broader audience was to do graphics."

Ray is a solo act. When he began designing for the Residents, he taught himself the computer, taking an extension course in graphic production to understand the basics (printing, mechanicals, and so on). Jobs at Tower Records and the City Lights Bookstore honed an appreciation for graphic design ("I've always paid attention to the marketplace, the street stuff, what's really out there for the general public"). And when City Lights published a book on performance artist and fellow outsider Karen Finley in the late eighties, Ray designed the cover and established a name as a book designer.

His work and life are seamless, centered on core issues of identity, choice, expression, and survival. "Mine is an isolated drive to combine potent images with powerful text in an incredible fusion." Along with traditional print graphics and multimedia projects, he shoots his own photographs, designs an entire line of book jackets for City Lights (up to twenty a year), and is responsible for the design and concept of an equal number of covers for the political and emotionally charged series of controversial writings known as High Risk.

"It can get wildly intense sometimes. Many of the High Risk authors have AIDS, so there's a struggle to get the books published before they die, but that immediacy and urgency of message is what drives me.

"I'm not eccentric, although I always deal outside the mainstream, but my book jackets are. The covers are as eccentric as the writing. I'm doing covers for a bunch of nuts! But seriously, I'm convinced some will become the classics of the future; what Burroughs or Kerouac were in the fifties."

But with the awards, the increased visibility, can he maintain an alternative position? With bigger jobs and clients, can he hold on to his freedom to express and control? "I think so. But you never know until you're standing there with your comps and they hate them!"

If, as the saying goes, the artist, like the idiot or clown, sits on the edge of the world, then where do designers dwell? Columbus, Ohio, is home to John Weber, the outspoken, self-styled, and self-taught design iconoclast, where he lives with his wife in a house (with design studio).

"I never had any rules," snaps Weber. "In fact, if there were a test for designers, I'd probably flunk. What could they possibly ask? Degrees? They mean nothing to me. I know a lot of people with degrees who shouldn't be designers."

His becoming a designer was pure serendipity, or fate. Either way, a local art supply store (where he worked during and after high school) figured largely in his future. "Career aspirations? You've got to be kidding. I was really confused."

He started small, designing the store's cut-and-paste-xerox monthly sale fliers after the person who did them left the company. "I took over and started looking at album covers and stuff. I remember seeing the design for Pink Floyd (it was the first time I ever remembered the name of a *company*). Soon, I was looking at design books in the store to see what other people were doing, not to rip them off, but to understand the thought process. From the beginning, everything I liked revealed someone's personality.

"So I learned the language of design through books. Meanwhile, I also worked in the shipping department and stuck a flier in every order that went out. The store got a tremendous response. Nobody wanted to hire me as a designer—my work was too weird—but everybody knew who I was."

That was ten years ago. Weber's first design job was a three-year stint with a major computer company in Columbus, where instead of apprenticing with a designer, he was the design department, and his style became the company's identity. (It also convinced him that it was possible to make a living in Columbus as a designer.) For the past seven years, he's built a singular practice with a network of clients (VH-1, TV graphics, *Ray Gun,* etc.) that relies heavily on FedEx and long-distance phone calls. Team design? "I don't play well with others."

Weber walks a fine line between self-promotion and being obnoxious, a cross between "an enigma or a pariah" even in his hometown. "I've always taken advantage of situations and am convinced that no one really knows what you're doing unless you tell them." Like the time he sent samples of his work with a note to Rudy VanderLans along with a subscription form to *Emigre.* "Rudy liked the stuff. Could I do it on the Mac? It was the start of a great association."

Tenacity, passion, and immediacy push Weber's highly personalized expression. "My work didn't jell until I began using the computer. Then I taught myself to shoot the images I needed, and these days I'm doing more photography and illustration than design. It's a great way to work with other designers. David

Carson doesn't need me as a designer, but he does need illustration so I can work with him that way. It's kind of nice."

But few things hold more personal meaning for Weber than his use of found objects: the cast-off, overlooked, and rejected are given new life in his work. Weber, his wife, even Laverne, the neighbor across the street, take part in treasure hunts around Columbus, collecting flea market finds, a peculiar rock, stopping the car to run back for a rusted twist of scrap metal. A snatch of faded embroidery shows up later on an album cover Weber did for British designer Vaughan Oliver. It all works. "Any preconceived notions of what a design should look like are dispelled by the elements in front of me. I could never make this shape if I thought about it, but I found it and I've got to use it."

His adopted objects find a second home in the studio, arranged as a shrine on an altar beside the computer. "I look at the stuff all the time . . . while waiting for the computer to redraw. . . . The digital and the trashy . . . such a contradiction. . . . I'm learning to see beauty in everything . . . beyond face value. . . . I see the results and remember where each piece came from . . . It's a way to incorporate my life into my art . . . into everything. . . .

"I feel I've been handed this way of working with the understanding that if I want to do this I'll be given the means, but I'll be on my own.

"My next big thing is to learn how to weld."

"You're only here once so express yo'self," the gangsta girl raps from a boom box as a skating streak of Lycra whizzes by. Lower Broadway elbows its way downtown, cutting a deep swath through Union Square, the East Village, and SoHo as crowds converge on the beat of street culture. One block north of Houston, several down from Tower Records, is the second-floor, one-room studio of Mike Mills Diversified Design. For Mills, born some thirty years ago in Santa Barbara, it's a long way from the beach.

Downing an iced cappuccino between bites of a blondie, Mills recalls bits of his California youth. No stranger to culture (his father is director of the Santa Barbara Museum of Art and his mother is an art historian), Mills grew up in the rarefied world of famous people and frequent dinner guests. The art world, not his world surely, but that of his parents. A young boy sitting on painter Richard Diebenkorn's knee? He was nonchalant. "I ignored the oldsters. They were my parents' friends who drank too much and crashed cars in the driveway.

"I already knew in high school that I wanted to do a bunch of different things." (Mills grew his hair long, played in a band, and hung with skateboarders.) But a book by Herbert Bayer literally saved him during a parental inquisition into his plans for the rest of his life. "Bayer was someone who did everything—graphics, environmental design, products, painting. Not only that, he was successful. I could point to that book as proof and say, Look, Mom and Pop, you can make a living and get respect by being undisciplined."

Bayer was a family friend who didn't suffer fools gladly. After dinner one evening, when Mills (who had written a paper on the Bauhaus for high school English) approached Bayer with a question, Bayer brushed him off with the gruff suggestion that Mills read his book on the subject. But when told Mills had applied to several design schools and was still uncommitted, Bayer recommended Cooper Union. Why? Because "I wouldn't have to declare a major in any one thing. I was a punker with dyed hair at the time. That was the extent of his tutelage."

After Cooper Union, Mills studied media, semiotics, and film theory at Hunter College, and ran with the rebels (he worked for Tibor Kalman at M&Co and Marlene McCarty at Bureau) before becoming Mike Mills Diversified Design.

"But I started doing graphic design back in high school, before I realized I was doing graphic design: fliers for my band or graphics for my skateboard. Today, when I do something I like, it's re-creating that experience. Not that I think about this every day or that it's a ruling force or anything, but board graphics do represent my first excitement. It was my first experience designing something that became part of the public style, part of my public being.

"That's why I'm interested in design. I'm not interested in communication or legibility and not even that much in aesthetics or being an artist. What I am interested in is being out in the public and playing around with public signs and public connotations and public styles. I hope I'm a pop cultural stylist more than a designer. A sociologist of surfaces."

What of this anti-design stance? A nondesigner with one of the world's largest corporations (Time Warner) as a client, who would rather read *Sassy* than any design magazine? "It's not that I reject the label of designer, I like the idea of the little guy working at the desk drawing stuff, it's just not that interesting to me, nor is it an accurate description of what I do" (loopy graphics for the band Deelite, skateboard videos, an identity for X-girl fashions).

"Am I eccentric? Subconsciously, I would never try to be. Even Paul Rand is eccentric; when he's not doing corporate logos, he gets away with being a witty artist who does commercial work. I don't follow the concept of 'what a designer is' that I learned either from school or from the design community, so, perhaps in that way, I'm eccentric.

"Eclectics, on the other hand, use a variety of value systems. Their thinking doesn't just come from their own design education or from one part of design history. They have an interest in a variety of cultures.

"Diversity: like the Herbert Bayer book. I hope to do the same thing in the world of popular culture. Bayer was more interested in art. He was very much a modernist and wanted to reach people, to bring an enlightened, rational sensibility of design to the masses. I have no lofty hopes. I'm more of a bottom dweller, an entertainer, an educator. I'm most content working with base materials and doing something unexpected with them. I get paid for mumbling just right."

Wrapped in the familiarity of my own surroundings, amid ticket stubs and tape cassettes, scribbled notes, scattered disks, book jackets, Syquests, and samples from those I met along the way, I begin to parse yet another language of selves.

I'm convinced. There is a serendipity to selfhood not unlike the act of creation: chance/choice, nature/nurture, passion/reason, deconstruction/disorientation. From birth, we run an odd course between fitting in and standing out, between doing what we want, what we must, and what we can.

For some, the expression is a temporary trip, a raw race outside the lines in an "I am who I am, I do it because I can" phase chalked up to rebellious youth or wistfully wanton midlife crises. Reason is often erratic, the ego notoriously elusive. But when identity is an end in and of itself, it becomes a sustained pursuit, a personal and professional path, and clearly the individual's choice.

Is the desire unreasonable? I think not. And if it were? A lusty individualism on the part of designers does not automatically diminish the influence of the profession nor signal a slide into a self-serving slurry of designspeak. That irascible curmudgeon (and vegetarian) George Bernard Shaw observed that while reasonable people adapt themselves to the world, unreasonable people try to adapt the world to them. Progress, therefore, is created by unreasonable people.

*Originally published in Volume 12, Number 4, 1995.*

# DESIGN AND BUSINESS: THE WAR IS OVER
*Milton Glaser*

**W**hen I first came to Aspen, the mantra "good design is good business" was the guiding assumption of our professional lives. Although it sounded beneficial to business, like all true mantras it had a secret metaphysical objective: to spiritually transform the listener. We were convinced that once business experienced "beauty" (good design), a transformation would occur. Business would be enlightened and pay us to produce well-made objects for a waiting public. That public would, in turn, be educated into a new awareness. Society would be transformed, and the world would be a better place. This belief can only be looked on now as an extraordinary combination of innocence and wishful thinking.

After forty years, business now believes that good design is good business. In fact, it believes in it so strongly that design has been removed from the hands of designers and put into the hands of the marketing department. In addition, the meaning of "good" has suffered an extraordinary redefinition. Among an ever-increasing number of clients, it now only means "what yields profits."

While we might agree that all of life is an attempt to mediate between spiritual and material needs, at this moment in our work the material seems to have swept the spiritual aside. Hardball is now the name of the game, and the rules have changed. This, of course, is nothing new. The struggle between these issues is as old as humankind. Through the years, as the power of official religion declined, the source and receptacle of truth and morality became "the arts"—and all those who were involved in them formed a new kind of priesthood. Designers very often perceived themselves as being part of this alliance against the philis-tines, whose lack of religiosity had to be opposed in order to produce a better world. Now this conflict seems to have resurfaced with a vengeance. One might say that what we are experiencing is merely a question of atmosphere, but the atmosphere is the air we breathe, and it has turned decidedly poisonous. Let me use a recent contract I received from a record company to illustrate this change in spirit. The contract reads, in part:

"You acknowledge that we shall own all right, title, and interest in and to the Package and all components thereof, including, but not limited to, the worldwide copyrights in the Package. You acknowledge that the Package consti-tutes a work specifically ordered by us for use as a contribution to a collective work. You further acknowledge that we shall have the right to use the Package and/or any of the components thereof and reproductions thereof for any and all purposes throughout the universe, in perpetuity, including, but not limited to, album artwork, advertising, promotion, publicity, and merchandising, and that no further money shall be payable to you in connection with any such use. Finally, you acknowledge that we shall have the right to retain possession of the original artwork comprising the Package."

The first thing one notices is the punishing tone. This is not an agreement between colleagues, but the voice of a victor in a recently concluded war. It reinstates the principle of work for hire, a concept that presumes that the client initiates and conceptualizes the work in question, and that the designer merely acts as a supplier to execute it. It destroys the relationship between payment and usage so that, although the work has been created for a specific purpose (and paid for accordingly), the client is free to use it anywhere, and forever, without further payments. This violates the most fundamental assumptions about compensation of professionals: i.e., that what something is being used for and how frequently it is used is the basis for determining how much should be paid for it. It also claims ownership of the original art, marking the reintroduction of a mean-spirited and unfair doctrine that we all assumed had been legally eliminated. The overall posture, of course, reflects what is seen in the larger culture—a kind of class warfare that occurs when societies lose their sense of common purpose. The collegial sense of being in the same boat, pulling toward a common shore, has been eroded and replaced by the sense that the rowers are below decks and the orders are coming from above.

The Aspen conference itself was founded in 1951 by Walter Paepcke and Egbert Jacobsen, his art director, to promote design as a function of management. It became, for a time, the preeminent symbol of the modern alliance of commerce and culture. They were joined in this adventure, at least spiritually, by such remarkable figures as Josef Albers, Herbert Bayer, and László Moholy-Nagy, the last of whom was active in Chicago's New Bauhaus, a school committed to the principles of modernism and the reconciliation of art and consumer capitalism. It is not an overstatement to say that design education in America began here. It is important to remember that the Bauhaus was not simply a trade school, but represented nothing less than the "transformation of the whole life and world of inner man" and "the building of a new concept of the world by the 'architects of a new civilization'" (Walter Gropius in *The New Architect and the Bauhaus*). Cultural reform was at the center of Bauhaus thought, as it has been in many art movements.

In the United States, the social impulses that characterized Bauhaus thought began to be transformed by our pragmatic objectives, such as the use of design as a marketing tool and the elevation of style and taste as the moral center of design. The primacy of individual opportunity and capitalistic efficiency replaced many of the mildly socialist impulses of the modern movement. The metaphysical objectives and the ideal of civic responsibility went underground or were swept partially away. The pressures of professional practice and breadwinning left little room for theoretical inquiry into social issues. Nevertheless, the feeling that the arts, in general, and design, in particular, could improve the human condition persisted and informed the practice.

In the struggle between commerce and culture, commerce has triumphed and the war is over. It occurred so swiftly that none of us was quite prepared for it, although we have sensed that all was not well in our world. Anxiety, frustration, humiliation, and despair are the feelings that are revealed when designers now talk among themselves about their work. These are the feelings of losers, or at least of loss. The two most frequent complaints concern the decline of respect for creative accomplishment and the increasing encroachment of repetitious production activity on available professional time. These are linked complaints that are the inevitable consequence of the change in mythology and status that the field has gone through. The relationship of graphic design to art and social reform has become largely irrelevant. In short, designers have been transformed from privileged members of an artistic class or priesthood into industrial workers. This analogy partially explains why the first question now asked about designers by clients is more often not how creative or professionally competent they might be, but how much they charge per hour. If screws are being tightened on a production line, it scarcely matters that a worker might be a brilliant poet. He or she still earns only $15 an hour. The same assumption makes it understandable how a person with six weeks of computer training can become a designer with significant responsibility in a corporation without having any knowledge of color, form, art history, or aesthetics in general. We once thought of these as essential to a designer's education.

But why now? What brought us to this unhappy circumstance when there is more design interest, more graphic designers, and more schools teaching the subject than at any time in history? Overpopulation, in fact, may be one of the problems, particularly when combined with the downsizing that the sense of a contracting economy and the computer have caused. Economic forces and technology have always driven aesthetics, although sometimes the relationship is not obvious.

In the past, the design process seemed esoteric, highly specialized, full of internal rituals, and hard to understand from the outside. These characteristics are all typical of spiritual or artistic activity, and serve as a means of protection. The computer, with its unprecedented power to change meaning, has made the process transparent and therefore controllable: and, as we know, control is the name of the game. The argument within the field about computers has been mostly concerned about whether they are an aid or a hindrance to creativity. These concerns resemble the semiconscious babblings of someone who has just been run over by a truck. The phrase "it's only a tool" scarcely considers the fact that this tool has totally redefined the practice and recast its values, all within a decade.

Clients can now micromanage every step of the design process, and production has become the central and most time-consuming part of every design office's activity. The overriding values are efficiency and cost control.

The use of the computer encourages a subtle shift of emphasis from the invented form to the assembled one. Imagery is now obtained increasingly from existing files and sources more cheaply than it can be produced by assigning new work. Electronic clip books have become the raw material for a kind of illustration we might call computer surrealism.

The computer appears to be an empowering and democratic tool. The operator can achieve results that previously were obtainable only through the long process of study and skill development. This partially explains its addictive effect on the user. For myself, someone deeply shaped by old value systems, all expressive forms that are easily achieved are suspect. There are many more bad examples of clay modeling than stone carving: the very resistance of the stone makes one approach the act of carving thoughtfully and with sustained energy. This may also be a small and passing issue. History has shown us that technologies develop their own standards.

There is something else to consider that may help us understand where we are: the relationship between the victory of entrepreneurial capitalism, the fall of world communism, and the almost universal collapse of liberal ideology. Here, we can see the connection between reduced ecological and social programs, the attack on "soft-headed or subversive do-gooders" (like the NEA and public broadcasting), and our own sense of loss. Flush with success and in the midst of its validating triumph around the world, business is in no mood for accommodation. Recent history has proven to business that unyielding toughness pays, and self-inquiry is a form of weakness. Unfortunately, with the elimination of an external threat, those same convictions have been turned inward. Once again, the wisest phrase in the language comes to mind—Pogo's immortal words, "We have met the enemy and he is us." The tendency of unconstrained business to produce a sense of unfairness and class warfare has emerged dramatically, and most of us have been affected by it.

We may be facing the most significant design problem of our lives—how to restore the *good* in good design. Or, put another way, how to create a new narrative for our work that restores its moral center, creates a new sense of community, and reestablishes the continuity of generous humanism that is our heritage.

The war is over. It is time to begin again.

*Originally published in Volume 13, Number 2, 1995.*

# THE END OF ILLUSTRATION (OR THE WAR IS OVER, PART 2)

*Milton Glaser*

Some months ago I received a call from a businessman who was interested in talking to me about the future of digitized illustration. To be specific, he wished to put illustration on disks and sell them in the same way as stock houses do today. He expressed specific interest in my viewpoint because he had read an article I had written for the *AIGA Journal* and realized that many designers were feeling vulnerable and exploited—especially in regard to unfair contracts (work for hire) and the prevailing dog-eat-dog business atmosphere. He suggested that he had come up with an idea to protect artists economically and maintain the quality of their work.

Last week, the businessman and his partner took me to lunch to explain the details. The scheme was breathtaking. Illustrators "only of quality" would be identified and chosen to submit a hundred salable images to be digitized and put on a disk. In the event the images were not quite right, modifications would be made by the producer. In some cases, the images would be specially commissioned for the CD to be created by the artist, guided by the producer's judgment and experience. These might include such visual situations as a man looking at a computer, a man and a woman (young) looking at a computer, a man, woman, and a dog looking at a computer—you get the idea. I interrupted the descriptive flow to inquire, "When you say these images are commissioned, how do you arrive at a fee?"

"This is a co-venture," one of my companions explained. " We are putting up the money for the digitizing, the distribution, the catalog, and so on. We look at this as a partnership."

For some reason I found myself almost embarrassed to ask, "Isn't this a kind of speculative work?"

"We don't look at it that way," he replied, expressing some mild irritation for the first time.

"What does the artist finally get out of this?" I persisted, realizing that I was about to enter a mean and treacherous world.

"Twenty percent of the sale of the disk," the entrepreneurs said proudly and simultaneously.

"Who handles the continuing royalties on the sale of individual images?"

"That's the beauty of it all," the boys responded. "There is no follow-up, no tracking, no worry about whether anyone is using the images without authorization. Once they buy the disk (and it won't be a cheapie—these CDs will go for as much as four or five hundred bucks each), they can use any image they wish forever without any limitations."

My head began to swim. "Let me understand what you are saying," I gasped. "Someone buys a disk and afterward can use any image, for any purpose, modified as desired, combined with any other images, recolored, reshaped, reconfigured, and the purchaser can do this forever (and to borrow a term currently very popular in work-for-hire contracts) throughout the universe?"

"You got it," the boys said, nodding enthusiastically.

"But stock houses and photo services always charge on the basis of use," I said, "Isn't that why Bill Gates is buying up all the world's image supply?"

"That's a business," the boys responded. "We're talking about protecting artists." The lunch ended badly soon after that, and I returned to my studio.

Since then, I have not been able to get the conversation out of my mind and found myself deeply troubled by its implications. It is troublesome for a variety of reasons. First, it creates enmity and resentment within the field of illustration by dividing those who benefit financially from the situation from those who suffer from it. Every job employing a recycled image means that a new illustration will not be assigned. Given the current money-driven nature of the field, it is difficult to imagine that a client would willingly pay for an illustration when a similar one could be obtained for nothing. A friend recently observed that really talented illustrators would always find room at the top. This may be true, but I find the idea analogous to the notion that great hunters can always find an elephant even in hard times; meanwhile, the rest of the tribe starves. As the

opportunity for assigned illustration shrinks, the further commodification of the
activity will produce increasingly generic images suitable for generalized application. The emphasis of the field will shift from the imaginative to the decorative, a
short-term triumph for the ethos of business. Illustration, an activity with an
extraordinary history of reflecting the human condition and making ideas clear,
will no longer attract a generation of bright young minds eager to find ways to
express their skills and imagination. As spiritual and economic rewards diminish
simultaneously, the profession of illustration will virtually disappear—except for
a handful of practitioners able to find room in the cracks.

There is another divisive characteristic that this new development creates.
By and large, designers and art directors don't view the availability of disk imag-
ing as a threat. In fact, many of them welcome it, since one of the emerging
models of the designer is that of a skilled computer operator, gathering all the
visual resources of the world and reassembling them at will. On one hand, this
eliminates most of the requirements for art direction, since true art direction is
about most efficiently encouraging the skills of others. On the other hand, it
places all the creative satisfaction in the hands of the person who does the assembly. The makers of the images—photographers, artists, or illustrators—are
reduced to the level of anonymous image providers. If our definition of a healthy
ecology is one that produces species diversity, this new paradigm creates the
opposite climate.

All this is not even the worst part of this development. By separating
payment from usage and art from its maker, a nasty and cynical atmosphere is
created that ultimately harms us all. Within the assumptions of capitalistic
enterprise, the idea that artworks have integrity and should not be arbitrarily
fiddled with has persisted with remarkable tenacity. This is more about property
rights than aesthetics, but nevertheless the idea has protected us. Now, with the
technology of the computer, the avarice of some businessmen, and the uncon-
sciousness or indifference of the field, we may be entering a new and crueler
period. Paradoxically, there has never been more agitation about intellectual
property rights by the business community. Just try to fool with some
company's logo.

Perhaps there really is no paradox. As old Karl Marx might say, we may
simply be witnessing a new method of controlling the means of production.
Business is well aware that the most important property of the future is intellectual property; in order to control this property, a shift of perception and definition
has to happen. Business has to position itself centrally as the creators of these
ideas, and the role of the artist/maker has to be downgraded. This philosophy is
the underpinning of the work-for-hire doctrine, suggesting that those who
actually produce the images are merely acting as "hands" for the true creator—the
client. In short, business has to effect the transformation of artists into laborers
and artwork into a commodity.

This separation of the maker from the object that is made undermines one of the basic tenets of the humanist tradition: that the maker and what is made have a relationship that should be respected. It is true that most material produced by the graphic arts field does not fall even remotely under the category of "art," but the new ethos doesn't care whether it does or doesn't. A recent catalog of free images available for manipulation includes everything from van Gogh to Bolshevik posters. Incidentally, the explosive growth of the multimedia conglomerates and their attempt to own and control all the world's images would give these organizations the most monopolistic control over human values and culture in history. All for the sake of the bottom line.

As usual, it is difficult to resist the velocity of cultural, technological, and social change, but some changes deserve to be resisted. The first step is to recognize the social and economic consequences of this new and destructive pattern. The next is to make it professionally and culturally reprehensible to participate in its proliferation.

*Originally published in Volume 14, Number 3, 1996.*

# TRUE CONFESSIONS: WHAT CLIENTS REALLY WANT
*Ellen Shapiro*

As the recession deepens and economic indicators continue to drop, many designers are feeling new, and uncomfortable, pressures. Business has been slow all around. More and more projects are being put on hold. It's harder than ever to set up a meeting to show your portfolio. It's easier to get the idea that the business world wishes you didn't exist. Even "good" clients are making things tougher.

I recently asked principals of several top, small- to medium-sized New York City graphic design firms, "What do your clients want of you these days?" Not surprisingly, I got a fair amount of grousing. Next to "Asking for work on spec," and "Not paying bills on time," the major gripe is, "Clients want everything for nothing." Designers report that although budgets are tighter, clients continue to want the same quality and amount of work they got accustomed to in prerecession days. Arnold Wechsler, whose firm serves the financial services industry, says, "This isn't the freewheeling eighties anymore. You've got to be able to deliver more, for less." Eric Baker, whose clients include publishing and fashion accounts, agrees, "The median job today is more involved than five years ago. What you used to charge $5,000 for, people now want for $3,500."

"Clients know they're in the position of power and are more likely to take advantage of it any way they can," adds Carla Hall, who, with four employees, was recently required to absorb 33 percent of the agreed-upon fee when a large insurance company misbudgeted a project.

"They argue with us more," says John Waters, "even about trivial things like type size and choice of photographs." Jan Uretsky adds, "They used to trust me to get the best printing price. Now, not only do they want everything cheaper, they want more numbers: 'How much will it cost in this version or that, with this feature and without?' Sometimes I feel more like a printing estimator than a designer."

Designers are sounding concerned, but not quite discouraged—yet. The feeling is that it's time to roll up our sleeves and work even harder. Designers admit, "You've got to hold on to existing clients as if they were gold. You've got to spend more time educating prospective clients, especially people who are new to their roles. You've got to make sure those contracts are signed." Alexander Isley, who left *Spy* magazine in 1988 to open his own shop, advises, "Spell out everything in advance. Everything. Agree on the number of designs, delivery, payment. Then there'll be no misunderstandings." He says that once the business aspects are clearly established, he's not afraid to push for a design he believes in. "I speak up, sell it aggressively. If you seem to waffle, they'll lose confidence."

Jan Uretsky agrees. "You do have to play hardball these days. But cover your hardball in velvet. In other words, it's too easy to get cynical. Remember, you still have to be a good guy and do good work."

It looks like the days of seven ink colors and three varnishes are truly over, and that designers in New York, at least, are adjusting to the new austerity with some aplomb. The hope is that the client for whom you've gone the extra mile will remember you when times are flusher, and will give you good referrals. It's a given that when your projects are successful, your name gets around.

And, say clients, those relationships can and will happen—if designers approach prospects properly, provide consistently good service, and avoid the pitfalls, the things some designers do that almost all clients dislike. "Number one, don't send a salesperson to see me," advises Kathleen Zarin, marketing communications manager for James River Corporation, who chooses designers for plum paper promotions. "I want to meet with you, or the person who's actually going to be doing the work."

"Don't spend money on fancy capabilities brochures for yourself," many clients say. Sandra Ruch, formerly responsible for cultural programs at Mobil Corporation, now at New Line Cinema, says, "Just show me your work." The approach that many clients think is most effective is summed up by former longtime IBM design manager Jonas Klein: "Send a new prospect a package containing two or three quality printed samples that are specifically relevant to his or her industry and needs. Don't bother with anything that won't hit home."

"And don't try to wine and dine me. No lunches, dinners, or anything like that are necessary," adds Ruch. "Don't try to impress me with fancy offices, amenities," concurs Diane Cory of AT&T, "I'm not impressed by a lot of status baloney, only by what you do. That other stuff doesn't mean diddley."

Then, when you get the job, clients warn, "Be there for me. Stay in constant touch. Meet your deadlines. Treat my project—no matter how small— like you really care about it." "Don't ignore my phone calls," declares Robert Moulthrop, a senior marketing director at KPMG Peat Marwick.

"Don't try to snow me with a thousand design ideas," recommends John Dietsch, a communications director at Booz-Allen. "Usually, one good one is enough."

This is what clients say separates the designers who know what they're doing from those who don't (and what separates the really professional clients from those who aren't). They know a good concept when they see it.

Finally, don't try to dangle awards like carrots. Winning awards is given pretty low priority by most clients, who see them as a nice bonus, but certainly no reason to make a decision. "Forget it," says Pelican Group president Ed Simon, who has produced over twenty top corporate annual reports. "CEOs don't know what the standards are for these awards, and aren't going to take the time to find out. It's irrelevant."

Not ignoring counsel like this, New York designers have been developing new strategies. "Before anything else, get to know the client's business," recommends Diana Graham. "Read the business pages, the *Wall Street Journal.* Clients are looking for designers who can tell them what they should be doing."

"Pay attention to details, even if you aren't asked to," says Craig Bernardt. Care about the project, find the typos, suggest improvements, even in areas that weren't supposed to be your responsibility. Figure out how to do it better, cheaper, faster. Then keep the client informed." "No surprises," adds David Vanden-Eynden. "Doing good work goes without saying. Timeliness in getting it done is what really counts." Carla Hall lauds flexibility. "Maneuver around the client's needs and don't stay rigidly attached to your own preconceptions. Listen, really listen. And make sure you, the principal, are always available."

Not surprisingly, not one designer I interviewed advised, "Give them beautiful type," "Pick great colors," or "Use the best photographers." And no one said, "Quote a low price."

Thus, many experienced design-firm principals aren't selling "great design" these days, even if it's what the client is ultimately getting. And although they may bid competitively for jobs, they aren't selling low price, either. Perhaps, to the chagrin of those who still emphasize "art," they're selling business smarts and problem-solving skills.

"Sometimes I think our chief role is to protect clients from themselves," says Kenneth Carbone, of Carbone Smolan Associates, which recently bucked the downward trend by expanding to twenty employees and moving to luxurious new 10,000-square-foot offices. "I don't let them choose something that might not be in their best interest," he explains. "I never push a design because I love the design. I push a design because it will work for the client. And I always clearly explain the reasons behind the decision. That's been one key to our success."

*Originally published in Volume 9, Number 2, 1991.*

## PROFESSIONAL PRACTICE: MODERN BUSINESS SKILLS FOR THE GRAPHIC ARTIST

*Ross MacDonald and James Victore*
*with apologies to Charles C. Nelson, USMC Ret., our mentor and business adviser*

I n the dog-eat-dog rat-race of nineties design and illustration, underhanded backstabbing business practices are commonplace. Knowing how to react can mean your survival. It behooves us all to take ten minutes out of our busy schedules to practice a few simple and possibly life-saving techniques. Whether you're a designer or illustrator, work freelance or hold a staff position, these easy lessons can give you the upper hand in negotiations, and prevent you from becoming the victim of a bad business deal. Remember, what you don't know *can* hurt you.

### THE EDITOR THROW

When it's time to let them know where editorial ends and design begins, this trick comes in handy. Following through with a knee to the groin is essential to completing the throw and reestablishing your editor's respect.

## DEFENSE AGAINST A WORK-FOR-HIRE CONTRACT

A common and dangerous situation unwary freelancers can find themselves in is the hidden work-for-hire attack. The proper response is to first block the attack. As you move into a basic wristlock, the client can easily be disarmed. Take care not to come in contact with the contract itself, which could be legally binding.

## THE 10 PERCENT KILL FEE CHOKE HOLD

In an effort to increase profits, clients can use unreasonable measures. The 10 percent kill fee is as financially debilitating as it is humiliating. The best defense is to bring your hand up between your attacker's arms, smearing his or her face backward and causing the client to reconsider your terms. This trick can also be used when haggling for a raise.

## THE THERE-WILL-BE-NO-CHANGES BAR-HAMMERLOCK

It's important to nip in the bud a client's tendency for changes. But when you're confronted with a barrage of revisions, a good persuasion technique is the always popular bar-hammerlock. By grabbing the back of your client's arm from underneath, then applying pressure downward, you can easily shift your assailant into a less recalcitrant position, i.e., his or her knees.

### DEFENSE AGAINST BACKSTABBING

The most cutthroat snipes are usually delivered as sneak attacks. Also known as the Quid Pro Throw, this maneuver can defend your reputation from half-truths, innuendos, aspersions, slander, and outright lies, lies, lies. Always follow through with a firm, but convival handshake.

While no single hold or throw can solve every business or legal issue, these simple tricks may be adapted to any emergency. Designers and illustrators need never feel intimidated, helpless, or victimized.

Next month: Using simple office tools to increase your negotiating power.

*Note: Any resemblance to clients living or dead is purely intentional.*

*Originally published in Volume 12, Number 4, 1995.*

# PUBLIC WORKS

# SISTERSERPENT: A RADICAL FEMINIST ART COLLECTIVE

*Victor Margolin*

SisterSerpent periodically blankets walls in the Chicago area with posters that express its rage at male oppression. Unlike ACT UP, which directs its graphics to specific AIDS-related events and issues, SisterSerpent confronts broad misogynistic attitudes deeply embedded in American culture. A SisterSerpent manifesto states, "Our struggle hopes to bring the demise of the system that allows for our brutalization. Our hostility is now in the streets, at public meetings and events, and in the media. We are guerrillas in the war against sexism."

The collective began in the summer of 1989 at the time the U.S. Supreme Court was considering the Webster Decision, which would give the states more freedom to regulate abortion. Originally a group of four or five, SisterSerpent now has members in San Francisco, Atlanta, Cleveland, and Seattle. There are also SisterSerpent supporters in England, France, and Germany. For the most part, the members of the collective prefer to remain anonymous and concentrate on their message, rather than draw attention to individual personalities.

Jeramy Turner and Mary Ellen Croteau, both artists, are among the few identifiable members of SisterSerpent. They show their own paintings independently, but use the SisterSerpent persona for their collective work. Jeramy Turner says that Berlin Dada has been a big influence on the group, and one sees this in their photomontages that appropriate fine art or media images and give them a new twist. The Dada influence is also evident in the ironic or sarcastic slogans that SisterSerpent attaches to appropriate images or prints on stickers.

Reminiscent of the Berlin Dada Fair of 1920, which featured Rudolf Schlicter's stuffed police uniform with a pig's head, SisterSerpent also organizes art exhibitions such as *Rattle Your Rage,* which went up in April 1990. Here, among other works, one could see *Fetus Wall,* hung with large pictures of fetuses to which spiky teeth or sinister eyes were added.

But SisterSerpent wants its messages to be seen in the streets, and, to this end, the group has designed about seventy posters that are mostly reproduced in cheap xerox form and then plastered on public walls with wheat paste. The initial members chose the serpent as their logo and the name to go with it because they wanted an image that was strong but humorous. As they began to create collages and xerox them, they also made several rubber stamps with winged serpents, and they continue to stamp these in red ink on their posters.

The themes of the posters are powerful statements of their anger. One of their strongest images, produced several years ago by offset and mailed around the world, is *Fuck a Fetus,* which shows a photograph of a fetus below the words "For all those who consider a fetus more valuable than a woman." Surrounding the image are statements such as "Have a fetus work for you," "Cry on a fetal shoulder," and "Have a fetus bear your ego offspring." Another poster shows a xeroxed image of the Supreme Court justices combined with a text formed of crudely cutout letters reading: "Men don't die from illegal abortion." Other posters play off works of art such as Goya prints or nineteenth-century illustrations. A poster showing a turn-of-the-century image of a woman in a long gown, playing the violin, bears the message: "Poor men, we no longer care about your guilt."

A series of stickers printed in neon pink and orange backgrounds carry such statements as: "Misogyny: Look it up, stamp it out," "Rapists are the boys next door," and "Dead men don't rape." Another sticker, to be affixed to the appropriate object, says: "This sells rape. Don't buy it."

SisterSerpent uses guerrilla tactics to distribute its posters, which are usually illegally pasted on buildings, newspaper kiosks, or elevated train stations. I first saw these images at my El station in Evanston. Within a day, they had been ripped off or painted over by the Chicago Transit Authority officials.

According to Mary Ellen Croteau, SisterSerpent messages sometimes engender powerful responses, most likely from men who don't like women speaking out so forcefully. But as she and Jeramy Turner stress, SisterSerpent aims to empower women rather than sensitize men. To this end, they continue to speak out and gather supporters. In a society where there is so much resistance to the expression of women's anger, guerrilla warfare seems the only way to go.

*Originally published in Volume 10, Number 2, 1992.*

# BARBARA KRUGER: SMASHING THE MYTHS

*interview by Steven Heller*

For fifteen years Barbara Kruger designed magazines; now she creates billboards, postcards, and posters with images that question assumptions of power, gender, and human relations. Her work is shown in museums, art galleries, on the street, in subways, and on walls. In pushing the boundaries of art, Kruger also reveals the potential power of graphic communications. In this interview, she discusses her need to question convention and counter prevailing stereotypes in art and society.

**Steven Heller:** Your work is significant for what it says about cultural and social stereotyping, but also for busting art-world convention. What are your roots? How did you become an artist?

**Barbara Kruger:** My first job was as a telephone operator at an ad agency. It was then I put together a portfolio of comp book jackets for books that I had read or wanted to read, took it to Condé Nast, and at nineteen was hired to work on *Mademoiselle*. I began by doing back-of-the-book turns. After about four years, I left the full-time life and worked freelance for almost eleven years, starting as a designer for *House & Garden*. At *Mademoiselle,* Alexander Liberman [the editorial director and chief designer of Condé Nast] pretty much left us alone, but he involved himself with *House & Garden*, making trivial changes which were merely exercises in power and control.

**SH:** Did the material that you were dealing with in these magazines have little to do with the real world?

**BK:** I had no delusions. These magazines are vehicles to sell color advertising. Nevertheless, I think Condé Nast had an important place early on. It offered the first generation of wealthy, white, college-graduated women a place to work. Where else could they get hired? Most women could have master's degrees, but would only get jobs making coffee for their male bosses. Condé Nast offered a kind of refuge from that.

**SH:** What kind of formal education did you get from that experience?

**BK:** Despite the fact that I studied at Parsons for a year with Marvin Israel and Diane Arbus, I didn't know anything about design until this experience.

**SH:** Was anything learned during those years that you applied to your later work?

**BK:** There's no doubt that my job as a designer became, with very few major differences, my work as an artist. Indeed, I'd say 90 percent of what I do is informed formally by being a designer. What it means is another issue. But a lot of people writing about my work, coming from art history or the art world, don't know anything about design. Which, incidentally, I don't know either except that I worked in it, so what I know is basically in my hands. People look at my work and say Heartfield, because they know John Heartfield [the German designer and photomontagist], not as someone who learned his craft through designing magazines and book jackets but as one who has become an "art figure."

**SH:** Did you ever want to paint canvases?

**BK:** I remember saying to Marvin Israel, who had such a conflicted relationship to being an artist, "If I want to be an artist, can't I just work with photographs and Magic Marker? Do I have to paint?" And he told me I had to paint, probably because he was already working with photographs and a Magic Marker, and he had such a romantic and conflicted idea about the so-called division between art and design.

**SH:** That perpetuates the stereotype of the artist with smock and palette. But what problems did you face being an artist in an essentially male-dominated field?

**BK:** The art world was a very forbidding place for a woman who wanted to define herself through her work, or productivity. There were so few models. But I tried. I made paintings and very obsessively decorated objects. Making them was time consuming and definitely put my brain to sleep. I showed them at the Whitney and a gallery, but I also started writing poetry and prose, and doing a lot of reading. That accelerated everything. It was at this point that I started to rethink what it might mean to call myself an artist.

**SH:** Why and at what point did you decide to turn to photography and type?

**BK:** I just felt that in order to best visualize my ideas I should return to what I knew best, which seemed to be a kind of deeply skewed rendition of editorial design that altered meaning and pumped up scale.

**SH:** Given that painting is historically dominated by men, do you think that photography is a feminist medium?

**BK:** The medium itself is not implicitly feminist, but has been used to show and tell other kinds of pictures and words. This suggests that people who have been unseen and unheard have curious, and at times canny, ways of turning their exclusion around and creating a critique. Or as Roland Barthes said, there are some of us who are obliged to steal language. And if not language, then something else, like pictures. Because it's the vernacular of the world in which we live. Even though it's not necessarily ours, we begin to use it for our own devices and for our own needs. We are trying to create a kind of insistent commentary.

**SH:** What was your first attempt at making word-image combinations?

**BK:** I started taking pictures of buildings in Berkeley for which I wrote little texts. They simply grew out of a double concern—my desire to deal with demi-narratives of the everyday, and my ongoing interest in architecture and its power to order our lives in the most (literally) concrete of ways. I also did a series called *Remainders,* photographs of what people leave behind in their cars. And another called *The Hospital Series,* pictures of what happens when one becomes objectified by the healthcare system.

**SH:** The latter sounds like your concern with debunking myths and exposing folly.

**BK:** I'm also interested in ruining certain representations. I'm also interested in welcoming the female spectator into the audience of men. For generations of us, there have been problems with the way women or people of color have been depicted. And I'm not looking to replace one stereotype with another. I can't stand that kind of binarism. I prefer to do work that entertains doubt more than surety, that is about questions more than answers.

**SH:** How does one break down these old stereotypes?

**BK:** It's very difficult. Stereotypes are powerful because they always have a potent and unrelenting moment of truth in them. They have to be incrementally questioned and sooner or later vigilantly exposed.

**SH:** How were you accepted in an art world that was so tight? Was it an easy transition?

**BK:** Everything is social relations. Everything's a hierarchy. I consider the fact that certain people have become visible, especially if they're women, or people of color, as a confluence of thoughtful, hopefully effective work, cultural awareness of change, and fortuitous social relations. In the art world, like any other subculture, whether it's academia, the literary world, or show business— which is even worse, everything is temporal. It just so happened that when I started making work, certain people were supportive of it. You can count on one hand the number of people who believe in you because of what you can do, rather than what you've already done. And if we have just one or two of these people in our lives, we're lucky.

My work also evolved at a point when there was a really defined difference between photographers and people who used photography, like Cindy Sherman, Laurie Simmons, Sarah Charlesworth, and Richard Prince.

**SH:** What was that difference?

**BK:** We were willing to play faster and looser with the definition of an artist. We had grown up looking at images and watching television. That had to be the stuff of our work. We felt weird making paintings. Which doesn't mean it's wrong to make paintings, but for us it wasn't the way to go. Moreover, art has been so fetishized—it's about objects, not processes. I consider my work to be about the processes of social relations, about being bought and sold, about living and dying, about men and women.

SH: But the marketplace is obsessed with objects.

BK: And so, I'm afraid, is history. We are not going to change the market. But we can pluralize history. And that's what a number of us who feel we're working critically are out to do. Working critically means I have a questioning relationship to the constructions of power. I prefer questions to answers. And I want to make change. I am not a conservator. I also have a wary relationship to property and pictures—which goes to the heart of the multiplicities of the image.

SH: There is such a controversy about the ownership not only of the photograph itself, but the image in the photograph. Who owns an image?

BK: Photography plays havoc with the notion of the singular object. It's about multiples. And yet, the way that many artists who use photography got their voices and visions seen was sort of playing around with that. Some of my works are multiples, while others are one-of-a-kind. And the scale has also changed radically. This is not the kind of photography framed in white mats.

SH: Did you adopt this form so that millions rather than hundreds could see your work?

BK: I'm not deluded about this, so I can't say yes unequivocally. We all work within our developed fluencies. I know that there is no one way that I can reach as many people as *Married with Children,* or *The Simpsons,* which I think is critical work. I don't have the same access, but it doesn't mean that I want my work stuck in some art ghetto either. I hope I reach people. And, as a woman, I hope I've changed minds. I know that. As a teacher and as someone whose images are out in the world, I think I've had some impact even if only on a small scale. I think we do what we can.

SH: You spoke earlier about how historians view your work. How would you like to be written into history?

BK: As women start to enter the canons of art history, hopefully we won't enter them the same way the guys have. It depends on who writes us and how we're defined. But, most importantly, I would like to be included by someone who understands feminisms and the relations around them—which very few people who've written about my work do. They say the word *feminism* once or twice, and it gets them off the hook.

**SH:** What do you mean by "feminisms"?

**BK:** Feminisms are multiple ways of being in the world, not a single methodology, not a "correct" recipe. A lot of writers, historians, and journalists do not understand that.

**SH:** Your billboard art seems to be an alternative to the usually disheartening social or political advertising we're regularly exposed to.

**BK:** During the last presidential campaign there wasn't one successful ad by the Democrats, let alone a viable candidate! But there are important issues. The people in Hollywood know how to use the media and they have commandeered the ratings with their savvy mixture of liberalism, humor, and populist narratives. This way of working has not yet been reflected in the electoral process.

**SH:** There's a certain subversive quality to all of this; does getting effective work out into the world always have to be subversive?

**BK:** I don't think it's subversive at all! The notion of being subversive is a very romantic one. It suggests that you're getting away with something. And I think that's naive.

There are certain incremental displacements that one makes through the differences from convention, and when you get appropriated into the convention, you become conventional yourself. And you have to keep moving on and remain insistent. I think that's how things change.

**SH:** Raymond Loewy called it the MAYA principle—"most advanced yet acceptable."

**BK:** Every moment is inflected by our collision with others in the world. We are always sharing an experience, even down to the air we breathe.

**SH:** Isn't the gallery or museum an elitist environment in which to show socially relevant work?

**BK:** One tries to deal with as many sites as possible. A gallery is a public space that is simply another arena in which to insinuate visual assaults onto certain assumptions.

SH: Do you get federal money for your work?

BK: I applied to the NEA for twelve years before actually getting a grant for $15,000 some ten years ago. But I've stopped applying because I don't want to take money from people who might need it more than me.

SH: Are you making the impact on society—or individuals—that you hoped you would make?

BK: I hope so. I hope that my work can be enabling to women and, more generally, to those who are trying to understand how power and exclusion work.

I remember when I was a kid, watching the Johnny Carson show—having a good time, laughing with Johnny. And he's telling a joke to Ed McMahon about broads. I'm laughing until all of a sudden it occurs to me that I'm that thing he's calling a broad. The joke's on me. Most people internalize this kind of humiliation throughout their lives and it works to determine their notions of self-esteem and their productive capacities. But, if you start viewing these moments critically, you can begin to alter these conditions, you can begin to create a different kind of spectator: one who might be intent on beginning to represent himself or herself rather than always being represented. And there are certain viewers of my work who understand that.

SH: Your art empowers you, but do you have the power to change minds?

BK: Power makes a difference. It changes lives. It changes minds, it changes the world. I think it is important to try to conjure up different relationships to power, to try dispersing it rather than hoarding it, and to make for a liberating force rather than a crippling one.

SH: What about the term *morality;* how does that affect you?

BK: Morality has been appropriated by the forces of fear and mean-spiritedness. It might be handy to come up with new terms to describe a generosity of spirit and inclusiveness. These conditions seem to be the bedrock of a benevolent social relation: one that eschews the dictations of a strict and scolding morality, and which welcomes the pleasures of empathy, laughter, and hope.

*Originally published in Volume 9, Number 1, 1991.*

# WHAT PUBLICO? WHOSE BONO?

*Dugald Stermer*

In a fit of lunacy, back when the world and I were about a decade and a half younger, I helped to found and operate what was then, to the best of our knowledge, the first not-for-profit advertising agency solely devoted to *pro bono publico* work. It was called, appropriately if not imaginatively, Public Interest Communications (PIC).

A curious phrase, *pro bono publico* literally means "efforts for the public good." But, over time, it has acquired at least two further implications. First was that what the official government of the day meant by public good could be a very different thing from what was meant by those who used the phrase and did the work. Second, and most critically, the work was done for nothing, or right up next to nothing. One seldom hears the name Richard Nixon or Ed Meese in the same sentence with *pro bono publico* (this may be a first), yet I can hear their voices resonating with smug claims of tireless work in behalf of our welfare.

Public Interest Communications was founded, at least on my part, in desperation and folded in frustration a couple of years later. Putting this in perspective, in the wake of the 1960s, there were free clinics and storefront law offices in every urban neighborhood. There seemed to be scores of committed volunteers for every human goal, community effort, or national movement, especially if it was in some way an alternative to the prevailing winds from Washington. That is, every endeavor except advertising and other forms of graphic communications, from television spots to newspaper cause-ads to posters, brochures, and leaflets. And the Ad Council didn't and doesn't count; its idea of a hard-hitting issue is the promotion of motherhood over child abandonment. Wherever one finds a universally acknowledged abuse of the social contract, like homicide or littering, especially one whose blame can be shared by all but responsibility pinned on none, there also is found the courageous presence of the Ad Council.

On the other hand, if any real issues needed an airing in the public media, or if any of the hundreds of issue-oriented groups, local or national, needed to pass the hat and simultaneously raise our consciousness, there were only two folks to call on in the 415 area code: writer Jerry Mander and me. (Jerry, along with spectacular designer Marget Larsen and clients Alvin Duskin, a local businessman, Friends of the Earth, and the Sierra Club, had produced a series of beautiful and definitive conservation ads a couple of years earlier. Beyond their splendid content and style, they remain as examples of the finest typography ever to grace any newspaper anywhere.)

Not coincidentally, Jerry, Alvin, and I were the founders of PIC Speaking only for myself, I saw it as a way to institutionalize what was fast becoming a volunteer way of life. I believed, mistakenly as it turned out, that if we had an office and a staff along with some order and a modicum of income in the form of grants from foundations, that together we might turn out more and more effective work than I had been able to achieve by myself.

The theory was as follows. We would charge no fees whatsoever and would even rebate the commissions on insertion orders. The clients would be required to pay only the actual out-of-pocket costs. Our operating funds were to come from foundation donations. We hoped against experience that this source would carry a reasonable office overhead and a paid staff of five or six. I never took a paycheck, not out of an excess of altruism but because I didn't want to be obligated to regular office hours and all that goes with them. Again, I was mistaken on many, if not all, counts.

The point about charging no fees had two purposes. First, this way we were free to select our clients and their messages without being influenced, however subconsciously, by their relative inability to pay us. Second, I had found through long experience that it was far less troublesome in dealing with what were inevitably amateur clients—however professional they may have been in other areas of their lives—if I charged them nothing for my services, rather than the pittance such groups could normally afford. After all, my pittance might be their rent money, and that bought them the right to nitpick, and generally "disimprove" the results. If they paid nothing, they had no rights, except the right of outright refusal. It was simply an effort to keep the lines of authority and expertise clear: the message was theirs, the context was to be ours. Sure, and the check is in the mail.

Let me now admit that, notwithstanding my nightmare that hell for me may just turn out to be an eternity of working within a reincarnation of Public Interest Communications without a pencil sharpener as further torture, we did produce some damn fine work and beneficial results for causes and groups in great need of public support. (I have an enduring memory of unlocking the office doors one early morning to the wondrous sight of a disheveled Joan Baez, who had worked late overseeing an ad for Amnesty International and then curled up on the conference room floor. May she ultimately prevail.)

That said, on to the flip side. Groups are not, by definition, more efficient or imaginative than individuals. Ours certainly wasn't. It is unfortunately part of reality that most people willing to work for meager salaries in the communicating arts for any length of time aren't worth it. The reason they entered the related fields of advertising and design in the first place was decidedly not to toil in the interests of the disenfranchised and downtrodden. In short, we got what our hand called for.

Further compounding the confusion, this was, as some of you may recall, the age of participatory democracy, wherein everyone present voted equally on everything from lunch to revolution. This also meant meetings, made necessary in order for me to present my notions for discussion in a conciliatory, nonthreatening, nonmanipulative, nonelitist, nonsexist, nonexpert, nonskilled, nonexperienced manner so that I wouldn't be perceived as attempting to cram my white male macho approach down their liberated throats. At the same time, of course, it was up to us threatening, manipulative, elitist, sexist, and semiskilled barbarians to pry the money out of the foundations to keep on paying the others so that we could go on having meetings and keep them in bean sprouts.

If this sounds hysterical, it is intentional because I am reminding myself never, ever in life to become involved with that kind of lefty circle-jerk again. It is almost more harmful to the spirit than corporations. The final telling point of the whole experience for me was that I realized that I could do more pro bono work on my own, part time, than the whole group—including me—could do full time; and I could do it better and have more fun in the process.

However, my experience is apparently not that of some others. The idea, somewhat altered, lives on with great vitality in the work and spirit of Public Media Center (PMC) in San Francisco, under the guidance of Herb Gunther, a wonderfully bright and precise gadfly of advertising, and the fellowship and consultation of the aforementioned Jerry Mander. It is both a blessing and a relief that PIC died so that PMC could live.

*Originally published in Volume 6, Number 1, 1988.*

# HIGH STYLE, LOW STYLE, VILE STYLE

*Philip B. Meggs*

Over the course of this century, the corporation has been the American dream machine. It has provided jobs, technological advancement, stockholder equity, and philanthropy, such as supporting cultural programs, matching employees' charitable contributions, and funding inner-city scholarship programs. Examples of corporate good citizenship abound. Westvaco Inc., for example, protects bald eagles in western Kentucky and red-cockaded woodpeckers in South Carolina by setting aside preserves of timberland inhabited by these endangered species.

Many—though certainly not all—major corporations have proven to be patrons of graphic design. "Good design is good business," proclaimed fifties designers as the corporate image concept took hold and flourished. Yet, a curious "high style, low style" ethic has developed in some corporate boardrooms and marketing departments. Graphic materials produced for stockholders, institutional ads in prestigious business and news magazines, and sometimes even employee communications are high style, produced lavishly and with taste and imagination. By contrast, materials produced for the consumer public are often low style, strident and banal with little concern for design integrity.

One of the great folk heroes among corporate clients, Walter P. Paepcke, founder of Container Corporation of America (CCA), is lauded for his remarkable vision in understanding the contribution that design can make to a corporation. In the late thirties, CCA appointed Egbert Jacobson as director of the design department and gave him the responsibility for developing a comprehensive design program. Initiated in 1951, the "Great Ideas of Western Man" advertising campaign was one of the most high-minded institutional advertising programs ever produced. Paepcke wrote that these advertisements "have made people talk about the company; have given the organization a tone of quality; opened doors for salespeople; interested college students in pursuing a CCA career; and perhaps even induced investors to study the company's stock."

The component of CCA's design activity not publicized, however, was produced by regional design studios that create grocery store and other packages for clients of CCA's package manufacturing plants. There was a real cereal-box mentality operating that addressed the infamous "least common denominator." Paepcke probably never paused to consider the contradiction of hiring outstanding designers and painters to interpret the "Great Ideas of Western Man" in business and news magazines in CCA's institutional advertising, while filling America's grocery stores with some of the most banal cigarette, soap powder, and cereal boxes imaginable. Paepcke was a corporate aristocrat who possessed an exceptional understanding of the role that design could play in addressing the corporate audience, but his vision stopped short of the Bauhaus ideal of functional and aesthetic design for the working class.

Arguments that mediocre consumer graphics are necessary because "they sell" are dubious in product categories where the public is not provided a reasonable alternative. In some product groups, only low-sales-volume, overpriced specialty brands give serious attention to well-designed products and packages. The corporate defense, "This is what consumers want," fell into disrepute when the Japanese automobile industry caught American automobile executives with their pants down in the late seventies. These executives were producing luxurious, fuel-inefficient cars that appealed to themselves and their social strata. They were totally oblivious to the existence of a large segment of the American public that was rapidly changing its ideas about what an automobile should be.

More serious than corporate lapses in taste, or even misjudging the market with difficult consequences for workers and stockholders, is the problem of "vile style." When products defraud or injure customers, or do grave harm to spaceship earth, star-crossed designers sometimes find that they have clothed the vilest companies or products in effective graphics.

The logo for an overseas investment firm was outstanding enough to warrant reproduction in a major design publication. After investors were bilked of millions of dollars, the firm collapsed and its founder fled the country to escape prosecution.

The designer created an image of quality and reliability when the client was, in fact, a con man.

Environmental problems surface and cause serious soul-searching for graphic designers engaged in corporate design. An extensive list of toxic dump sites, which were required by law to close on November 8, 1985, and file a closure plan fifteen days later, was recently made public. The Environmental Defense Fund has discovered that many closure plans have not yet been submitted, that most of those which were submitted are of very poor quality, and that some sites may be continuing to receive toxic waste in violation of the law. Under the Reagan administration's Environmental Protection Agency, enforcement of these legal requirements has been lax. Designers working half a continent away can be totally oblivious to a client's toxic-waste dump. For example, the twenty-eight toxic-waste dumps required to close in the state of Louisiana alone include such corporate giants as General Electric, American Hoechst Corporation, Kaiser Aluminum and Chemical, Uniroyal, and Ethyl Corporation.

Allied Chemical caused one of the worst environmental disasters in history by dumping hundreds of tons of a highly toxic chemical, kepone, into the James River. After being convicted and slapped with a $13.2 million fine by Federal Judge Robert R. Merhige, Jr., Allied Chemical retained a design firm to develop a new visual identification program. It dropped the word *chemical* from its name, calling the renamed firm Allied Corporation. This is not unlike surgeons performing cosmetic surgery on criminals to give them a new identity.

A personal close brush with vile style occurred when I was art director of the A. H. Robins Pharmaceutical Co. Shortly before I left that position I had been briefed and was about to begin work on graphics for a new product, the Dalkon Shield IUD birth-control device. Its inventor, an assistant professor of gynecology at Johns Hopkins Medical School, made wondrous claims for his invention. Problems were being reported with birth-control pills, and the IUD was touted as a major advance in safe and economical contraception. Today, A. H. Robins is in Chapter 11 bankruptcy to preserve its solvency in the face of thousands of suits from Dalkon Shield users whose "problems" ranged from chronic infection to death. Had I stayed in that position another six months and developed graphics promoting the Dalkon Shield, a difficult ethical dilemma would have arisen years later when problems surfaced.

Corporations are like people: while most are law-abiding citizens, criminals do exist. Designers usually lack the expertise to assess the ethical value of their clients' integrity on faith. When graphic designers provide an image of style and quality for corporate clients, sometimes we unwittingly put makeup over melanoma. High style can turn distressingly vile.

*Originally published in Volume 5, Number 1, 1987.*

# FOOD FOR THOUGHT, LIKE APPLES, GROWS ON TREES

*Véronique Vienne*

I know how Eve felt when she reached for the apple. She felt the way I feel whenever I buy a newspaper, sort my mail, leaf through a magazine, open a package, or browse in a bookstore. She felt exhilarated, buoyant, venturesome—and slightly guilty.

Taking the apple—and cutting the tree—is the Original Sin. The way we waste paper products is a constant reminder of some of our worst shortcomings, and yet, driven by a relentless urge to consume—and be consumed—we keep doing it. As designers, our relationship with paper is passionate and sensual. Food for thought, printed material is also a major source of physical enjoyment. Words are associated in our minds with the texture of fine vellum, the touch of onionskin, the character of a coarse piece of cardboard or the patina of coated stock. In the beginning was the Word, but the Word was disembodied. It took shape only when it became accessible to our senses.

The symbolism of the apple and the tree is forever intriguing. You can think of it metaphorically, or, like me, you can also take it literally. With increased awareness of environmental issues, every time I use a wood by-product, I feel a tension between myself and nature. After I read the papers, for example, I wash my hands stained with ink—and scrub them hard to remove the sap as well. I pry junk mail out of my mailbox as if uprooting a young tree. I explore newsstands like a small mammal foraging in the underbrush. I rip at packaging the way some worms eat leaves. I pile up books around my home as diligently as a beaver builds a dam. The rain forests are disappearing? Their shadow over my life is constantly lengthening.

To make matters worse, I exploit paper for a living. If you are reading this article, chances are you too work with a chainsaw. Never mind your vice president, senior designer, or graphic artist title—you are, for all intents and purposes, a tough lumberjack. Forestry, like typography, is the backbone of your craft.

I have tried to figure out how many trees are cut, processed, and shredded each month to provide the paper on which my own work is printed. On a good month, I am afraid, I consume about ten thousand trees on one hundred misty acres of timberland in the Pacific Northwest, patiently awaiting their fate as I sit at my desk and stare at my computer.

To alleviate my conscience, I recycle—and every two years I make a pilgrimage to the AIGA Design Conference. The sponsors' evening is my favorite event. It is a three-hour-long bacchanal during which I celebrate the death and rebirth of invisible forest spirits that live in my imagination. Free food, free wine—and free paper samples—are served at this sylvan ritual. Graphic arts high priests, design professionals, paper suppliers, printers, students, and computer artists mingle together in the crowd. I stampede with the herd to gather as many complimentary paper samples, promotional portfolios, albums, collateral material, leave-behinds, and brochures as I can carry. From time to time, I stop to inhale deeply. The smell of paper and fresh ink goes to my head. I just wish I could sip at a glass of turpentine-scented retsina, the Greek wine with an aftertaste of coniferous sap.

This year, the AIGA revelers were as merry as ever, but the graphics, in contrast, were meditative, almost monastic and pious. Many of the paper samples were stone gray, beige, dirt colored, or dark green. Ropes, twine, plain cardboard, and simple typography prevailed. Most of the paper stock, and most of the creativity, came from recycled material. Numerous brochures claimed 10 percent postconsumer waste, 40 percent postindustrial waste, and 80 percent nonoriginal photography. Sometimes even the words were recycled, like the recycled wisdom of the Potlatch "Remarks" booklet or the quotes from the likes of James Joyce, Dylan Thomas, and Henry Ford compiled in a handsome Hopper Papers portfolio.

Austerity does not exclude sensuality. In general, the texture of the page was more interesting than the graphic treatment of the text. Embossing, debossing, engraving, silk-screening, and thermography were cleverly and sparingly used. The Engraved Stationery Manufacturers Association made this clear with a demure folded brochure featuring a delicately engraved fingerprint, while Weyerhauser demonstrated the tactile impact of these techniques with its "Paper Cut" brochure printed to replicate realistic three-dimensional Band-Aids. The complicated de-inking process necessary to bleach recycled paper had apparently sobered everyone's typographic ardor. Less ink—and thus less type—was the dominant trend. Fox River Paper Company even decided it was time to de-emphasize the importance of the written word, and published a deconstructivist exercise book for the phonetic pronunciation of vowels.

The more I studied the sponsors' brochures, the more I realized that the feeling was one of preservation, not so much of the trees, but of the paper itself. The printed word is fast becoming an endangered species. If people stop reading books, magazines, manuals, and brochures, we will lose yet another connection with nature—the comforting knowledge that food for thought, like apples, grows on trees.

I was jolted out of my reverie when I noticed that a book I had recently written was given away as a freebie at one of the printers' tables. Less than a month had elapsed between the book's launch party and its repositioning as a paper sample. Moving swiftly down the food chain, it was now compost for my colleagues. Like Eve, I reached once more for the apple—for a knowledge that only comes from a personal realization—and understood that recycling is not a secondary operation designed to salvage damaged goods. Recycling is the primordial process of life itself. The paper was cool and smooth against my face. The ink smelled of distant places—oil wells, moldy leaves, foreign money, wet varnish, and lost paradises.

*Originally published in Volume 11, Number 4, 1993.*

# CONTRIBUTORS

MICHAEL ANDERSON is an editor of the *New York Times Book Review*.

ROY R. BEHRENS, professor of art (graphic design/illustration) at the University of Northern Iowa, is a contributing editor of *Print* magazine and editor of *Ballast Quarterly Review*.

MICHAEL BIERUT is a partner in the New York office of the international design consultancy Pentagram.

SVEN BIRKERTS is the author of four books of essays, most recently *The Gutenberg Elegies: The Fate of Reading in an Electronic Age*.

FRANCES BUTLER is a professor in the department of environmental design at the University of California, Davis.

MATTHEW BUTTERICK is president of Atomic Vision, an Internet development company in San Francisco.

CHUCK BYRNE is a design crank who designs, writes, and lives in Oakland, California.

RALPH CAPLAN is the author of *How to Be a Client (Even Though You Don't Want to Be) and How to Be a Designer (Even Though No One's Asked You To)*.

MATTHEW CARTER, an AIGA medalist, is a type designer and principal of Carter & Cone Type in Cambridge, Massachusetts.

IVAN CHERMAYEFF, an AIGA medalist, is a partner in Chermayeff & Geismar Associates Inc., New York.

ROSEMARY J. COOMBE is an associate professor of law at the University of Toronto and the author of *Cultural Appropriations: Authorship, Alterity and the Law*.

MOIRA CULLEN is a design consultant and chairperson of the design department at Parsons Otis, in California.

RUDOLPH DE HARAK, an AIGA medalist, has been a designer and a photographer for nearly forty years, and was professor of design at the Cooper Union, New York.

DANIEL DRENNAN is a senior designer at Delphi Internet in New York City.

JANET FAIRBAIRN is a graphic designer in New Hampshire and assistant professor at CUNY, the college at Fredonia.

PETER FRATERDEUS founded Alphabets, Inc., in Evanston, Illinois, and design-Online, Inc., where he helps corporations develop Internet strategies.

DAN FRIEDMAN (1945–1995) was the author of *Dan Friedman: Radical Modernism* and an artist whose subject was design and culture.

STEFF GEISSBUHLER is a principal at Chermayeff & Geismar Inc., New York.

MILTON GLASER, an AIGA medalist, is president of Milton Glaser, Inc., and has taught design at the School of Visual Arts for more than thirty years.

JESSICA HELFAND is a graphic designer who works in partnership with William Drenttel. She is a contributing editor to *Eye* and *I.D.* magazines, and the author of *Six Essays (to 12) on Design and New Media.*

STEVEN HELLER, the editor of the *AIGA Journal of Graphic Design,* is a senior art director at the *New York Times,* and the author of more than sixty books on graphic design.

TONY HENDRA is a performer, humorist, author, and the former editor of *National Lampoon.*

MIKE HICKS is principal of HIXO, Inc. in Austin, Texas.

BRAD HOLLAND is an illustrator and a former board member of the AIGA.

RICHARD HOLLIS is the author of *Graphic Design: A Concise History.*

NATALIA ILYIN teaches cultural and design theory at the Cooper Union in New York and at Yale University. An art director and a writer, she is working on a book about mythic images of American culture.

JENNIFER KABAT is an editor at *I.D.* magazine.

JEFFERY KEEDY is on the faculty of the program in graphic design at California Institute of the Arts. He received an MFA from Cranbrook Academy of Art and is known internationally as an educator, writer, and type designer.

LARRY KEELEY is president of Doblin Group in Chicago.

JERRY KELLY is a designer and representative with the Stinehour Press and a partner at the Kelly-Winterton Press. He has contributed articles to the *AIGA Journal of Graphic Design, Papers of the Bibliographic Society of America,* and other books and journals.

ROBIN KINROSS is a typographer, writer, and publisher in London. He is the author of *Modern Typography* and *Fellow Readers.*

JULIE LASKY is the managing editor of *Print* magazine.

LEO LIONNI, an AIGA medalist, is a graphic designer, writer, and children's book author and illustrator who divides his time between New York and Italy.

GEORGE LOIS, an AIGA medalist, is the chairman of Lois/EJL in New York.

PAUL LUKAS publishes *Beer Frame: The Journal of Inconspicuous Consumption,* a 'zine that deconstructs consumer culture in excruciating detail, and is a columnist for *Fortune* and *Spin* magazines.

ELLEN LUPTON is the curator of contemporary design at the Cooper-Hewitt, National Design Museum and co-chair of the design department at the Maryland College of Art, Baltimore.

KEVIN LYONS, a designer for Nike Inc., received an MFA in graphic design from CalArts. He is a founding partner in the New York City design firm (((stereotype))) and is also writing a book on issues of cultural reappropriation in urban street design, called *Cease and Desist: The Low End Theory.*

VICTOR MARGOLIN teaches design history at the University of Illinois, Chicago, and is the author of *The Struggle for Utopia* (University of Illinois Press).

ROSS MacDONALD is an illustrator who lives in Connecticut and works in New York City.

STUART McKEE is a graphic designer living in San Francisco. In his current research, he is examining the ways in which graphic design contributes to the political identities of the American public.

PHILIP B. MEGGS teaches graphic design history at Virginia Commonwealth University and is the author of *A History of Graphic Design.*

PHIL PATTON writes design criticism for *Esquire, I.D., Wired,* and the *New York Times.*

SHARON HELMER POGGENPOHL teaches design at Institute of Design IIT in Chicago and is the editor of *Visible Language.*

PAUL RAND (1914–1996) was a designer, painter and author of *Paul Rand: A Designer's Art* and *Design, Form, and Chaos.*

FORREST RICHARDSON is a principal of Richardson or Richardson in Phoenix.

RANDALL ROTHENBERG is the editorial director of *Esquire* magazine and the author of *Where the Suckers Moon: An Advertising Story.*

FATH DAVIS RUFFINS is a historian and head of the collection of advertising history at the National Museum of American History, Smithsonian Institution. She is currently at work on a book and exhibition on ethnic imagery in twentieth-century American advertising.

RHONDA RUBINSTEIN is an editorial art director and pop culture design writer (who considers the two-line bio to be an undistinguished literary form).

PAUL SAFFO is a director at the Institute for the Future in Menlo Park, California.

GORDON SALCHOW is a professor of graphic design at the University of Cincinnati and a past president of the AIGA board of directors.

PAULA SCHER is a partner in the New York office of the international design consultancy Pentagram.

MARTHA SCOTFORD is a professor of graphic design at North Carolina State University and the author of a forthcoming book on Cipe Pineles.

DUGALD STERMER is an illustrator and writer in San Francisco.

ELLEN SHAPIRO, a graphic designer and writer, is president of Shapiro Design Associates Inc. in New York.

GUNNAR SWANSON is a graphic designer in Duluth, Minnesota, and the head of the graphic design program at the University of Minnesota, Duluth.

CHRISTIAAN VERMAAS is a visiting professor at the Universidad de Las Americanas Puebla in Mexico.

JAMES VICTORE is principal of Victore Design Works in New York.

VÉRONIQUE VIENNE writes about design, photography, and cultural trends. Her articles have been published in *Metropolis, Graphis, Print, Emigre, Eye, Communication Arts, AIGA Journal of Graphic Design,* and many general-interest magazines.

MASSIMO VIGNELLI is an AIGA medalist and a principal at Vignelli Associates.

ALINA WHEELER founded Rev Visual in Philadelphia.

LORRAINE WILD has been teaching at the California Institute of Arts since 1985 and also serves as a project tutor at the Jan van Eyck Akademie in Maastricht, the Netherlands. She has her own design practice in Los Angeles.

RICHARD SAUL WURMAN is the creative director of Access Press Ltd. and the president of the Understanding Business in New York and San Francisco.

# INDEX

## BOOKS FROM ALLWORTH PRESS

**AIGA Professional Practices in Graphic Design**
by The American Institute of Graphic Arts (softcover, 6¾ × 10, 320 pages, $24.95)

**Looking Closer 2: Critical Writings on Graphic Design**
edited by Michael Bierut, William Drenttel, Steven Heller, DK Holland
(softcover, 6¾ × 10, 282 pages, $18.95)

**Looking Closer: Critical Writings on Graphic Design**
edited by Michael Bierut, William Drenttel, Steven Heller, DK Holland
(softcover, 6¾ × 10, 256 pages, $18.95)

**Design Literacy: Understanding Graphic Design**
by Steven Heller and Karen Pomeroy (softcover, 6¾ × 10, 288 pages, $19.95)

**The New Business of Design**
by the International Conference in Aspen (softcover, 6 × 9, 256 pages, $19.95)

**Careers by Design: A Headhunter's Secrets for Success and Survival in Graphic
Design** Revised Edition by Roz Goldfarb (softcover, 6¾ × 10, 256 pages, $18.95)

**Selling Graphic Design**
by Don Sparkman (softcover, 6 × 9, 224 pages, $18.95)

**Business and Legal Forms for Graphic Designers**
Revised Edition by Tad Crawford (softcover, 8½ × 11, 208 pages, $22.95)

**The Copyright Guide**
by Lee Wilson (softcover, 6 × 9, 192 pages, $18.95)

**Electronic Design and Publishing: Business Practices**
Second Edition by Liane Sebastian (softcover, 6¾ × 10, 200 pages, $19.95)

**The Business of Multimedia**
by Nina Schuyler (softcover, 6 × 9, 240 pages, $19.95)

**Lectures on Art**
by John Ruskin (softcover, 6 × 9, 224 pages, $18.95)

Please write to request our free catalog. If you wish to order a book, send your check or money
order to Allworth Press, 10 East 23rd Street, Suite 210, New York, NY 10010. Include $5 for
shipping and handling for the first book ordered and $1 for each additional book. Ten dollars
plus $1 for each additional book if ordering from Canada. New York State residents must add
sales tax.

If you wish to see our catalog on the World Wide Web, you can find us at:
**http://www.arts-online.com/allworth/home.html** or at **http://www.allworth.com**